Sleeping in a Life Jacket

A Complete and Funny Guide to Cruising

Gail Gauvreau

Dedication

*To my mother Nevaida Howe
who taught me my first words.*

Contents

Foreword

Why Write About Cruising?

I am a writer who specializes in short humorous stories about travel. All kinds of travel. Having taken a number of cruises, and in light of the negative stories floating around about cruising (post covid-19 shutdowns), I decided that it was the perfect time to write a book packed with tips and filled with short, funny cruising stories that are intended to make you laugh and to specifically give you helpful information on booking and taking a cruise.

If I had found a good book about cruising before I took my first cruise, I would have been spared some basic rookie mistakes and certainly saved myself money. I am confident that I would have had a better cabin, secured onboard credit and probably enjoyed some type of all inclusive beverage package.

If you are thinking about taking a cruise and seeking some helpful information, or you are an experienced cruiser looking for some travel related laughs, this book is for you.

Welcome aboard our shared journey into the joys of cruising.

Acknowledgments

I wish to acknowledge and thank my husband Dan who always encourages me to write and never complains about the time it takes me to do so. I would also like to thank Annette Aucoin, Linda Post and Lynne Walker who read through some very rough first drafts of this book. Your patience and comments were invaluable.

A special thank you goes out to my many friends, fellow cruisers and family who have supported me in numerous ways and who permit me to write about them, quote their words and talk about their cruising experiences.

Finally, to my readers who share my passion for travel with laughter, you are the reason I put words to paper.

Thank You!
Gail Gauvreau

Introduction

The sea was angry, the waves huge and the rain slashed down upon the ship with increasing ferocity. I was in my element. Standing on our balcony, located off our cabin at the front of the ship, I was thrilled as the bow rose with each towering wave and then suddenly crashed to the sea below. It felt like a giant, wet, roller coaster ride. Now THIS was my idea of cruising. I loved each and every minute of the storm. Dan, my husband, was inside our cabin with the balcony door opened about ten centimetres. He was holding out a life jacket. I had asked him to join me on the balcony so I could take a video of us braving the storm together, but he had declined.

> *"Get in here. You are going to be swept overboard and you will never be found"* he yelled over the noise of the storm.

> *"Come inside, or at least put on this life jacket. It's not safe!"*

> *"Are you worried?"* I asked with a laugh.

> *"Only about the increased time it will take me to collect the life insurance because they can't locate your body"* he shouted.

1

I did not want to step away from this unexpected benefit of a sudden, fall storm that engulfed our ship.

This entire trip had been amazing. I had forgotten about the cruises I had enjoyed in my twenties and the associated fun. Too much time had passed and I had taken land vacations around the world that had become my norm. I had been reluctant to go on the cruise as I had feared boredom and tedious days trapped on what I thought of as a floating hotel. The fact that once on shore, we would be restricted in port time and guaranteed crowds at all the popular tourist spots, left me less than enthusiastic. However, I found that I loved the entire experience, and the storm was just the icing on the cake. I had met interesting, fascinating and downright weird people on the cruise, eaten some awesome meals and participated in captivating events. Cruising was far more than I had envisioned.

In addition to my own reservations, I was concerned about setting sail with my husband who had never taken a cruise and who had experienced sea sickness on the short, sunset cruises we had booked on previous vacations. We were starting off with a voyage of approximately two weeks and if he did not like it, or was seasick, there would be no escape. Little did I realize when we took our first cruise together, that our cruising days had just begun, and we had entered a new phase of vacationing: Cruising!

Join me on this adventure into the ins and outs of cruising, along with tips to help you choose the trip, ship and cabin best suited to your wants and budget. This book is designed to help you learn about cruising as you are entertained by stories and real-life onboard experiences.

The title *Sleeping in a Life Jacket* is based on a joking comment by a friend who apparently suffered under the misconception that watching disaster movies about ships at sea, would be a great way to prepare for her cruise.

> *Most people get ready for their cruises by planning their shore excursions and deciding what to pack. I planned for lifeboat drills and sleeping in a life jacket. Needless to say, the cruise was all smooth sailing. There was no drama and the closest I came to a disaster was slopping crème brûlée on my best dress.*

Why Cruise?

The woman looked at me with suspicion when I asked her how and why she chose to take her first cruise. My question was innocent enough, I am always curious as to why people choose to start cruising. Was it the romance of sailing the high seas? How about the excitement of visiting exotic locations? The charm of floating luxury offering up entertainment, fine dining, relaxation and pampering all within easy walking distance?

> *"I take a cruise so someone else has to cook and clean"* She finally responded.

Well, that was not the glamorous answer I had been expecting but she was only one person on a ship of 2500, so I decided to expand my research to see what other answers were on offer. The second person I asked, told me that he was a bit of a hypochondriac and the fact that a cruise ship has a fully equipped medical facility onboard, staffed with medical professionals, was his reason for sailing. He followed that up with a detailed explanation on how to properly sanitize a cabin. I figured a man with a hand sanitizer dispenser conveniently attached to his belt might be an expert on getting rid of pesky germs.

The third person told me that she took cruises so she only had to unpack and pack once while visiting various locations. Another response that left me underwhelmed.

Where were the answers relating to the allure of the oceans, the thrill of the adventure, the glamour?

"I did the math. A Mediterranean cruise would get me to six countries for a certain amount of money and I could not afford to travel to the same countries by land or air." said the man who was sharing a table at breakfast with my husband and me.

At least that was an answer that touched on an advantage to cruising.

"My in-laws paid for it." said another cruiser.

Well, that was an honest answer.

A choice line came from a fellow we met at one of the bars: *"They had me at free beverage package"* he commented as he indicated to the bar staff that another martini was required.

Once I decided to find out why people cruise, I was like a dog with a bone. For the next couple of years, I continued to pose the same question to people I encountered on various cruises. I then posted the question on cruising related websites and on my travel website.

I learned that some people decided to take a cruise based on the look of a ship. One of my favourite answers that fell into the "look of the ship" category, came from a fellow sitting beside us at trivia. He explained: *"On one of our Caribbean Island trips, we were staying in a less than stellar three-star hotel and we both had spent a couple of days in bed with food poisoning. By the evening of the second day, we finally felt well enough to drag ourselves out to sit on our balcony. We could see a cruise ship in the nearby port, all lit up and looking amazing. We saw people dining and heard the music playing. It looked so inviting that we decided that we might as well give cruising a try. We thought we would take our chances with seasickness, which at that particular moment, seemed preferable to food poisoning.   We never looked back once we took our first cruise."*

When I asked him if he ever worried that he might get food poisoning on a ship, he seemed surprised at the question and responded that it never entered their minds.

He was not the only person to tell me that seeing a ship arrive in a port or leave in the evening with the music playing and the lights twinkling, acted as an enticement to take a cruise. One couple told me that they had a time share in Puerto Vallarta and whenever they were on their balcony and saw that a ship was leaving, they would wave. To them, people on the ships were always toasting those onshore with their drinks and smiling. *"The people we could see at the ship's balconies always looked like they were having fun."* they told me, hence they decided to give it a go and see if it was indeed as enjoyable as it appeared. Apparently, it was, as by the time I spoke with them they had completed several cruises.

As time passed, and I obtained more and more responses to my question, I heard many similar responses. Based on a totally unscientific recording of replies, I have found that there are a large number of people who chose to take their first cruise because of a television show in the late 70's and 80's that focused on the romantic side of cruising. I was told by a number of individuals that they booked on cruise lines that offered singles activities or gatherings. This allowed them to meet other single people who had the money and the desire to travel.

I also found that there are three common responses:

1. People they knew were going on a cruise and they wanted to join them;
2. They saw an advertisement that was enticing (flyer, newspaper, internet, advertisement etc.); or
3. To celebrate a milestone event (wedding, honeymoon, anniversary, birthday, retirement).

The common thread responses were informative, but I was especially entertained by some of the more colourful answers:

1. *My ex-wife always wanted to go on a cruise and we never did, so when we divorced, I took a cruise and posted pictures galore on social media where mutual friends were sure to see them and comment;*
2. *My husband liked to camp with his parents so I booked a cruise knowing it was the one vacation they would not want to join us on;*

8

3. *Our neighbours went on a cruise and never stopped talking about it so we decided to go on one so we could brag about our cruise;*

4. *We heard they had activities and people onboard to look after kids. Since we had run out of people on land who would babysit our hyperactive kids, we took a cruise. We figured we could get one cruise under our belt before the cruise line banned our family. Surprisingly, the kids enjoyed cruising, were well behaved and we loved that we could relax when they were off doing activities geared to entertain children: and*

5. *I won the trip at a conference and being the winner, I had to be the one to go. I had a blast. I am now on my fourth cruise in six years. Fourth girlfriend as well so if you ever write a book about dating, shoot me an e-mail.*

No matter what the motivation, the basic reason for taking a cruise is because you have decided that it is the right vacation for you.

Starting to Cruise

Don't just pick any cruise, do a little research and select a sailing that meets your needs. Demographics and ship dynamics matter.

The first time I took a cruise was many years ago when planning a vacation with a friend. She suggested taking a cruise would be the perfect holiday. We were in our 20s and the idea arose from watching a television show where everyone seemed to find love on a cruise. Yes, as mentioned in the previous chapter, we fell into the category of people who chose to cruise because of a television show. We were single and based on what we saw on the program, cruising seemed to be a great way to meet people and to be an enjoyable holiday. We booked with high expectations and loads of anticipation.

This cruise, occurring pre-internet time, obviously should have been researched, or at a minimum, booked through a travel agent who could have offered us advice about cruise lines and their target demographics. We were young, anxious to take a cruise and not savvy enough to know we should do some type of research on cruising before booking. We assumed all cruises and cruise lines were the same. We packed and repacked with care and ensured we had the right mixture of clothing for those parties and dances we were sure we would be enjoying. I can say without doubt, I spent more time focused on my wardrobe than any other aspect of the cruise. Imagine our surprise when boarding, we kept encountering people our grandparents' age. At the check-in counters, the hallways, the elevators, the buffet and finally in the dining room, we were running into the senior crowd. Not a person under 60 was in sight unless they were part of the ship's crew. We searched bow to stern and within a relatively short period of time it became apparent that we had ended up on a senior's cruise. Pretty much everyone we met was in their late 60s, 70s or 80s. Amidst the sea of white and blue haired people, we stood out like sore thumbs. There was one flaming red-haired woman we knick-named Zelda who at age 67 was also on the hunt for a single man so we sometimes joined her at the bar. She was entertaining, witty and she enjoyed more action than we did.

By 10 pm each night the ship was quiet and there was not much in the way of nightlife. There were times we were the sole participants at late night events so by virtue of being the only guests awake, dressed and at the event, we won a number of give-away prizes. I became the proud owner of numerous cruise ship promotional pens. We were soon on a first name basis with many of the crew and even though the cruise was not what we had expected, we had a great time.

We were seated at a table for eight in the dining room and we found our dining companions to be much older than us. Our initial disappointment soon gave way to the pleasure of their company as we found them all to be well travelled, knowledgeable and the table conversation was interesting and lively. We may not have met any people in our age bracket, but we ended up being entertained and learning a lot. Bright and engaging, our fellow diners made the trip enjoyable, and we finished the holiday better informed than when we started. Best of all, we had developed a whole new appreciation for travelling with people outside of our age bracket.

At the end of our cruise, we both agreed we had a good time and the money spent had not been wasted. The scenery was amazing, the food excellent and the entertainment enjoyable. Overall it was a great experience. We committed to taking another cruise at some point but made a mental note to do advance research on the cruises we would take and ensure that the cruise fell within all our expectations. We had learned our first cruising lesson, it is not just about the destination and affordability, it is also about the on-board dynamics and demographics.

Check Out the Cruise in Advance

No matter how many times you tell yourself you will never forget, you might just forget. Worse still, you may make the same mistakes.

Having read the preceding story about my Alaskan cruise with a friend of mine, you would think I would remember the lessons learned and ensure that I did a little more research before my next cruise. But the recollection of my pre-cruise research failure had faded and when I was ready, and could afford to take another cruise, the passage of time had dulled my memory. Three girlfriends and I decided a short cruise around the Hawaiian Islands was in order. We were planning a vacation in Oahu and decided to tack on a short three-day, two-night cruise at the end. We would get to see the other islands, enjoy fabulous sunsets, music, dancing and dining. It sounded perfect. Best of all, the price was affordable since cruises of a week or more would have been a hardship on our wallets. To be honest, there is a lot to be said for short, inexpensive cruises that offer all inclusive food and beverages.

This time, before booking, my friend Bobbi, called and asked about the age group of the average cruiser on the cruise we had selected.

We were told that there was no guarantee but for this particular cruise, 30 to 40 was most likely the average age. Perfect!

Once again, this cruise was booked before the days of the internet. We had made our arrangements over the phone before we left on vacation and we were to pick up the tickets at a travel agent's shop in Oahu. After a few days of vacation, we went to the agency and met up with the fellow who sold us our packages. He gave us a flyer that had been printed for the cruise. The photo of two good looking, aged 30ish fellows standing at the railing of a ship pointing at an orange and red sunset assured us that this was the cruise for us and that we were going to have a blast.

As he was completing the last of the paperwork, he seemed a bit distracted by our joking about meeting guys and finally suggested that maybe there was a different cruise that would better suit us. Brenda, who having passed what she called the magical age of 30, wanted to meet someone and get married. She asked if there were going to be lots of guys on the cruise and he responded in the affirmative. Good enough for her said Brenda. He hesitated and looked like he wanted to say more, but then completed the paperwork. As soon as it was finished, he handed it over and we left.

As you may now suspect, the cruise was geared to same sex cruisers so clearly it was not the demographics we were anticipating. The cruise was not a disappointment as we had a fabulous time and many a laugh over the mix-up. Some of our fellow cruisers said the agent should have been a little clearer with us but I felt the cruise had in fact lived up to its billing. The ship was nice, the food excellent, the company convivial, the entertainment great and even the sunsets were as promised. It had been up to us to seek more information.

In response to people asking me how we could not have known, I usually confirm that this cruise predated the days when pamphlets advertised a cruise as gearing towards same sex cruisers and the advent of the rainbow flag on advertising. All I can say with certainty is that we enjoyed the cruise, met some fun people and we were reminded that researching a cruise in advance is always helpful. As for Brenda, she met a fellow in a grocery store seven months later and they were married within the year. They honeymooned on a cruise.

One last story about checking out your cruise in advance before I move on to the next topic.

When on a cruise and talking about lessons learned, a woman from Washington told me that she and her husband took a cruise with a line that geared its sailings to children. Not only was the ship they took a magnet for families filled with under 18 offspring, but they also booked their cruise for a July sailing, thereby ensuring that plenty of families would be onboard for their summer vacation.

"*Never again*" she sadly told me. "*There were little ones everywhere.*" The buffet was a disaster and she expressed great sympathy for the employees who spent a lot of time cleaning up messes that poorly supervised children created. She described the pool as a "*packed zoo*" and said all the public areas were filled with running bodies that always seemed to be crashing into people. She also spoke of constant noise and indicated that the ship never seemed to be quiet.

They had booked an inside cabin with the idea that they would seldom be in the room and could enjoy seating in the common areas (outside on deck or inside in public spaces). Unfortunately, those seats and/or loungers were always occupied either with a person or personal effects left to save chairs. Her dreams of lounging on a sun filled deck, quietly catching up on her reading, never came to fruition. They spent more time than intended in their cabin and regretting their lack of private balcony space.

She told me that prior to the cruise, she never gave a thought to the possibility that many children would be present, and lamented that when making their booking, she and her husband were careless about examining various cruising options. They should have known better. They had heard from friends that cruises gave good value for money and focused their attention on prices and port stops. "*I really should have done more research*" she said. I knew exactly what she meant.

Type of Cruise

I like the itineraries that have numerous port stops. This is the perfect vacation. You unpack, make yourself comfortable in your cabin and overnight the ship takes you to each new place. You get off for the day, do your sightseeing and then get back on the ship to get taken to the next place in style and comfort. It is the perfect way to travel.

Ronald – USA

***

Our family booked a cruise for us to celebrate our 40th anniversary. It was a surprise and meant to be a special treat since we never had a honeymoon. They booked us on a Mediterranean cruise that had lots of calls at ports. We were exhausted at the end of it. We felt like we never got to enjoy the ship.

Beverly – USA

We completed a trans-Atlantic sailing for our first cruise. We had a great time just enjoying the many sea days. It spoiled us. Now we prefer cruises that have lots of sea days with only a few ports of calls thrown in.

Glenda – England

***

We don't bother to get off the ships when we cruise. Why would we? The cruises have everything we need to enjoy ourselves. Great food, entertainment, onboard activities and more. We pay to cruise and that is what we do.
Conrad – England

As you can see from some of the comments I have received, people have distinctive feelings on what they want or will enjoy, from their cruising vacation. When examining your options, ask yourself what you want to see and do. For example, if you are looking to visit numerous European cities, a Mediterranean cruise that is port intensive would be just the ticket.

If you want to relax and enjoy the beauty of the ship without the hustle and bustle of numerous shore excursions, then look for an itinerary that offers up plenty of sea days.

When it comes to mapping out your vacation, be realistic about what you want to accomplish on your holiday. If your desire is to visit numerous European cities, focus your search on only those cruise itineraries that include the places you want to see. Don't be the person that looks back on your vacation with regret because you failed to see the places that really interested you. By narrowing your field of search, you can focus on the most suitable itinerary, price and cruise line.

If you want to try cruising but have no specific itinerary or activity in mind, then engage in a little internet sleuthing. There are many websites, groups and blogs that discuss all aspects of the cruising industry. Check some of them out and see if any of the comments offered provides information that will aid you in your decision.

When examining cruising options, it is also important to remember that you don't have to get off the ship at a port stop unless you choose to do so. There are always activities onboard to entertain you.

Travelling with Children

If you are looking to take a child friendly cruise, there are lines that either gear their sailings to families, or have a number of facilities onboard that include activities and entertainment for children. Ask about discounted or half fare prices for children, the availability of family cabins and whether there are clubs for children onboard. Also examine the port stops with an eye to what family activities and excursions might be available, affordable and of interest. Check as to whether babysitting is available.

You Are Special

My husband is a police officer and because of that we get a discount with some cruise lines. My sister is in the military and she seems to get discounts on ALL the cruise lines. Why is there a difference among cruise companies when it comes to giving out discounts?

Penny - USA

Penny's question is a good one as there is not one policy across all cruise lines on which professions qualify for a discount. Seniors, firefighters, police, military personnel, previous cruisers and groups are often given special rates. These specific percentage discounts, or onboard credits, are not always the same. Some cruise lines do not offer discounts to certain professions such as firefighters, while other lines do. Additionally, some lines may offer a discount to persons who have served in the military but attach a certain criteria to that benefit (such as they must have served for a specific period of time, honourable discharge, retirement, medical discharge etc.).

Cruise lines offer discounts for a wide variety of reasons so before booking, always check to see if you are eligible for a fare reduction. As a friend of mine always says *"If you don't ask, you don't get."* It is a simple matter of enquiring if you are eligible for a discount or other type of special when you are booking your cruise.

Age

Yes, there is a benefit to getting older and once you reach 55, you may be eligible for a senior discount. In fact, there may be times when mature discounts are offered for those 50 and over. Here is a random sampling of some cruise lines that offer senior discounts on various sailings:

Azumara	Carnival	Celebrity
Costa	Crystal	Cunard
Holland America	MSC	Norwegian
Oceania	Royal Caribbean	Silversea

(*Note: This list is not intended to be exhaustive.*)

As to what value a senior discount affords you is dependant upon the cruise line and the specific sailing. Generally, I have found that cruise lines will offer discounts between 5 and 15% but that can vary. Some offer a flat dollar value discount. There may even be themed cruises that offer up specials for lower or higher age groups such as diamond seniors at age 75 and up.

Employment

Another avenue to savings may fall under your current employment or work history. If you have worked in the military, had policing or firefighting careers, cruise lines have been offering special discounts for your service. Additionally, there may be other careers that cruise lines decide to honour. Personnel who worked during the covid crisis (such as hospital workers), are often touted as being personnel deserving of special treatment.

Repeat Cruisers

Brand loyalty deserves recognition, and you may be the beneficiary of discounts and specials if you have previously sailed with a cruise line. However, it is important to register for the loyalty program of each cruise line after you have taken your first cruise with that particular company. Each loyalty program is specific to that brand and cruises on other lines do not normally count unless there is a designated affiliation between plans.

Generally, you cannot register for a loyalty program until you have completed your first cruise with that line. Consequently, once you take your first cruise, make sure to register with the loyalty program as registration is free and you will receive benefits if you take another cruise with that same company. The benefit levels escalate with the number of cruises you take with a specific line. I am a fan of any free dry cleaning and/or clothes pressing, that may be part of a repeat customer reward while my husband favours the exclusive social gatherings.

Groups

Family or school reunions, weddings, celebrations of some type, work type affiliation cruises (such as military, police or firefighter sailings) etc. may be beneficial to you if you plan on booking a certain number of cabins for an event. If you have a group, you could be eligible for a group discount. The discounts vary according to the cruise lines and are always subject to change so I cannot list them here and be assured that the information will not change or be applicable to all sailings. Consequently, I mention the discount as it is absolutely something you should check into if you are booking a cruise. Verify directly with the cruise line by contacting their groups reservation desk or have your travel agent enquire on behalf of your group. In addition to possible savings on cabin prices, you may receive other benefits such as use of a private room for a meet and greet event or other perks.

Large Group Bookings

Always enquire as to what may be possible when booking for a large group. Such group bookings can garner cash back and free cabins so it pays to do comparisons as to what each cruise line will offer your group. For example, a large group of 100 cabins could generate almost $20,000 dollars and a number of free cabins. The money can be used to fundraise for your specific group. The cabins can be used as prizes for future events.

Once again, the rewards and benefits vary according to cruise lines, so I recommend that you and your group determine what type of cruise you want to take and then obtain quotes from various companies. It will be helpful to go to the cruise line armed with the information as to how large you anticipate the group to be and the type of cabins you will want. Try to book as far in advance as possible so that you have a choice of cruise lines and cabin availability. Additionally, there are some cruise lines that have a very small number of single cabins and you will want to have some of these available to your group.

Paying for Your Cruise

Many people express an interest in taking a cruise (or any vacation for that matter), but then lament that they cannot afford the cost. There are obvious solutions to this and paying for a cruise in installments is one of them. Available cruises are often posted several years in advance which gives you time to research where you want to go and what you want to see. You will also be able to price out your trip so you know the general overall cost.

Good news, you don't have to pay for your entire trip at the time you book unless you are booking within a 90 day of departure window, or the cruise is a special event (charter etc.). You will need to pay a deposit when you book and this deposit may be fully refundable or not, depending on the type of booking you make. I write more about the refundable/non-refundable deposits further on in this book.

Once you have put a deposit and booked a cruise, you can then decide whether you want to pay so much a month or put a certain amount of money into a travel fund and pay the remainder of the cost when final payment is due. Obviously other related costs, such as flights cannot be booked several years in advance but a general rule of thumb is to look at the current airline ticket cost and add 10% per year.

Final Payment

Final payment on your cruise is normally due within 90 days (or a 3-to-4-month window), of the cruise departure date.

I booked a Mediterranean cruise two years in advance and paid a little every month so that the cruise was fully paid for by the time the final payment was due. I also asked my family to give me cruise line gifts at Christmas and on my birthday. That way I had onboard credit on my cruise account. I had two years of planning and getting excited about my trip and the anticipation made the cruise all that much better.

Nicole – USA

Will I Get Seasick?

I choose the method of preventing seasickness based on whether or not it will work with the booze package I have purchased.

Melinda – Australia

Have you been invited to join your friends on a cruise but were reluctant to give it a try due to sea sickness concerns? What about ship-board wedding invitations or those reunion specials that sound like they will amount to a fabulous vacation? Are you interested but concerned that you might not do well onboard a moving vessel? You are not alone. I understand why people may have reservations about booking a cruise if they believe that they might get seasick. One of my friends is prone to motion sickness on any type of moving vehicle and although she would like to take a cruise, she does not want to spend the money only to find herself suffering from what the French call "mal de mer". Booking a holiday that might trigger your propensity for motion sickness seems to be the height of lunacy.

My friend is not alone in her concern about spending money on cruising when one already knows they are prone to motion sickness. Why book a holiday that might trigger your motion sickness and consequently turn out badly? As one person so succinctly put it: *"Who enjoys a pukefest?"*

But are there steps that can be taken to reduce, or eliminate the possibility that you will be seasick? In this chapter I try and answer this question and offer suggestions that may help you make a decision whether a cruise will work for you.

First let's define Sea-Sickness – what is it? It is basically motion sickness caused by the movement of the ship or boat. Symptoms can be feeling queasy, vomiting, dizziness, headache, burping, vertigo, dehydration, sensitivity to smells and generally feeling unwell. It sounds a little like a bad hangover without the enjoyable night before.

None of these are symptoms you want to experience when on vacation and certainly not things you find listed as cruising benefits in travel brochures. In my opinion, there are three scenarios that relate to people having concerns about a predisposition towards motion sickness:

1. Persons who have never cruised but who suffer/have suffered from any type of motion sickness (predisposition to motion sickness);

2. Persons who have cruised and suffered from motion sickness on the cruise; and

3. Persons who cruise because they have proactively taken preventative measures to prevent motion sickness before they even board the ship.

I will address those three categories in order.

Predisposition towards Motion Sickness

There are two types of people who suffer from motion sickness, those who almost always have problems and those who sometimes have problems. If you, like my friend, are prone to getting sick when riding on, or in, any moving vehicle, your fears are real and should not be dismissed. Your concerns stem from experience. Be it a car ride or other device that is tied to some type of motion (such as a swing), the prospect of going from feeling great to queasy is not something to embrace.

The second type of person is one, who like my husband, has been known to suffer from motion sickness but not all the time. This type of person may take a hundred trips and become ill on only a few of them. The possibility is there but the probability is an unknown.

Many years ago, we were in Puerto Vallarta during the month of February and my husband booked us onto a sunset cruise for Valentine's Day. It was a smaller boat with a total of 12 guests and a crew of three. Dan had been on a few smaller boat trips on that vacation, so he had no concerns. The trip started out well but the water was choppy and the boat was definitely rocking as we moved away from the sheltered shoreline and into deeper water. Dan was soon feeling the effects of the little boat's swaying motion and fortunately there was a washroom onboard with a huggable toilet. He spent most of the cruise being sick while I and our fellow guests downed margaritas and feasted on surf and turf. As the rest of us made merry, Dan was wallowing in abject misery, waiting for it all to end. At the conclusion of the cruise, I am not sure if he cared whether he returned to dry land or just died. Our memories of that Valentine's Day are distinctly different, and our enjoyment level sat at opposite ends of the fun spectrum.

Two years later, while in Acapulco, we went on a day cruise on a larger boat holding about 100 people. The turquoise sky offered up a delightful contrast to the blue green of the ocean which was calm and smooth as glass. As the sun shone down upon us, we enjoyed what most would deem to be perfect boating conditions. Shortly after leaving the dock, my husband began to suffer from increasingly strong waves of queasiness. Although in this instance he was not throwing up, he spent an uncomfortable time on the water. Once again, while I feasted, drank and participated in the revelry of the day, he delicately sipped water, nibbled on dry crackers supplied by the crew and anxiously awaited our return to land. If Dan always suffered from motion sickness, we would plan our activities to avoid it, but his onboard nauseousness tends to be intermittent with no discernable triggering factors other than he is on a boat.

Suffered from Motion Sickness on a Cruise?

When posing the question as to whether people have suffered from seasickness while on a cruise, I have encountered few people who answered in the affirmative. Since I met most of those on a cruise, I asked about their experience and what made them decide to cruise again. Some said that sufficient time had passed that the memory had faded but ALL of them stated that times had changed, and they had boarded the ships armed with modern medicine and greater knowledge about cruise ship stabilizers. I will cover these considerations a little further in this chapter.

I have met two people who had taken cruises and having suffered from seasickness, opted not to cruise again. In both those cases, their experiences were decades in the past. Neither was willing to give cruising another go.

Preventative Measures Against Motion Sickness

There are people who take cruises even though they have had negative experiences with motion sickness outside of cruising. I met one such woman on a trans-Atlantic sailing during the fall, when there is a higher possibility of inclement weather. She was sporting dual wrist bands and informed me that they came in assorted colours so she could colour co-ordinate with her outfit of the day. She further explained that she and a friend had wanted to try cruising but because both were predisposed towards motion sickness, neither wanted to risk booking such a holiday.

Eventually they attended a travel expo and were enthralled by the cruises on offer at different booths. When they expressed reservations about cruising to one of the travel agents handing out information pamphlets, he suggested that they visit a nearby booth that offered homeopathic remedies to combat seasickness.

I was curious as to whether the offerings of that booth were the incentive that led them to finally book a cruise. *"No, not at all"* she said laughing. Apparently, while discussing possible treatment/prevention options, the operator of the booth had told them that if they didn't want to try the homeopathic remedies, they could always ask their doctors to prescribe something. Armed with the knowledge that there were preventative options available, the woman and her friend booked a cruise as a holiday. Before they left on their trip, they each consulted with their doctors and boarded the ship armed with both prescription medication and assorted homeopathic remedies." *We were well prepared."* she told me. They fell into the category of persons who have proactively taken preventative measures before they even board the ship.

I was told that both loved their experience and the cruise I met them on, was their second cruise in that year. Her friend soon joined us and when I commented that she was not sporting any wrist bands, she told me that she preferred the much more discreet patch behind the ear. Both women indicated that they had encountered no adverse health problems on their first, or current, voyage.

If Seasickness is a Concern

As evidenced in the preceding paragraph, there are things that you can do or medication you can take that will help ensure you will enjoy your cruise. The season you cruise, the size of the ship, your cabin location, the food you eat and your level of preparedness are all important factors to mitigating a possible bout of motion sickness. The length of your first cruise is also something you can control.

Worried about how you will fare? Select a short cruise of three, four or five days. If you can, try and book your short trial cruise in the same type of water you might want to sail in on a longer cruise. For example, don't book a short river boat cruise if you want to try a longer ocean crossing as river and ocean sailings offer vastly different cruising experiences.

The Time of Year Can Impact Weather Conditions

Book your cruise for a geographical area and season when weather conditions are usually favourable. For example, do not book a Caribbean cruise during hurricane season. Fall storms in the Caribbean, Atlantic or along the North American eastern coastline, can develop and lead to course changes and rougher water. I may love towering waves and the thrill of a ship's bow rising and falling, but there are many who do not.

People have shared horror stories of storms at sea and almost all of them are tied to weather patterns that could easily have been predicted. One couple, who we met on a land vacation in the Mayan Riviera, told us about their one and only cruise experience. They booked a Caribbean cruise for their September honeymoon. They were enticed by the low cost of the cruise fare and the promise that if there were any hurricanes on the radar at the time of their cruise, the ship would simply reroute to avoid the problematic weather. What they were not told is that although the cruise line would reroute to avoid storms, the ship might still encounter rougher than normal seas and inclement weather. Their voyage was a series of rough waters and rerouting that ultimately resulted in them missing two port stops that they had really wanted to see. Their honeymoon memories are ones of seasickness and disappointment. Had they deferred their Caribbean cruise to the winter months; they would have found much better weather and less chance of rough waters.

Here is some general information regarding favourable weather conditions:

Africa East Coast	-	March to May and September to November
Africa North	-	March to May
Africa West	-	November to May
Alaska	-	July to August
Asia East	-	November to March
Asia West	-	November to March
Australia	-	November to February
Caribbean	-	December to April
Hawaiian Islands	-	May to June and September to mid December
Mediterranean	-	April to November
Northern Europe	-	May to September

You should also note that there are areas that will usually have choppy waters and it is expected that there will be greater movement on the ship. For example, the Tasman Sea or the Drake Passage are both known for rough seas so they may not be high on your list of potential destinations if you are worried about being seasick. Choose a geographical area and cruise itinerary that is most likely to have smooth sailing.

The Size of the Ship

Large cruise ships are quite unlike small boats so don't expect to feel the same type of movement or motion. Each offer a different experience when it comes to possible travel complications due to motion sickness. Wherein a small boat will roll and shift with the waves, cruise ships tend to be far more stable with less motion felt. There have been times after leaving a port, where we had no awareness that the ship had left the dock as the sailing was that smooth.

Larger cruise ships are equipped with stabilisers that will significantly reduce the motion of a ship. This is not to say that selecting the largest ship possible is the best option. Any cruise ship will have the capacity to reduce motion be it one with a tonnage of 228,08 or a medium size of 65,000 tons as most cruise ships have stabilisers. Having taken ship tours, I recall being told that these stabilisers extend on either side of the ship to prevent the rolling motion. On one tour, when asked the question of whether these stabilisers had the capacity to totally eliminate the motion, the crew member told us *"No, not in really rough seas, but it will significantly reduce excessive motion"*. He spent considerable time talking about the measures that cruise lines take to ensure passenger comfort and much to his credit, he spoke about all cruise lines in general working towards a common goal of a smooth sailing experience for their passengers. The take-away message was that the cruise lines do whatever they can to avoid rough seas and mitigate excess rolling and pitching on their sailings.

It is important to note that the weather and ship size can, and will, impact on the motion of a ship. You can't control the weather, but you can control the size of the ship you book for your vacation. If you have chosen a destination and season when there is the expectation that the weather and water will be calm, and you have likewise chosen a ship that has stabilizers and other mechanisms in place to help reduce the pitching and rolling of the ship, you have set yourself on a path towards a nausea free voyage. But there is more that you can do such as choosing your cabin location.

Location of Your Cabin

A lot of people cannot ride in the back seat of a car or bus and as such their placement in a moving vehicle is important to them. They still have to ride in the vehicle to get to where they are going, but they make sure they are in a front location to help them avoid being nauseous. Much like being a passenger in a car or bus, there are areas of a ship that are more suitable than others.

If you have experienced motion sickness on a ship or expect that you will be susceptible to being ill due to motion sickness, choose a cabin mid ship and mid deck level. As already mentioned in this book, cabins at the front or back of a ship tend to experience more motion while mid ship cabins are noted for being more stable.

Eating and Drinking

Modifying your behaviour is another way to put yourself on the road to an enjoyable cruise. Feasting and drinking are two activities people associate with cruises. The food served on cruises is generally excellent and quite often you will find that formal dining room meal selections, is very much like eating at an upscale restaurant every evening. Although the temptation to eat as much as you want may be strong, if you are prone to motion sickness, try and stick to smaller meals. You can eat a number of small meals throughout the day rather than three large meals.

Avoid the hard to digest foods or meals that are prone to giving you heartburn. Fried and/or fatty foods may upset your digestion so stick with the grilled, poached or broiled. These are not hardship meals; you will still be eating excellent gastronomic offerings.

Avoid strong smelling or spicy foods. Maybe this is not the best time to try raw oysters, kippers or that smelly cheese you heard so much about.

I love foods that have sauces and foods sporting hollandaise or bearnaise sauces are top of my yummy list. But those types of heavy cream sauces may not mix well with a delicate stomach. It is best to stick with lighter foods and if you really are prone to stomach upset, steer yourself toward foods that you know suit you well and have not previously caused stomach upset. If you do start to feel queasy, nibble on some crackers to help settle your stomach.

As tempting as making full use of your beverage package might be, boozing and cruising may not mix well for those prone to motion sickness. For people who may have a story or two about the room spinning after a night of drinking, the same feeling may come over you with less alcohol if the ship is moving through some choppy water. If you are anticipating a night of rough seas, avoid a night of heavy drinking.

Aids to Combat Seasickness

I was once on a Cunard cruise where the subject of sea sickness came up while we were in the pub playing trivia. The ship had enjoyed smooth sailing and one of my fellow guests had talked about how pleasant the trip had been in contrast to a previous cruise they had taken with another line. This guest attributed the velvety sailing to the captain and crew for their ability to keep things on an even keel and smooth. This prompted a gentleman from a nearby table to weigh in on the subject. "*Sea sickness has nothing to do with the ship and everything to do with the mind.*" he stated authoritatively. "*It is simply an issue of mind over matter. Tell yourself you are not sick and you won't be!*" Sharpish comments were traded and I, as the observer to the exchange, decided that as much as he might believe that the mind can control the body's reaction to movement, I would rather place my faith in modern medicine.

I have seen it all from the promotion of herbs and vitamins to help reduce nausea to over the counter or prescription medication. There is a plethora of anti nausea aids available and on a ship, you will find a number of people sporting wrist bands, earrings or patches, all of which are designed to eliminate or reduce motion sickness. If you did not bring anything with you, a trip to the ship's medical facility will usually result in you being given some medication to aid you. I have seen nonprescription anti nausea medication freely available on board a cruise ship with no cost to the passenger and going to pick up such medication did not result in a charged visit to the medical facility. The one downside to taking prescription medication is that it may make you drowsy so always look at the list of side effects when faced with various medication options.

Rest and Relaxation

This may sound like a given when on a cruise that is supposed to be a vacation, but a lot of times people go from activity to activity and do not make time to simply relax. If you start to feel unwell, try some deep breathing exercises and a little rest and relaxation. Sometimes just laying down and focusing on a focal point in your cabin may help you.

If you start to feel panic for any reason, place a light object in your hand and extend your arm out to the right as if pointing to something in the distance. Slowly bring your arm back to the front of you and switch the item to your other hand. Then extend that arm out to the left as far as it will go. Slowly bring it back to the center in front of your body and switch hands again. Repeat the entire exercise for ten to fifteen minutes. Keep switching the item you are holding from right to left and back again. This should help calm your feeling of panic.

Travel Agent Angst

Having had an unfortunate experience, I learned firsthand that a bad travel agent can ruin a trip before it even begins.

You have now chosen to take a cruise and it is time for a decision as to whether you want to book your trip directly with the cruise line or use a travel agent. How you book your trip is a personal choice and generally relates to your comfort level in making travel arrangements and specifically, your personal knowledge about booking cruises. If you decide to use a travel agent, make sure that you choose an experienced specialist in cruise bookings.

Most people who have used travel agents have formed an opinion about their experience. I have heard everything from glowing recommendations to less than flattering assessments. I once received a rather ambivalent recommendation from someone who wrote the following about their travel agent: "*She manages to get the job done and to date, she has not screwed us over.*" Hardly a ringing endorsement that the agent may have hoped for, nor a comment designed to have me quickly put that agent on speed dial. Over time, I have come to learn that not everyone holds travel agents in high regard and some people are just undecided. I believe that there are great travel agents working in the field of cruising and if you find one, use them and recommend them to others.

Excellence deserves recognition.

For the most part, I like to handle my own travel arrangements as I research places and travel options extensively and I am extremely particular about my transportation needs. However, I am always happy to seek the knowledge of those who have broad experience and industry expertise. Therefore, I am not averse to booking through a travel agent or transferring a booking I have already made to an agent, if I feel it will be beneficial to me. In addition to finding deals, cruising travel agents will often give incentives for booking with them. Onboard credit, a bottle of wine in the cabin, flowers, chocolate covered strawberries or other onboard treats have all been offered up for booking through certain agents or their affiliated travel company.

You may ask when, in the booking process, is it advantageous to use an agent? The answer is simple: at any time. For example, in relation to cruising, booking with an agent from the beginning, can help snag preferred cabins, or garner group rates because the agent has put together a group. But if you want to start by making your own booking and consider transferring it to an agent later, that also works. One word of warning though, some cruise lines have time limits as to when a cruise booking can be transferred so always check for time restrictions (such as transfers within 30 days).

In my case, I specifically like to check out options such as changing or upgrading cabins when final payment dates get closer. This is the time when people, who have placed a deposit on that cruise, start to cancel their bookings before cancellation penalties kick in, thereby releasing cabins previously unavailable. I write more on this subject later so I will not delve into the upgrading cabin process at this time. Suffice to say, about three months or so before the cruise departure date, there is a good possibility that you will be able to upgrade your cabin at a reduced cost. In order to take advantage of this opportunity, I need control of my booking to make a change, or, I need to be working with a really great travel agent who will keep on top of possible upgrades or sale events. In short, I want an agent who will contact me immediately, or follow-up quickly when I notify him or her that I have found a special, as these types of last-minute deals are time sensitive.

Because this book focuses on cruising, my comments re travel agents refer specifically to cruising. There are specialists in all areas of travel from the simple all-inclusive Caribbean get-a-ways to the more exotic African safaris. Finding an agent who is experienced and knowledgeable in the type of trip you want to take, is simply being smart. You want to ensure you get the best advice and information possible and be confident in the booking process. Cruise specialists can be a treasure, and in my opinion, they are worth their weight in gold.

When I speak of a cruise specialist, I am referring specifically to a travel agent who focuses on cruises and/or cruise tour combinations. I am not describing someone who merely processes cruise bookings along with a myriad of other travel. Rather I am speaking of an agent who understands the cruising industry, is knowledgeable about the way cruise lines operate, and they know when to look for sales and discounts. They have taken courses or information sessions offered by cruise lines and they also have training certificates issued by various cruising companies. Usually, these are people who like and take cruises themselves, so they have both work and personal experience on which to draw upon when rendering their services. Most importantly, they have working relationships with staff who are employed by various cruise lines. This is important as they will be notified in advance of upcoming sales and promotions. They can, in turn, check to see if those promotions would apply to existing customers. Specifically, they will know whether these new deals or specials could be pertinent to their currently booked clients or to new bookings only.

Cruise prices can rise and fall like the tides and specials can be added as booking incentives at any time. Beverage packages are a prime example. I have been booked on cruises and seen specials advertised by the cruise line offering "free" beverage packages. Most often, those types of specials can be added to your existing booking at no extra fee with a simple call to the cruise line by you (if you booked directly with the cruise line), or by your travel agent. A great agent has a listing of people and cruises she/he has on the books and seeks out the deals before their customers even know that a sale is taking place. As mentioned, I write more on sales and booking the cruise later in this book but for now, I will focus on the importance of choosing a travel agent you believe has the cruising knowledge and skill to suit your interests. I had a horrible experience with a travel agent who was chosen based on a family affiliations/friendship with one of my fellow travellers and it was a learning experience.

When Things Go Wrong with an Agent

I once took a cruise with a small group. We met prior to booking to jointly decide on the itinerary most attractive to us, the price range and which cruise line to use. Armed with booklets we had all picked up from various travel agencies, we spent an enjoyable evening of dinner, drinks and discussion. Our gathering was convivial, and we reached a consensus as to which cruise best met our needs.

It was at that point that one individual announced that they had "*promised*" our cruise booking to a certain travel agent. I had no feelings one way or another about travel agents, so I thought nothing of the announcement. Although we subsequently agreed we would all obtain quotes from different agents and go with the lowest price, it later came to pass that to avoid conflict, we went with this person even though the price quoted was not the lowest.

I subsequently learned that this suggested travel specialist, who I will call "X", was loosely tied through a marriage to the person who had proposed them to be our agent. I was also told that as opposed to being experienced in the travel field, "X" had recently graduated from a tourism and travel program at a local college. I never confirmed the accuracy of that information because hearing about their reported relationship or background set off no alarm bells with me. At that time, I thought that a travel agent, if trained and licensed, would have the necessary expertise or interest to get us the best deal and cruising perks. I was wrong.

I would like to say that our booking and trip went smoothly but that was not the case. There were several issues that arose, and I could spend the next one hundred pages detailing the problems and frustrations that became associated with this holiday. Problems that had nothing to do with the cruise line, ship or itinerary and much to do with the actions of the agent and the person who recommended them.

By simply being handed the booking, "X" appeared to have no incentive, nor inclination, to do price matching with the lower deals we had found. Additionally, as cabin sales and specials arose, nothing was offered to us. As the whole booking process started to unfold and problems arose, I questioned why we had gone with "X". I was informed that the person who had proposed "X" would be "*upset*" if we went with anyone else. By the actual cruise date, there were a number of issues that surfaced but I will refrain from detailing them all in this chapter because my emphasis is on choosing an agent that will focus equally on all the clients in a group and with an intended goal of getting the best deals possible.

This incident affected the way I book travel. To this day, I have not experienced that lack of professionalism from any other travel agent, but the occurrence presented a learning opportunity. I choose my travel agent based on my knowledge of their skills and not because someone decides they want to use a certain person. There have been times I have booked with a travel agent someone else has chosen/recommended, but I only do so if I am satisfied with that agent's knowledge and skill level. Thankfully, most of the recommendations made by friends, are based on previous experience with knowledgeable agents and not some nebulous family relationship.

Why am I rehashing a story from over a decade ago? I want to ensure that people spend time choosing the method of booking a cruise that best suits them. If you want to manage your own booking, book your cruise directly with the cruise line. If you want to book through a travel agent, ensure you book through an agent who specializes in cruising or who works for an agency that has specialists available to guide them. If you have doubts about a travel agent, change your agent. Remember, you can remove your cruise booking from an agent (if no time or booking constraints exist).

An experienced travel agent will ensure that they are on the lookout for travel deals and sales. On board credit, beverage packages, gratuities, better cabins, free wi-fi, all are possible if you and your agent work together to search for, and take advantage of, deals that arise. Things that I do:

1. Never pay for your cruise in full until shortly before the final payment date;
2. Monitor the cruise line's website and cruise related chats sites for news of deals or specials. If you see a special, take

a screen shot and call your travel agent (or the cruise line if you booked directly), and see if you qualify for the deal;

3. Never be afraid to call your travel agent to ask about specials or price drops;

4. The cabin category you initially book, does not have to be the cabin you end up in. I have gone from a regular balcony cabin to a suite and on two occasions, a two-bedroom family suite for a small increase in fare;

5. Know the differences in cabin categories and what amenities are associated with each category;

6. I like to electronically save images of the deck plans of the ships on which I am booked. That way I can easily reference different cabins and locations when rooms become available;

7. I examine those deck plans and make a list of preferred cabin numbers which I then keep handy. There are times that cabins in the same category have slightly better positioning or larger balconies;

8. Pay attention to the location of your cabin (more on this point to come);

9. Never be afraid to question advice, a decision or request a second opinion about the availability and eligibility of a cruise perk; and

10. If you are dissatisfied with the actions (or inaction), of your agent, talk to their supervisor and if possible, move your booking.

Choose Your Travel Companions Carefully

I travelled with a woman who was an absolute horror. At the end of the cruise, as we were all saying our farewells, the only thing that got me to a polite goodbye was my inner voice telling me "I never have to travel with this bitch again".

The most common problems encountered on a vacation are things that can be prevented or avoided by a little pre-trip planning and a great deal of communication. In this chapter, I address one of the most important elements of a successful trip: your travel companion.

If travelling with an immediate family member you live with, you are pretty much aware of what their interests are and what you anticipate doing. These are people you know. But travelling with friends or relatives with whom you do not live, needs a little more thought and a lot of communication. Your cruise vacation is your holiday. It is your time to do what you want to do and generally relax. Make sure you take the necessary steps to have a strife free vacation.

At the top of my trip list to prevent having your vacation going to crap is knowing the person/people with whom you are going to cruise. In my opinion, it is one of the most important components of a successful trip. I hear stories about cruise companions who drove each other crazy and ruined trips due to interpersonal conflicts. You may not be able to do anything about the annoying person interrupting a show in the theatre or the loudmouth on your shore excursion, but you can choose your cruising companions and thus you have some control over your own destiny in this regard.

Know the Person

The party animal who likes to get wasted and then get naked might be hysterical at an isolated cottage party but a huge embarrassment on a cruise ship. The book worm who parks their butt on a bed in the cabin and buries themself in the latest best seller is hardly the fun companion you envisioned if you anticipated a friend to join you in ship-board activities or on various shore excursions. Conversely, the person who dreams of a vacation where they can just sit, relax and catch up on their reading will hardly enjoy being on a whirlwind, port intensive, cruise with little down time. Are you a museum dweller or a speedy gazelle who runs to as many points of interest as humanly possible? Nature lovers versus urban explorers. Night owl or early bird. It is critically important to talk through your expectations and how you see your vacation unfolding.

On a 2007 cruise, while sitting by myself eating breakfast, I was joined by a woman and we struck up a conversation. Her story was tragic, and I was moved by her situation. She and her husband had always wanted to take a cruise, but they were farmers and over the years, they spent their disposable income raising their family and making improvements to their farm.

Their children were grown and had left the nest when her husband was diagnosed with cancer. As he was undergoing treatment, they decided that they would book their dream vacation, a cruise, to coincide with the projected end of his treatment. She told me that they realized the circumstances surrounding her husband's health had shown them that time was limited, and they needed to start doing the things they always dreamed of doing *"in the future"*.

Sadly, eight weeks before the cruise, her husband passed away. The cruise was paid for and involved a non-refundable fare but due to the circumstances, the cruise line would allow another person to take the place of her husband. The woman invited her sister-in-law to go on the cruise with her. Unfortunately, they were not compatible travellers and the woman relating the story to me was clearly not having a good time. She was an early bird who liked to rise at dawn, have breakfast, and partake in many of the onboard activities. Her sister-in-law was a night owl who liked to rise mid morning and did not enjoy group events. She took pleasure in being solitary and preferred late nights in the casino. It was clear that although they were both on a trip that they should be enjoying, their different personalities and interests were causing conflict.

Communicate Your Expectations

Telling your travel companion(s) what you want to do and see will help establish expectations. Even when you know the people with whom you are travelling, it is essential that you are up front about what you anticipate for the cruise and specifically, costs associated with the cruise and shore excursions. Talking about physical limitations, phobias or fears will also provide clarity. There is no point booking that spelunking shore excursion with someone who has a phobia about caves or signing up for horseback riding on a beach with a person who fears horses.

Be Honest – Just Say No

If I had a dollar for every time I heard a person say, "*I did not want to do* [something] *but I did not want to say no*", I would have a lot more money and taken a lot more trips. Just because you want to go on a vacation does not mean you have to accept a cruise or shore excursion that will have you doing and seeing things that you do not want to do. Do not go along with an activity if you are going to resent the location, time and/or money spent. Decide if you are comfortable with the compromise or feeling coerced into an activity.

> *Some friends and I decided to take a Caribbean cruise. Three of us wanted to do an ABC cruise (Aruba, Bonaire and Curaçao), but our fourth friend talked us into a different cruise that had only two port stops. Neither stop was one we wanted to visit. The cruise was fun but we felt like we had*

been cheated by not going to the places we wanted to go. Next time my best friend and me are picking our cruise and sticking with it.

Melodie - USA

You are Not Attached at the Hip

I love to visit art museums. I could spend an entire day in a museum that specializes in portraits. Once in the gallery, I may focus on a painting that captures my attention and I can easily spend an hour examining a particular work of art. I would consider that a perfect shore excursion. My husband and many of my friends, would judge such a museum visit to be a form of hell, to be avoided at all costs.

If you don't share a passion for an activity, it would not be an enjoyable outing. If you really wanted to visit some specific place, and missed out on it to engage in an activity that you were not keen on, you will regret your choice. Do what you want to do even if you may be doing a shore excursion without your travel companions.

That segues to my next point: Choose travel companions that will understand if you decide to engage in an individual activity. Travelling together does not mean that you must do all your activities together.

Be Prepared to Compromise

In the previous paragraph I talk about doing activities (that you would really like to do), on your own if necessary, so you can look back on your holiday without regret. In this paragraph, I speak to the difference between surrendering and compromising. Don't give up something that you really want to do, because you feel pressured to do so. But reaching a compromise about an activity, whether it is on the ship or on a shore excursion, is a different situation.

I once attended a conference in Northern Ireland and invited my husband to join me. He arrived in the city with a list of the 100 best pubs of Northern Ireland while I had a booklet identifying the famous churches of Belfast. Prior to the start of my conference, I wanted to get some touring in and obviously, churches were on my mind while Dan was focused on pubs. Clearly our interests were not aligned, and a little give and take was necessary. I chose my top "must see" churches based on architectural design while my husband selected his choice of pubs based on historical importance. We visited the major buildings on our respective lists and then went our separate ways. Later on in the week, when I was at my conference, Dan continued to visit the places he wanted to see. At the end of the week, I had seen twelve churches and five pubs. Dan had visited an impressive twenty-eight pubs and five churches. We were both happy.

Beware of the Divisive Travel Companion

Divisive travel companions are stress boosters. They create havoc and division in a group. They are unhappy if they don't get their way and spend a great deal of time and energy behaving badly. Whether they engage in making passive/aggressive comments, controlling conversations, giving you the silent treatment or simply speaking negatively about you to others, their actions can ruin your vacation. If you find you have someone in your group who is feeding negative energy, you have three choices. You can:

1. Ignore their behaviour;
2. Speak with them about your concern; or
3. Avoid them.

Never let an individual actively ruin your entire trip. Once you identify the problem, decide how you want to handle it, so the remainder of your vacation does not disintegrate. It is also important to remember that conflict between two people can negatively impact on other members of your group.

> *I was on a cruise where we had one woman who had a hate on for me. Her constant sniping made things awkward for me and made the rest of the group feel like they needed to take sides.*
>
> *(Name Withheld)*

***

> *We were regularly seated at a table for ten in the main dining room. One of the women at the table was clearly annoyed with another. Her animosity towards that other person made the rest of us feel uncomfortable and her snide comments and nasty looks made us think less of her as opposed to the woman she was talking*

about. When the cruise was over, we stayed in contact with the woman she talked about but not her. People don't realize the impact their behaviour has on others, especially if they create an unpleasant atmosphere.

Jackie - Israel

Ship Size - a Matter of Preference

This ship is so big, I lost my wife this morning and still have not found her. With any luck this will continue until we dock.

(Overheard on an elevator of a cruise ship).

There are times that the size of the ship is determined by the itinerary that you have chosen. For example, an exploration of the Galapagos Islands pretty much assures you that you will be on a small ship. However, there are popular itineraries, such as Caribbean or Mediterranean cruises, that will offer you a wide variety of ship sizes to choose from and you will always enjoy a greater selection of itineraries.

All ships are not created equal. Larger, smaller, older, newer, traditional, innovative, the list goes on. Cruising ships come in all sizes and shapes. When making a decision on what cruise you want to take, you will be faced with all kinds of choices about the cruise line and the size of the cruise ship. I don't expect anyone to immediately know what type of ship they want to sail on, as in my opinion, you should experience various sized ships.

How do you determine the size of a ship you want to book?

Some people look at the physical size of the ship, while others look at the number of passengers carried. Determining the physical size of a ship is fairly easy. The overall length of a cruise ship is established by measuring the maximum length between the bow and stern of the ship while the width is determined by measuring the widest point of the ship. Therefore, you have a set amount of space in which to put passenger cabins, restaurants, shops, facilities, crew accommodation etc.

I am going to provide examples, selected at random, to demonstrate the difference in the sizes between cruise ships:

Ship	Length	Width
Crystal Mahler	135m/443ft	12m/39.37ft
MS Koningsdam	285m/935ft	32m/105ft
Queen Elizabeth	293m/961.29ft	32m/105ft
Carnival Breeze	306m/1004ft	37m/121.29ft
Celebrity Edge	306m/1004ft	39m/128ft
MSC Seaview	324m/1059.71ft	43m/141.08ft
Norwegian Escape	326m/1069.55ft	42m/137.80ft
Disney Dream	339m/1,112.0ft	41m/134.51ft
Enchanted Princess	330m/1083ft	47m/154ft
Allure of the Seas	360m/1181.10ft	64m/210ft

As you can see, there is a noticeable difference in size. The *Crystal Mahler* has a fairly intimate passenger capacity of approximately 106 while the *Allure of the Seas* can host an impressive 8565 passengers or more. That makes a distinct difference in the conditions on the ship and how busy it will be embarking and disembarking.

Bigger ships offer up more space in common areas and usually have a greater variety of things to see and do onboard. Waterslides, go carts, zip lining etc., the cruise lines have come up with impressive and diverse activities to keep their passengers entertained. The bigger the ship, the more things to do and the more people doing those things. If you like variety, the larger ships will usually provide the greater number of activities. Consequently, these ships can also be busy with many people getting on and off the ship on embarkation day, port stops and at the conclusion of the cruise. You will also find larger crowds at the shows, buffets, pools, spas and common areas.

Smaller ships usually provide a more intimate setting and there are people who swear by them. They enjoy getting to know people and seeing the same faces around the ship. One couple we cruise with, prefer the smaller ships as they feel it gives them a sense of community and the crew working in the different venues can get to know them.

On the other side of the coin, a fellow cruiser from New York, told me that the bigger the ship the better he likes it. He says that he feels uncomfortable on a smaller ship. He knew from his first cruise that bigger was better and liked that he was sailing with thousands of other people. After he had five or six cruises under his belt, he tried a small ship cruise and although he acknowledged some obvious benefits, he told me that he did not enjoy the cruising experience as much as he had on the larger ships. He liked the anonymity of a larger vessel and the array of offerings with respect to onboard activities and shopping.

At a recent family party, I was speaking with family members who told me they also preferred bigger ships. They informed me that they had just sailed on a smaller vessel and found it to be more intimate. They kept running into and chatting with the same people. Lovely at first but after awhile, they longed for the privacy associated with being unrecognized. As one explained to me, she had left the cabin to find a quiet place to read as her husband was watching a movie. She said that on larger ships, there are always nooks and crannies to tuck yourself away or best of all, a library/reading area to enjoy. Trying to read in a public place on a small ship proved to be more difficult than she had anticipated: "*I am not unfriendly, but on a smaller ship, people see you as a familiar face because they keep running into you. They feel like they should talk to you, even when you are trying to have a little quiet time. It is difficult to be inconspicuous.*"

Another factor to consider when deciding on what size ship to take, is the ability of the ship to dock at a port. Some smaller ships are able to dock closer to a city center while larger ships may end up being berthed/docked further away or tethered offshore. We recently had a stop in Bora Bora removed from our ship's itinerary when the country decided to restrict the size of the cruise ships visiting.

I confess to having no preference as I find there are benefits to both large and small cruise ships. But I suggest that people think about what they enjoy in general and translate that to what size ship will most closely match their expectations.

People often post pictures and comments about their cruising experiences. A little internet research should secure information on what people thought of the ships and the activities that are offered. Photographs and deck plans will also demonstrate facilities that are available. Photos of chairs packed by a pool versus photos of a smattering of deck chairs in a small decking area of a ship with no pool can help with the decision making. Before I get inundated with e-mails from people who state that you can't always trust internet reviews, I acknowledge that what one person finds enjoyable, another may not. That is why I suggest you spend a little time doing your research and visit more than one site. Pay particular attention to photographs that are posted.

Sometimes sorting through conflicting information can be confusing. When helping a friend look for information as to the best size ship to help with claustrophobia, I asked experienced cruisers for their take on the most effective size ship to consider if one was claustrophobic. Here is an example of some of the advice I received:

Response #1

If your friend is claustrophobic and finds large crowds problematic, then he should choose a smaller cruise ship with fewer passengers and less crowded venues.

Response #2

Regarding your claustrophobic friend, he should consider booking a larger ship where he will have plenty of space and the surroundings give the feeling of openness.

Response #3

I don't think ship size matters as much as cabin size. Tell him to check out the cabin sizes and pick the ship with the biggest cabins.

Response #4

If your friend wants to feel less crowded, tell them to book a cruise on a medium to large ship and then keep on a late schedule. Eating in the second sitting of fixed dining is less busy. Going to the casino or bars late at night means a lot fewer people. Deck loungers under the stars are plentiful. Think late, late, late.

Response #5
I have tried all the different sized ships from the biggest to the smallest and each have their good and bad points and no matter the size, if someone feels claustrophobic, they will feel that way on any size of ship.

Tell him to pick the size of ship that suits him. If he likes a huge ship with all the bells and whistles, tell him to book on a big ship. Those giants of the waters always have a ton of things to do with numerous eateries and bars. If one space is too crowded, he can move on to another.

The smaller ships have less activities and usually don't have multiple restaurant options for their passengers, but they offer calmer, quieter venues and to me, they feel less frenzied and busy.

Both large and small sized ships support different offerings so it will always come down to what he finds in any given space on the day, and at the time, when he goes there.

All Cabins Are Not Created Equal

Most people can talk about the usual cabin choices of inside, ocean view, balcony or suites. But in reality, cabins also vary according to location and services attached. Think carefully on your cabin choice.

"Come on in and have a drink." said our hostess. We had met her and her husband on a cruise at one of the port information talks. We struck up a friendly conversation which continued after the talk. We ended up going for coffee and eventually, we decided to dine together later in the week. They invited us to their cabin for a pre-dinner drink.

Entering their cabin, I was amazed at the spaciousness of it and astounded by the larger size of their angled balcony. What type of cabin was this? Over drinks I learned that it was the same category cabin we occupied. Further discussion revealed that we had paid the same price. How can that be I wondered? This was my aha moment when I discovered that all cabins in the same category are not necessarily created equal.

From that pivotal moment, I came to the realization that selecting a cabin was not as simple as it first appears. Obviously, a little research is involved beyond the basic "want".

What is a basic want you ask? It is the minimum you will accept in a cabin. For example, I like to relax with a book when sitting on a balcony and my husband, a retired firefighter, always ensures he has two methods of exiting from the cabin in event of an emergency. As such, we understandably gravitate towards cabins that have balconies. Pretty simple want: we must have a balcony cabin.

Having learned that all cabins or balconies in the same category are not identical, I now take a look at the deck plan before booking and decide what looks biggest. Cruise ships are not all shaped the same with many having transition areas that change the lines of the ship. This usually occurs mid ship and I jokingly refer to this as the battle of the bulge. Cabins at the juncture of where the ship is increasing or decreasing its width, might have odd shapes or differently configured balconies. Consequently, a row of cabins may have slightly differing sized cabins and balconies.

On a long cruise, that extra 10 square feet might make all the difference in your comfort. That angled balcony may just give you the extra space to have four chairs and be able to enjoy outside private space with friends. Having a small sofa versus a chair can transform your cabin interior from minimal seating comfort to a great place to lounge or recline.

There are other considerations when choosing your cabin and those are categories of balcony cabins that you pay more for in order to have "perks" such as a concierge service. Your cabin is the same size and has the same look as other cabins but you also get priority boarding, afternoon hors d'oeuvres, your shoes shined, first choice for dinner reservations and other considerations. For me, I want the largest room I can get for the best price. I am not sure the upgrade in service will actually enhance my vacation as I have found the cabin service on almost all cruise ships to be very good to exceptional. That being said, I have friends who swear by upgraded services and I respect their choices. So, for more money, they get the same size and outfitted cabin but a more enriched experience in relation to the personal services offered.

Location, Location, Location

Let's talk about where your cabin is located on the ship. I like the cabins at the back of the ship. Often referred to as Sunset Veranda or Aft cabins, these balcony rooms allow the cruiser to view the wake of the ship unencumbered by any blockage or restrictions imposed by being situated in a balcony cabin on the side of the ship. I love to sit out on a lounger and watch the wake of the ship. The downside is there is supposedly more movement at the rear and for those who suffer from motion sickness, you may want to seek an area closer to the middle of the ship, where experts say there is less movement.

In the Introduction of this book, I wrote about being in a storm in a forward cabin and that cruise is, to this very day, one of my favourite sailing experiences. We had managed to upgrade from a balcony cabin located on deck 8, to a two-bedroom with living room, family cabin on deck 7. Our cabin was huge and the cost to upgrade at the last minute was very reasonable. Being very near the front of the ship, meant we experienced more motion and so the bow rising and falling in rough weather was very noticeable. As mentioned in my chapter entitled *Will I Get Sea-Sick*, if you feel that motion sickness might be an issue for you, avoid the cabins in the front and rear of the ship. Once again, cabins with the same price and category, offer up different experiences due to their location with mid ship cabins noted for being less prone to noticeable motion.

If you have mobility issues, and require an accessible cabin, almost all cruise ships offer those type of cabins. However, if you are mobile but not comfortable walking long distances, please take time to look at the deck plan to see how close your cabin will be to the stairs or elevators. Cabins located in certain areas of the ship may mean you have a bit of a distance to walk to get to stairs or elevators so choose your cabin according to your physical abilities. For me, one of the side benefits of a sunset cabin at the rear of a ship is the additional exercise I get walking to the stairs mid ship. I sometimes get my 10,000 steps in by walking to and from the cabin numerous times during the day.

Port or Starboard

Cabin placement on port or starboard side of a ship is also a consideration. For those unfamiliar with those terms, the port is the left-hand side of the ship if you are standing on the ship facing the bow, and the starboard is the right-hand side of the ship. If you have two cabins, equal in size, category and price, but located on different sides of the ship, take a look at what you may be facing and/or seeing when in port or sailing.

Previously, when sailing into Venice, I would always take a cabin on the starboard side of the cruise ship as the view sailing past the famous St. Mark's Square was excellent. There was always so much to see. Likewise, sailing into most ports, the starboard side of the ship is most often dockside. If you like to watch the happenings ashore, a cabin on the starboard side would be your choice. But those cabins will be noisier so if you prefer a water view, and quieter location, the port side might be your location of choice. Of course, this only holds true if there is not a massive ship docked right beside you on the port side. If that happens you will find yourself staring at people on the ship "next door" and possibly be hearing noise emanating from activities on the neighbouring ship.

What is Near Your Cabin?

The cabin proximity to certain venues is also a consideration as our friends learned on one cruise. They were both light sleepers and prefer absolute quiet. They had taken a cabin that was located under one of the ship's restaurants and every morning they were greeted to the sounds of moving chairs scraping along the deck and the conversations of those early risers. They felt they had no privacy when on their balcony and declared that they would never book a cabin on an upper deck that was located under a restaurant, bar or lounge. Similarly, another couple contacted me to tell me that they had inadvertently booked a cabin near a smoking area and vowed that would be the last time they made that mistake. They complained that there was always noise and the occasional whiff of smoke.

Keep a List of Cabin Experiences

I keep a list of the pros and cons of each type of cabin I occupy as it comes in handy when booking future cruises. For example, in the fall of 2022, I booked a forward family cabin in the bow of a ship. It was a very large, but noisy cabin as the sounds of banging was constant. My husband is a light sleeper and he kept waking to the persistent, loud, battering sounds. I made a note to ensure I never booked that cabin again.

I cannot stress strongly enough that location is a key consideration in ensuring you enjoy your cabin. Once you have decided on the class of cabin and the deck you prefer, have a look at what facilities are located around your cabin. For example, some cruise lines offer up self serve laundry rooms and those are always high traffic areas and busy. On a positive note, those ships with laundry rooms usually have operating hours to ensure people occupying cabins nearby are not treated to the sounds of washers and dryers operating 24/7.

Asking people the type of cabin they like and why, is likely to get you 20 different responses as the reasons for their choices are tied to their tastes, preferences or budget. I mentioned that we will always book a balcony cabin while we have friends who routinely book inside cabins because they find them cheaper, quieter and better for sleeping. The savings on booking an inside cabin can be considerable and if you are not bothered as to whether you have a balcony or window, then take advantage of the savings.

While on the subject of interior cabins, check to see whether the cruise line you are considering has virtual balconies in their inside cabins. Although not actual step outside balconies, these offerings are HD displays that mimic balconies or windows and offer up outside views. You can even enjoy the sounds of the great outdoors by way of a sound system with self controlled volume. The "view" is usually a feed from a camera placed on the ship (front or back), and allows the viewer to see what the weather is like, port entry etc.

Cabin type must always be paired with cabin location. I recommend that people go online and look at the ship's deck before selecting a cabin. NEVER allow a travel agent to select a cabin for you unless you have absolute faith that they know your likes and dislikes, or you have had a fulsome discussion about cabin options. A good travel agent will always review cabin preferences with you and be able to talk to you about the location and benefits of potential cabins on offer. Never be too shy to ask questions about the different type and locations of cabins and ask your agent or cruise line representative to list the benefits or concerns associated with the various cabins.

If you are part of a group and cabin selection is limited, or the ship is almost full, you may not have a lot of cabin options available to you but at least you will have exercised due diligence and examined what is on offer.

Here is a summary of things to think about when making your selection;

1. What type of cabin do you want and what can you afford;
2. What location on a deck do you want your cabin to be (forward, middle, aft, stern);
3. What deck level do you want your cabin to be on;
4. Is there any venue near your cabin that will adversely affect your enjoyment;
5. Is your cabin near the elevators, stairs, smoking area or service elevator;
6. What is the square footage of your cabin (size);
7. Is the balcony included in the square footage;
8. Do you want special perks attached to your cabin; and
9. Are you willing to do follow-up searches for possible cabin upgrades or do you just want to select and confirm a cabin.

Selecting a cabin also involves a few other considerations and I cover some of those in the following chapter. As you can tell through my comments, I spend a lot of time and effort selecting my cabin. A room you are dissatisfied with, can adversely affect the quality of your cruise. I highly recommend that once booked, you spend time looking to see if you can enrich your experience by improving your cabin. My advice is that at the time you first book, you choose the best cabin available in your price range. Later, if you can move up, do so, if not, then you know you have the best selection that was available to you.

Veteran cruisers will not make payment in full until almost the time when final fees are due to be paid so they are not locked into a specific cabin. They know that as the date of final payment approaches, cabins are freed up and people can upgrade and possibly get better deals. They also know that for some cruise lines, they can bid on a room upgrade and possibly get a better location for a fraction of the listed price difference.

Accessible Cabins

Almost all cruise ships have accessible cabins and if you require such a room, you should book one as soon as possible as they can sell out. Ask the cruise line what the accessible cabin has by way of special equipment and facilities and determine whether it will meet your needs. Usually, these cabins will have wider doors, grab bars, roll-in showers, higher toilet seats and more room to maneuver a wheelchair. An accessible cabin can have flashing lights to alert the occupant if there is someone at their door or if there is a telephone call. These rooms may also have telephones with captioned messaging capability.

The cruise line may verify at the time of booking, that in event of an emergency, the individual requiring assistance, has a travelling companion to aid them. If the passenger is travelling by themself, the cruise line may assign a member of staff to aid the passenger in case of an emergency but this is dependant upon available staff, the level of aid required by the passenger and the nature of the emergency. Ensure the cruise line is aware of your specific needs at the time of booking.

In addition to requesting an accessible cabin, you should also let the cruise line know of any other accommodation required to meet your needs. Do you need a table in the dining room suitable for wheelchair seating or a spot in the theater? If your needs involve other considerations, such as placement in an area of the dining room with less ambient noise, or if you are accompanied by a service animal, make sure you are specific as to your requirements. I also recommend you check with both guest services and the dining room once you have boarded to make sure your request(s) have been recorded against your reservation and conveyed to the appropriate venue on the ship.

Finally, it is important to remember that although cruise lines endeavour to accommodate the needs of all passengers, accessible cabins may sell out and suitable space in certain venues might be limited. Additionally, if the special needs of a passenger are too great and prove to be a hardship to the cruise line, it may not be possible to make a booking.

Service/Assistance Animals

I have a friend who is blind and uses a working guide dog. As a result of her questions as to whether a cruise line will allow her guide dog to accompany her on a cruise, I completed some research on her behalf. Some cruise lines will allow certified service animals to accompany their passengers on a voyage. The animals must be on a leash or harness when outside of the cabin and they cannot be left alone.

The care and feeding of the animal are the responsibility of the owner as is the provision of their food. Cruise lines must be made aware in advance of the sailing, that the animal will be onboard and a spot for the animal to relieve themselves will be designated. As the policies of cruise lines vary slightly, I recommend that individuals contact the cruise line directly to obtain a copy of their service animal policy and what documentation they will require to prove that the animal meets the test of being a bona fide service animal.

It will also be necessary to determine whether the service animal can accompany an individual when at a port stop and what documentation may be required by the country being visited.

A Honking Big Lifeboat Blocks View

They said that our cabin had an obstructed view but the last time we had a cabin that had an obstructed view, there was a skinny pole at the end of the balcony and we certainly did not consider that to be obstructing anything. The next time we booked, we had zero concerns when told that our cabin had a partially obstructed view but this time, we found a honking big lifeboat right smack in our line of sight.

Vivi and Burton

Ouch, the couple who made the above comment learned that obstructed views come in all sizes and shapes.

I used to laugh when my grandmother would photograph the hotels and hotel rooms she stayed in. She would happily show us her holiday photos and talk about the room and location. She would make comments pertaining to her room choice such as "*There was no closet space*" or "*We could hear all the traffic noise*". In truth, we wondered as to the purpose of her note taking as they had already stayed at the place. But clearly she was ahead of her time when it came to reviewing accommodation and keeping a record she could refer to at any time. In the event that she had to stay in the same place again, she could authoritatively speak about the good and the bad of the hotel and related services.

I travelled for decades and never photographed a hotel room, or even a hotel exterior. The same for cruises. Cabin photos did not interest me as I was sure I would recall what the cabin looked like and the general layout. I was wrong. As with everything in life, it was a learning experience, and I came to see the value of taking cabin photographs and including general cabin comments in my travel journals.

I now examine cabin floorplans on the cruise line site. I will also look at customer reviews on various internet sites. I can pick up a lot of valuable information or better still, see photos or videos of prospective cabins. Enjoying a visual as to what the layout of the cabin is, and specifically getting an eyeball on any advertised obstructions, is extremely helpful. After all, a lifeboat in front of you is different than a skinny pole. Noisy machinery nearby or a busy venue immediately above, or below, your cabin can interfere with the peace of your room.

When you are about to book a cabin, look for possible obstructed views or notes that a cabin may have some oddities. Let's start with the example provided of the couple who had booked cabins that had reported obstructed views. On the first sailing, they found that there was little in the way of an obstruction. On a subsequent voyage, they found a large object blocking their view and they were not impressed. Obstructions come in all shapes and sizes so clarity as to what you are getting is critical to your decision making.

When you are told there is an obstructed view attached to a cabin you are considering, at a minimum, do the following:

1. Ask what the obstruction is and what percentage of the view is affected.
2. Check the internet for comments about that cabin or for photos or videos.

Once you have an idea of what the obstruction is, you can make a decision as to whether you can live with the obstruction or not. Some may ask why anyone who wants to book a balcony cabin would book an obstructed view cabin and the answer is simple: price. Obstructed view cabins can be less expensive than regular balcony cabins. If you want to enjoy some degree of outdoor privacy not afforded you in the common areas of the ship, your own balcony is the way to go.

One couple told me that they book obstructed view cabins if the view blockage is 50% or less. Others hold the opinion that a blocked view of less than 25% is acceptable and there are those who favour minimal view interference which represents 5% to 10%. Hence, examining any photos of that cabin, that can be found on the internet, will be very helpful to you.

I have asked people I know who favour certain cruise lines or specific ships, if they have any tips or photos they want to share. One friend had pictures of the rear of a ship I was considering booking and his shot gave me a clear view of what the aft cabin balconies looked like and whether they decreased in size as the decks rose higher. I could also see from the photo, how much of those balconies were covered. Balconies that are large enough to allow me to sit closer to the railing to enjoy sunshine or nearer the door to be covered if it rains, are always attractive to me.

Another consideration to note, is whether your cabin window, also faces a walkway or promenade instead of facing only the water. You will want to make sure you and your cabin mate are dressed before you open your curtains, especially if there is a possibility that there are people on the deck outside. I am always amazed at cruisers who are surprised when they find people standing on the deck just outside their room because frankly, it is a given that it will happen throughout the day and into the evening. Although shipboard etiquette generally frowns on standing outside someone's cabin and talking, or worse, looking into their room, it happens. Privacy is not assured when people can walk by your door or window.

Guarantee (guaranteed), cabins are rooms in any available category that you book but you don't get to select a specific cabin. Basically, at the time of booking, you select the category, and your cabin is guaranteed to be in that category or higher. The actual physical cabin will be assigned later by the cruise line. Booking a guaranteed cabin is not something that I have experienced as I prefer to personally select the location of my cabin. I have talked to people who regularly book guarantee cabins and they are quite content with them. The timing of when you are assigned your cabin varies with cruise lines and I have heard of people not receiving their cabin assignment until shortly before they leave on their cruise.

On one cruise, the couple in the aft veranda cabin next to us, told me that they had originally booked a guaranteed veranda cabin and at the time of cabin assignment, they had been upgraded to an aft veranda cabin. They claimed that guarantee cabins are sometimes less expensive and that is the reason that they always select those as an option.

They theorized that since these types of cabins are assigned around the time of final payment or close to the date of sailing, there are always choice cabins that suddenly become available as people opt out of taking a cruise. Cruise lines assign those now vacant cabins to passengers in the unassigned cabin category and our cruising neighbours informed me that on a few occasions, such as the cruise we were on, they were offered the upgrade to a better cabin category. They were on back to back sailings and unfortunately could not remain in the same cabin for both voyages so their upgrade was only for the one trip.

It is a risk, we know, but one we feel usually works to our benefit. We have generally been assigned great cabins and at a slightly reduced price. If we luck into an upgrade, it is just a bonus.

Let's examine the opposite side of the guaranteed cabin coin. When researching this book, I received the following in an e-mail:

We booked a guaranteed cabin because we wanted to save a few dollars and we had heard about people being upgraded to higher level cabins. Well, an upgrade did not happen for us. In fact, I have never met anyone who got a higher-grade cabin through this process.

In our case, we booked a guaranteed balcony and we ended up in a balcony cabin that had to be the worst one on the ship. It was in a shit location and the balcony was the smallest on the ship. We complained but we were told we had been assigned a cabin in the category we had booked. From now on we pick our cabins. No mystery and no leaving it up to chance.

Since I have not done the research to determine how often upgrades do or do not materialize, or have a realistic measurement as to how happy cruisers are with this method of booking, I cannot offer an opinion on the practice of booking a guaranteed cabin.

Cruise lines do continue to offer up these types of bookings so clearly there is a market for them. If you want to select your cabin category and you are not bothered about the exact location of that cabin, then you are a suitable candidate for the guaranteed cabin option.

Watch for Sales and Other Perks

Once you have booked your cruise, your trip research has just begun. Time to start watching for price drops and special offers.

Following our usual Friday afternoon golf game, one of the ladies in my golfing foursome offered to host us for post game dinner and drinks. During an evening of congenial conversation and excellent food, the topic turned to the issue of an upcoming cruise two of us were taking.

The hostess and her travelling companion, were booked into a similar sized cabin to mine, and in order to try and upgrade to large sunset suites, we had both dedicatedly stalked the sales and cabin availability. Just before final payment was due, we had seen several mini suites open up and we pounced. Much to our delight, we were both able to secure the much-desired rooms and we would also enjoy oversized balconies. All for a modest increase in costs. Shortly after upgrading, the date for final payment arrived and I paid in full.

However, our hostess had not completed her payment. Usually, she booked through a travel agent who managed her bookings and reminded her when final payment was due. This time she had booked directly with the cruise line which gave her the option of handling her own booking. Consequently, she had successfully obtained the upgraded cabin and then waited to be contacted about making final payment. She was aware of the final payment date and during our dinner, had casually mentioned that the cruise line had not contacted her or her cabin mate about final payment and wondered if the cruise line had forgotten about them. I told her that the final payment date had passed and that the obligation to make final payment before or on the deadline was up to her. The cruise line was under no obligation to remind her to make the payment nor request it. The booking confirmation instructions were explicit, if she failed to make final payment, she might just forfeit her cabin and down payment.

Following dinner, our hostess hurriedly contacted the cruise line and made final payment on the cabin. This example of a situation is one that covers two areas of cruising. The first, and one previously mentioned in this book, is to ensure you keep looking for the best deal, even if you have booked the cruise and made your downpayment. Don't make payment in full until the date of final payment. Just because you have a confirmed reservation and price, does not mean your deal searching is done unless you want it to be finished.

The second point I want to address regarding self booking is the responsibility you bear to know the booking rules/limitations and payment schedule. If you make your booking yourself, directly with the cruise line, know the rules and conditions that relate to your obligations. Read the fine print of your booking confirmation. Know what you are responsible for and what may hinder your ability to travel. You do not want to be the pregnant woman who is refused boarding because you are near term. You need to know what documents you must present on check-in. Did you ask for any applicable discounts such as the military, police or firefighter price concessions? If so, what proof do you have of your service if requested upon embarkation day.

Even the most seasoned cruiser will make mistakes. I had rented a place in North Carolina for three months during the winter of 2020. While there, I had found a good deal on a Baltic Sea cruise, and I decided to book it. I never make non-refundable bookings and, in this case, as usual, I booked a fully refundable cruise. However, I called the cruise line back the next day because there was a sale that had popped up on the cruise line site and I wanted to find out if that Baltic Sea cruise was eligible for the sale deal. It was. The person I spoke with, rebooked the cruise and sent the new documentation. I received the revised booking but as it was on my phone, I did not open it up to look at it and since I was not at home, I did not have a printer to print out the documentation. It was not until several months later, when covid shutdowns were in full swing, that I realized that the rebooking was a non-refundable fare. I knew better and should have checked when the revised booking was sent to me. The cruise was cancelled due to covid shutdowns so it became fully refundable, but I learned a lesson. ALWAYS check the paperwork as soon as you receive it so that discrepancies and/or errors can be corrected.

Tell your readers to check the spelling of their names. I booked a cruise and on the cruise documents they spelled my name Brain. I get that it was a typo but I did not notice it until I was trying to check in for my cruise seven months later. I could not complete the check-in process because the first name did not match the name on my passport. I was on the phone with (the cruise line) for a couple of hours to get it changed and straightened out.

Brian – USA

The Beverage Package

When asked what is the worst thing that ever happened on a cruise, one woman told me: *"We booked our cruise 18 months in advance and decided to splurge with the best booze package. The day before we left on the cruise, I found out I was pregnant. Talk about sucky timing."*

You have decided to take a cruise and now you are looking at what you want to add to your sailing experience. One of the add on possibilities is a beverage package. Cruise lines offer assorted beverage packages which can either be included in the price of the cruise or as an add-on for an additional cost.

In my chapter entitled *"Security and the Smugglers"*, I address the issue of bringing alcohol onboard a ship, so in this chapter I will define what a beverage package is and speak only about the pros and cons of the beverage deals.

Beverage packages are not all the same. There are non-alcoholic, alcoholic (assorted types which may encompass basic or premium liquors, or specialty types of a specific type of liquor), and wine packages. Different cruise lines have different names for their beverage packages and rather than name them all, I simply refer to them in the generic descriptive form of beverage package.

First, I will address whether you even need a beverage package.

Ships will offer coffee, tea and soda fountain drinks as part of their inclusive meal services. In response to the question of whether you can have beverages without a beverage package, the answer is always yes. The same holds true for water. You can get water without paying extra however, you should be aware that although dispensed water is free, bottled, sparkling or flavoured water is invariably an extra charge. Some cruise lines offer bottled water as part of their beverage packages while others sell water separately.

If you want to get a soft drink package, which usually includes juices, brand named soft drinks (such as specific colas), you might consider a non-alcoholic beverage package. These are normally the least expensive beverage packages you can buy and great if you are travelling with children. If you prefer a specific brand of a soft drink, then this might be the package for you.

Some cruise lines offer more than one type of package involving alcohol while a few offer only the one package (which is all inclusive). In this chapter, I provide you with a generic overview of the general packages and advise that for precise details as to what is offered by your cruise line of choice, check their website or consult with your travel agent.

Alcoholic beverage packages usually include all the items offered up in the basic beverage package and comprise of specifically named spirits, wine and beer. This is the type of beverage package that would normally suit me. I like to drink bottled water throughout the day, but I will have wine with dinner. Brands of wine that are palatable, and that I enjoy, can usually be found within this package. This type of beverage package is the one most commonly included in specials offered by cruise lines whether they are all inclusive or presented up as a cruise perk.

A cruise line's higher level of beverage package will include upscale brands of spirits, wines and often include the drink of the day. If you enjoy premium spirits, specialty coffees/teas, cordials or after dinner liqueurs such as brandy, this package is for you. It is the most expensive package so before you decide, have a look at the drinks pricing for your chosen cruise line and decide which package would best suit you.

On some cruise lines, all beverages are included in the purchase price so you don't need to concern yourself with any specific "package".

Pro Tip Regarding Beverage Packages

Always check to see what is included in the beverage packages. I usually prepare a list of the types of drinks that are included in the packages and provide that to my travel companions. It helps them understand what is and is not included. On one cruise line, a premium package is the highest-level package you can enjoy while on a different cruise line, a premium package is on the lower end of the scale. Know what you are getting with the package you have bought.

Most cruise lines will offer wine packages. You buy "X" amount of bottles in the package which can be drunk at dinner (or throughout the cruise depending on the cruise line). If you do not finish your bottle, it can be recorked and served at the next meal or when you ask for it.

On one cruise, my friend and I, being wine drinkers, bought such a package. A bottle, when requested, was delivered to our table which we could then enjoy during dinner. At the conclusion of the meal, if there was anything remaining in the bottle, we would take it with us to the theatre where we could enjoy another glass while taking in the entertainment.

Deciding on Whether to Buy a Beverage Package

I have been on cruises with people who have opted not to buy a beverage package and lived to rue the decision. I have also been on cruises with individuals who have purchased top of the line packages, only to discover the amount they drank did not make the package worthwhile. Consequently, a little honest self reflection about what will best suit your needs is required.

As an example, I offer up the story of two people who were a part of a group I was sailing with on a transatlantic crossing. These two friends opted to forgo the purchase of a beverage package in favour of paying on a drink-by-drink basis. Their rationale was that they would never drink enough to justify the cost of a beverage package, which on that cruise was a little over $50 per person, per day. Once on the cruise, they opted to buy the drink of the day everyday (around $14 each). As explained to me, they wanted to try a different drink (and I don't blame them as those specialty drinks always look delicious), and they wanted to get the souvenir glasses. In addition to those specialty drinks, they also had a few drinks around the pool in the afternoon ($8.50 each), a couple of glasses of wine with dinner ($8.75 each) and an evening liqueur $7.50). They freely ordered bottled or sparkling water whenever they were thirsty. They were averaging $70 - $80 a day in beverage costs (both alcoholic and non alcoholic). Consequently, at the end of the cruise, they discovered that for them, the beverage package would have represented a savings. Unfortunately, they did not track their cruise bill and as mentioned, did not discover their daily costing until the end of the cruise. At the conclusion of our sailing, they each had a collection of souvenir glasses that could not fit in their luggage and a hefty, unexpected bill. They ended up taking one glass each and left the remaining glasses behind. They subsequently learned that they could have had the drink of the day without the special glass and saved themselves some money.

I ran into one of them at guest services the night before our cruise concluded and she had just finished paying her account. Clearly shocked at her bill, she told me she should have done the math on the costing of the drinks as she would have saved money with a package.

One other important note regarding a beverage package, it is not always about alcohol. Bottled and sparkling water will cost you extra on most cruise lines. If you drink bottled water throughout the day, you too may find that a package will save you money.

Which Package is Right for You

As mentioned, think about your drinking habits and what, and how much, you normally like to drink. My husband likes a specific brand of diet cola that is usually only available at an extra cost. In other words, he does not drink the generic fountain soda. His choice of soft drink automatically translates to an extra cost on most cruise lines.

I know couples who can easily enjoy a bottle of wine with a meal and then order another. If they don't specifically care if they drink a certain brand of wine, a beverage package wherein they get wine by the glass, might actually be the more cost-effective option.

My husband always likes to get the beverage package that includes every type of drink as he says he does not want to have to worry as to whether the drink he is ordering falls within a certain price range. He simply gets the top-of-the-line package and orders without worrying. This segues into my next point: Don't buy the beverage package if you are not going to need it.

People assume that they will need to buy some type of beverage package but I urge you to do the math when making a decision. If regular coffee, fountain sodas and drinking water (always potable on a ship), will suffice, then you do not need a package.

I have long since discovered that for me, I don't drink enough premium alcohol to warrant paying for a top-of-the-line package.

However, I like specialty coffees and I always have a bottle of water with me throughout the day. I clearly need to have some type of package that allows me to order my preferred coffee and water. Bottled water is particularly handy if travelling to a hot climate area and when getting off the ship for a shore excursion. I weigh the cost of the beverage package against what I realistically think I will spend on drinks on a cruise.

Once Again Look for Specials

From the start of any booking I make, to the time I set foot on a ship, my goal is to have a beverage package included in the cost of the sailing. There are always special deals and incentives going on that can secure the inclusion of some type of package. In the rare event that I am unsuccessful in getting a drinks package, I take a look at the cost of the drinks for that cruise line and focus on the drinks that I know I would order. I then do the math. Whatever works out as the best deal, is the route I choose to go.

When considering your needs, take into account the length of your cruise and whether you want a package for the entire cruise or only a portion of the time you are on the ship.

Also in the *"Security and the Smugglers"* chapter, I refer to the option for each adult passenger to bring a bottle of wine on-board. If you wish to take advantage of this opportunity, check to see if the cruise line is going to charge you a corkage fee (even if you drink the wine in your cabin). Will bottles of wine be delivered to you in your cabin for any reason?

For example, some loyalty programs will have a bottle of sparkling wine awaiting customers who have achieved a certain level of loyalty. I have also seen travel agents arrange for a bottle of wine to be put in their customer's cabins as a thank you for booking with them. On one cruise, we were celebrating my husband's retirement and our anniversary. The cruise line gave us a bottle of champagne for each event and had greeted us with a bottle of wine upon our arrival on the ship as we had previously sailed with that line and were repeat customers.

Friends or family may also arrange to gift you with wine or other spirits. On one occasion, a couple we know were celebrating a milestone anniversary and our group of friends arranged for a bar set up in their cabin as an anniversary gift. For another family member, who was trying cruising for the first time, we arranged for champagne and chocolates to be waiting for them upon their arrival in their cabin.

Onboard Accounts

When I was in my early twenties, my older sister decided to get married on a ship and to ensure we got to go, my parents cut a deal with my brother and me. They would pay for our cabin and we would pay for our extras like our drinks, wi-fi and anything else we purchased.

Seven days of sailing around the Caribbean was a pretty good deal and there were several of the wedding events that the groom's family were paying for that had all the drinks included such as the wedding party meet and greet and then a reception in their suite.

For three days we had a blast and hung out at the pool, different bars and partied late. We did not even bother getting off the ship at the first two port stops because we had everything we needed. No cash changed hands, we just showed the bartenders our magic cards and drinks would appear. We both looked pretty sick in the designer shades we got at one of the shops.

On the fourth day, on the advice of my mother, we checked our onboard account on our room TV and we saw how much we had already spent.

The onboard account total was already higher than the

cash we had. Thankfully my mother covered the excess on our bill but our free spending had ended.

Robb – location unknown

Every cabin has an onboard account attached to it that will update daily to let you know how much you have spent. If you are sharing a cabin with a friend, ask if the spending can be separated. Some cruise lines will be able to separate the accounts of individuals in the same room while other lines cannot.

Depending on your spending habits and what packages you may have against your cruise, there may be zero additional charges. But if you don't have a beverage package and drink beverages that have an additional charge, all drinks will be listed and may have automatic gratuities added. On some cruise lines, basic gratuity charges are added daily. The same for specialty dining or shore excursions you may purchase onboard.

Like all technology, there can be glitches so ensure your account is accurate and reflects your spending.

Pro Tip - Onboard Account

You should check your onboard account everyday. Most of the cruise lines allow you to do this in the privacy of your cabin via your television or on the cruise line's app. If you find that your costs are higher than anticipated, you can either adjust your spending or you can purchase some type of package and it will be prorated on the number of days left on your cruise.

Yes, that is correct, if you did not buy the beverage package before the cruise, you can buy it onboard at the start or during the cruise and the price will be modified to reflect the days you will enjoy the benefits of the package.

In response to a question I received about buying a beverage package for sea days only, I have not found a cruise line that sells a beverage package that applies only to certain days. The packages that can be bought during the cruise, normally apply to all the days remaining on that sailing. As such, you cannot pick and choose which days to have a beverage package.

You can also attach any onboard credit (known as OBC), to your onboard account to pay for some of your purchases. Always use your OBC as it does not carry forward to any future cruise and normally, cannot be cashed in if it was given by the cruise line as a booking incentive for that cruise. The saying "*Use it or lose it,*" applies in this case.

Specialty Dining

If the food on cruises is reported to be so good, why are cruise lines always trying to up sell specialty dining packages?

This is a question that was posed to me at a talk I gave on cruising.

People considering taking a cruise often ask me this question and it is also a recurring one among experienced cruisers. Cruise lines are always advertising great food and touting gourmet meals served in elegant settings. If the menus are prepared by award winning chefs and the food top notch, why would any cruiser need to pay extra to eat in a specialty restaurant?

I normally respond that specialty restaurants offer food and service that is a cut above the normal dining room experience and may have selections that are not offered elsewhere on the ship. Steak offered in the dining room might be Ribeye or New York Strip while a specialty restaurant might serve Filet Mignon or a Porterhouse.

French cuisine, Italian or Japanese foods are often offered up in specialty restaurants but there can be other types of food and themed places that are designed to titillate your taste buds and entice you into paying that extra fee. The big question is whether they are worth it or not and there is no one size fits all answer.

96

I can only share my experiences. The first time I opted to splurge on a specialty restaurant, was on my third or fourth cruise. I had been on a few cruises and delighted in the meals in the main dining room. I had enjoyed excellent dinners and always found something on the menus to my liking. The service is generally very good and I had gotten to know the wait staff. I too thought "*Why pay extra?*"

Eventually it was time to see what all the fuss was about and I made a booking for my husband and I to enjoy a specialty restaurant that served French cuisine. Our experience was delightful, and the food was exquisite. I would liken it to a Michelin-starred restaurant meal. We enjoyed the event so much we booked again the very next night. That second meal was just as superb and the service flawless. We were hooked on specialty dining.

Our love affair with specialty dining continued for the next few cruises until we sailed with a different cruise line. With that cruise line, we had regularly enjoyed outstanding meals in the dining room and we had been in no hurry to book a specialty dining night. However, we figured that if the meals were so fantastic in the dining room, the meals in a specialty restaurant must be marvelous. We made two bookings and looked forward to our reservation in the French restaurant. When we arrived, the décor and ambiance did not disappoint. We were directed to a comfortable window seat that offered an outstanding view of a burning red and orange sunset. The table linen was pristine and the service was excellent. Then it all went wrong. The food was abysmal. The appetizers were well presented but tasted off. The main course was no better. For the first time ever in a specialty restaurant, we sent one meal back as the steak was over cooked and unpalatable. The second attempt was no better. The experience was such a disappointment, that we cancelled our next reservation and ate the rest of our meals in the main dining room where the food continued to be brilliant. That experience was our first encounter with a specialty restaurant wherein the food was not worth the extra cost.

Since that time, on different cruise lines, we have encountered mixed outcomes. Some reservations have resulted in experiences to rival our first specialty dining encounters and we were left feeling spoiled and pampered. Other experiences have fallen short of expectations; often in the same restaurant. For example, on a recent cruise, we ate at one particular restaurant three times. The first two times it was excellent while the third time, the service was poor, and the food could best be described as mediocre. It may have been that on that night, staff were in short supply due to illness, but there was a marked difference in the quality of both service and food.

This chapter is not designed to warn people off trying specialty restaurants; indeed, I encourage you to book a specialty meal. For the most part, the food is excellent, and the service is generally quite good. Remember, if you book a specialty restaurant, and they are not included in your cruise price, you will pay extra for the meal and most often, the cruise line will add an automatic gratuity to the cost.

Themed Meals

Some cruise lines may offer special dinners with food associated with a specific culture. These dinners usually have an additional cost and can be held in a certain section of a specialty restaurant, in a sectioned off location in the main buffet or other designated location. They are not part of a regular menu in a specialty dining restaurant or main dining room. These meals are often excellent and good value for money. They encourage diners to try foods associated with different cultures.

Specialty Restaurants with a Theme

As mentioned, specialty restaurants usually have a theme with respect to their offerings. French, Italian, Indian, Japanese, American, Thai cuisine etc. might all be on offer in themed specialty restaurants. Sometimes the food itself is not the attraction but the whole dining experience. We have eaten in a restaurant that offered an interactive video experience where cartoon characters appeared on the tablecloth and prepared the food. As soon as the "meal" was done, a look alike real dish was placed in front of the diner. It was highly entertaining and fun. Such a dining experience is suitable for all ages.

Injury or Illness Pre-cruise

Did you ever have one of those vacations where something goes wrong before you even leave on the trip? It has happened to me a few times and I put it down to bad luck but upon exploring the topic in more depth, I found that it happens more than we think.

I had already settled into my airplane seat, ready for a long, overnight, trans-Atlantic flight. Contrary to the common travel warning about leaving shoes on to avoid swelling feet, I had taken my shoes off and I was minutes away from falling asleep. If my normal travel pattern held true, I would be asleep before the plane pushed back to begin taxiing.

Just as I was about to drift off, I was disturbed by a little kerfuffle taking place in the aisle beside me. The aircraft was a wide body jet with a 2-3-2 seating configuration in the economy section. The dispute involved the passengers' holding tickets for the three seats of the middle row. Apparently one passenger had numerous bags which he had placed in the overhead bins above the seats of that row. I had seen him get on the plane and had been surprised that the airline had let him board the aircraft as his numerous bags clearly exceeded the standard carry-on limit both in size and amount.

By placing his bags in the overhead bin, he had left no room for the baggage of the two other passengers holding tickets for the two middle seats in his row. They were among the last to board having just made the connection from another flight and they found that there was no room for their carry-on baggage. They checked for space in the nearby overhead bins without success.

The couple subsequently determined that all the bags occupying the bin in the area of their seating belonged to the man in their row. They wanted him to take one of his bags down and put it under the seat in front of him. That would have made room in the overhead bin for their two small pieces of baggage. But such an action would have meant the fellow would have to put one of his bags underneath the seat in front of him (if he could even get it to fit into that space). It would have resulted in little legroom for him and on a long flight, it would prove to be quite uncomfortable. He held the opinion that the first person on the plane, had "dibs" on the overhead bin space and the couple would just have to find space elsewhere or put their bags under the seats in front of them. They baulked at this proposal. He then suggested they check at the back of the plane or ask a flight attendant to find space for them. They objected as they wanted their carry-on to be easily accessible during the flight and they felt he was unfairly monopolizing the overhead bin space.

Just as a note to my readers, this type of problem is fairly common. The lack of overhead storage space and the actions of those who bring a lot of carry-on baggage is often the source of conflict. I have seen it played out numerous times over the years.

Once I had ascertained what the issue was, and realizing that it was a common problem, I tuned out the conversation, punched my little pillow getting it flight ready and once again started to drift off.

Suddenly something heavy landed on my foot, jarring me awake. Apparently, in an attempt to resolve the carry-on dispute, a flight attendant had pulled one piece of luggage from the overhead bin with the intent of moving it to the back. She did not realize the bag was extremely heavy and as she pulled it from the bin, gravity took over and she lost control of the bag. It swung down and landed on my foot. Several of my toes were broken in the mishap. Not an auspicious start to my trip. I had meetings set up in Europe over the next few days and then I was joining friends and family for a cruise. Consequently, getting off the plane to seek medical attention would have resulted in rescheduling the meetings and involved quite a bit of itinerary juggling. Knowing that there was little to be done with the toes, and not realizing the extent of the damage, I opted to continue with the trip. Thankfully, I had packed sandals and once at our destination and in possession of my checked baggage, I was able to access and change to that footwear. Given the cold weather, it was necessary to wear socks with those sandals. The rather odd footwear combination, aside from being a fashion no-no, was a conversation starter. Upon my return to Canada, I had surgery on the foot to repair the damage and to this day, if you look at my right foot, you will see the surgery scars and the crooked toes.

As stated in the introduction to this chapter, in researching this book, I became aware that accidents and illnesses happen just before a vacation, and many dedicated cruisers are not about to be deterred from taking a cruise when incidents happen to them.

A Slippery Tale

Karen related a pre-cruise mishap that did not dissuade her or her husband from their cruise. Here is a summary of what happened to her:

It all started the Sunday before Thanksgiving and stemmed from my love of ice cream. My husband and I had established a ritual of having a bowl of ice cream about eight in the evening and normally, my husband would be the one to serve up our frozen indulgence. However, on this occasion, I was on my own. I prepared my treat however as I was transitioning from the kitchen tile to our hardwood floor in the foyer, I fell. My fall was both hard and painful. It was very clear that I had sustained a serious injury that required medical help.

An ambulance was called and following an examination, I learned that I had a very bad ankle break that necessitated surgery. I was extremely worried that my accident would keep us from going on our planned back-to-back cruises which included a trip to Antarctica.

At the beginning of January, the doctor took my cast off on a Thursday and put me in a restrictive medical walking boot. With the boot and the use of a roller walker, I was set to go and that Saturday we boarded the airplane and were off.

Upon arrival at the baggage claim area, we met our cruise representative (rep) who was young, agile and oblivious to the obstacles facing someone who was wearing a medical boot and limping along pushing my walker. He set a blistering pace that was a challenge for the able body, much less me, to keep up. We were soon in danger of being left behind.

Since we had no idea where we were going it was imperative that we not lose sight of the rep so my husband, in desperation, said "Sit on the walker seat and I will push you." There is a reason this walking assistance device comes with a warning that says "walking aid not a transportation device."

I was sitting facing my husband as he was pushing me when the walker hit a crack causing me to go over backwards where I hit my head on the cement sidewalk. We were able to join the rest of the group but I was a little worse for the wear as a result of the fall.

When we finally got to the port of embarkation, I was able to secure the use of a wheelchair to board our cruise ship, but I instantly encountered a new challenge. The ship's ramp appeared to be a rather steep 45-degree angle and there was no way I could wheel myself up it. Walking was also out of the question. Consequently, cruise ship personnel came to my aide and helped me board.

I am not a large woman but I felt HUGE as it took 2 deckhands to push me in the wheelchair, up that steep ramp! My ego took a massive hit at the thought of what it looked like to anyone watching this boarding exercise.

Once on the ship it was fantastic! Everyone was so helpful and I was asked many times whether I had injured myself on the cruise. I simply told them the truth and said "Nope, just getting my bowl of ice cream!"

Karen - USA

Batting a Thousand

Raymond from England shared the story of his, and his wife's anniversary cruise. He stated:

My wife and I had saved for years in order to take a Mediterranean cruise. We never had a honeymoon as we had bought a house and then quickly had two children. Our third son was born eight years later. Money for vacations was not plentiful so it was only with careful planning and dedicated savings that we were finally able to book a cruise in time for our fifteenth wedding anniversary. We talked about nothing else for months. The day before we were to leave, while my wife was going over last-minute preparations, I took the boys out to the cricket pitch to spend some time with them.

My youngest, who was not known for his hand/eye coordination wanted help batting so I was instructing him. I was trying to get him to be more aggressive in his bat swing. On the third or fourth try, he took my advice and put a tremendous effort into his swing. His momentum swung him around and the bat hit me in the face, breaking my nose and resulting in my eye swelling shut. I knew immediately that this was not going to be pretty, but it was more important to calm my son who was in bits over "hurting daddy".

The next day we headed to Southampton and boarded our cruise. I sported two black eyes, one of which was still partially closed. My nose was a bit swollen and crooked, and I looked like a street brawler. My wife did not appreciate my joking response when I told someone who asked what had happened that "My misses had a go." I quickly opted to let her respond to all future questions about my injury.

We ended up having an excellent time on the cruise and my appearance did not hinder our enjoyment of our holiday. However, anyone looking through our photos, will see that most of the snaps are of my wife or the scenery as I looked pretty rough for most of the trip.

Heart Issues Just Before A Cruise

I was also sent the following story:

About ten weeks before we were due to leave on our cruise, I suffered from chest pains and was hospitalized. I ended up having a stent put in and I was sure that I could not go on our planned cruise. I talked to my doctor and since there were no flights involved, I got the go ahead but I had a few reservations about traveling. I had heard of people having heart attacks on holiday and I admit that I was nervous. I had gone from feeling like I had no health issues to suddenly being worried that something could go wrong.

My wife had let the cruise line know and the ship's medical staff called me in our cabin the first full day of our cruise to see how I was doing. It ended up that I did not need to go there at any time during the cruise but their friendliness gave me confidence that I could call down with any questions or concerns.

We had a great time and we cautiously proceeded to see and do pretty much everything that we planned.

George - USA

As evidenced by these stories, people do experience pre cruise injuries or illnesses, but choose to proceed with, and enjoy, their vacations.

Packing For Your Cruise

We packed about a week in advance of our cruise. Having overpacked in the past, we worked on packing everything in one large suitcase and we achieved success. Our carry-on bags were small and mostly contained our electronics, power cords, camera, snorkel gear and medicines. We landed at our departure city airport only to find our large bag was missing. We had packed little clothing in our carry-on. Our cruise set sail the next day and our big bag, with all our clothes, never caught up to us the entire time of the cruise.

Wayne – USA

***

We are going on a cruise in four months and my wife has already started packing.

Luiz – USA

***

We pack the day we are leaving. We have a border collie who gets separation anxiety when we leave so we try to keep his stress level to a minimum. We used to try and pack in the spare bedroom and shut the door so he would not see us but he quickly caught on to that trick. We would pay extra to a cruise line to be able to go on a cruise with our dog in our cabin.

Harry – location unknown

When You Should Pack

When should you pack? I get asked that question on a regular basis and my answer never changes. People should pack when they want to as there is no set timetable as to when one should start filling up their suitcase or bag. I only advise that people ensure that there is sufficient time in their schedule to actually get the packing done in event that there is a roadblock tossed into their life just prior to their trip.

There are many good reasons to pack in advance, such as being able to organize everything exactly as you wish and ensuring items you want to bring are ready. There are also good reasons to leave packing to a day or two before you leave such as a lack of space in your home to lay out the suitcase, or a pet that may have great interest in the contents of the bag. For example, my friend's cat considers an open suitcase the most desirable of sleeping locations while another friend has a dog who considers anything in a suitcase is a potential toy.

I know people who spend weeks packing, unpacking and repacking for a vacation. They enjoy planning what to wear, what to bring and how to put it all together in their suitcases. Some lay out each outfit and marry up the accessories with each one before placing the ensemble into individual packing cubes and labeling them. Others carefully roll each item to avoid wrinkling while several use packing techniques garnered from various internet videos. Prior to a pre trip packing disaster I experienced, I was never one of those people. I traveled extensively and frequently so I had adopted a rather blasé attitude toward packing, preferring to pack a few hours before a trip. I usually had an idea of what I wanted and needed to bring, and it was simply a matter of placing it all in my suitcase. An hour or two on the day of departure is all that was usually needed.

Leading up to a trip, I simply ensured the necessary clothes were clean and the toiletries were topped up. On the day of the trip, I would make decisions regarding shoes and other accessories as I packed the clothing I had chosen. I was the master of the quick pack and I had achieved a certain skill in ensuring my clothing arrived at my destination wrinkle free and ready to wear.

In 2015, we decided to enjoy a transatlantic cruise with a group of friends. The cruise left from Civitavecchia, the port near Rome. Having been to Rome a number of times, my husband and I decided to head to Germany for a pre-cruise visit to Bavaria. Packing to jaunt around castles in Bavaria and packing for a cruise required two distinctively different clothing considerations. For example, we were going to enjoy a minimum of three formal nights on the cruise, which meant that evening wear was a necessity. There was also a requirement to wear 'smart casual' outfits for the dinners. Had we only been vacationing in the mountains in Germany; casual clothing would have dominated our apparel choices. Because of our itinerary, we recognized in advance of the trip that packing would require careful consideration.

As usual, I left my packing to the day of departure knowing that I would have a full six hours or so to prepare my suitcase and carry-on bag. I cover that day in detail in my book, **Postcards to Alice**, so I will not revisit what transpired, but suffice to say that unforeseen events overtook the day and I was left with zero time to pack. I ended up taking five minutes to throw clothing, accessories and other assorted items into a bag and in reality, I did not have those five minutes to spare. By the time I opened my suitcase to pack, I should have already left for the airport and I was in perilous danger of missing my flight.

Normally, I would have ensured that my carry-on bag contained sufficient clothing to see me through a minimum of three days if my checked bag was waylaid but on that trip, clothing was tossed willy-nilly into the bags with no thought as to what went where. The cat's toy was scooped into the bag while only one sandal made the trip. My same day packing system was an utter fail due to the time constraints fate imposed upon me.

I confess that this was a one-time incident and that I had decades of same day packing experience with absolutely no issues. But once was enough. I now ensure that at a minimum, I start to pack the day before I leave on a trip. I still go through the process of thinking about what I might need and want to wear, well in advance of the trip, so that the clothing is ready to go when I want to start packing.

How You Should Pack

There is always a possibility that your checked bag might be delayed if you are travelling by air. I absolutely counsel you to ensure that your carry-on baggage contains any critical items (such as prescription drugs) and sufficient clothing to get you through several days and one quasi dressy event.

If you are travelling with another person, such as your spouse, and you are taking two suitcases, intermingle your clothing between those two suitcases. That way if one bag is lost or delayed, you will still have clothing for each person in the remaining bag. A word of caution, make sure that when you mix the clothing, that you do so in the form of complete outfits. When researching this book, I received the following from a fellow who contacted me through my website:

> *We followed your advice to mix our clothing in our two suitcases and lo and behold, one of our cases was delayed. We were not worried though until we looked through the clothing in the suitcase we had. We had packed all the pants, shorts and shoes in one suitcase and the shirts, underwear and other*

items in the other. It was a DUH moment. Next time up, we pack complete outfits in each suitcase.

Merv – Location unknown

As for the specifics of how you physically put your items into your suitcase, I leave that to you. Whether you use packing cubes, roll the items or utilize the bulk fold method, you will find the technique that best suits your needs. Everyone I have asked has had a preferred packing method. Personally, I combine two methods which involves rolling most of my clothing and then placing it in packing cubes. Suits and more dressy wear, I leave in the dry-cleaning bags.

Lastly, on the subject of how you should pack, I remind you to bag liquids in case of a spill. Two excellent examples come to mind. First up comes to us from Harry from Canada who packed a large bottle of rye whiskey in his checked bag without benefit of encasing it in bubble wrap or swathing it in clothing. When the bottle broke in transit, the entire contents of his bag smelled like rye and had to be cleaned. A similar story was provided to me by Alima from England who packed an almost full bottle of nail polish remover. She thought she would be OK as the bottle was plastic so there was little danger of it breaking, however, she failed to check that the top was secure. The bottle leaked and the remover solution discoloured all the clothing it touched.

What Should You Pack

When I pack on a trip, I always place a layer of bubble wrap at the bottom of my suitcase. It adds a layer of protection on the outbound trip and can be used to protect any delicate or fragile item I may purchase when returning. I also double bag liquids with the outside bag being a large resealable bag. It can double as a holder of wet items or ice (to form an ice pack if necessary), and the large size means it can be used for any larger liquid purchases.

For cruises, I always pack wire hangers that I have saved when I have clothing returned from the dry cleaners. I find that ship's cabins never have enough hangers and I bring the wire ones to use during the voyage and they can be discarded at the end of the trip.

In my opinion, another cruising must have, are magnetic hooks and magnets. The walls of a ship are metal and magnetic hooks that will hold some weight are valuable when hanging wet items. I bring the ones that will hold up to 15 pounds/6.8kg as they are great for hanging coats, hats, umbrellas and other assorted items. I use everyday magnets to hold the daily itinerary or dining reservations in place on the wall. Although most cruise lines now have apps for your phone that will have the daily itinerary, reservations and other items, my husband still uses the paper versions. He prefers looking at the daily schedule that is left in the cabin for each day and that lists all activities, weather and general port notices. According to him, he can see all the ship's offerings at a glance, and he does not have to scroll through the app.

Always check the average weather associated with your cruise destinations. On a multi port cruise, I look up the typical temperature for each and every stop on the cruise and plan my clothing choices accordingly. Additionally, a week before I leave, I check on the 14-day weather forecast for my destination and make any necessary clothing adjustments.

On multi day cruises, you should determine how many sea days you have versus port days as that will help with your wardrobe selections. Do you need to pay particular attention to your clothing choices at certain ports, such as dressing conservatively if it is the norm at one of the countries where your cruise may stop?

Determine whether there are any formal, semi-formal or themed event nights (such as white nights), on the cruise and pack the appropriate apparel. I cover these subjects in more detail later in this book so for now, I mention the need to ensure your packing includes any special dress/clothing requirements.

Remember, you are on a cruise and on most evenings, the ship is moving. That means there will be a breeze or some wind when you are outdoors and a jacket, sweater or wrap may be necessary. Pay attention to what the cruise line may recommend or what you will see by way of suggestions from other cruisers commenting on social media sites about their experiences in certain locales.

Pro Tip on Clothing

Every time I cruise, I buy something new to wear. Sometimes I buy more but the point of this section is to ask you to pay attention to what you buy and if it is suitable for the trip.

1. How often do you think you will wear the outfit?
2. Is it a piece of clothing that will travel well. Not to knock linen, but a few hours of wear can render it pretty sad looking.
3. Select clothing that you can mix and match and that travels easily.
4. Are those new shoes comfortable? If I had a dollar for everyone who bought new shoes for a cruise and then complained that those shoes hurt their feet, I would be cruising in suites most of the time.
5. Is it washable and drip dry? This will save time and money in washing.
6. Does the item of clothing "just" fit? Most people gain a few pounds on a cruise so tight clothing might get tighter.
7. If you don't love it, don't bring it. Many people over pack and bring items "just in case" they might need it.
8. Don't give in to the usual last-minute impulse to add more items.

Always make sure you have the essentials in/on your carry-on bag/purse/person. By essentials, I am referring to your passport, picture identification (such as a driver's license or Nexus card) and any prescription medication.

I also double check to make sure I have my valid credit and bank cards. I keep a separate credit card and bank card specifically for travel. Both are associated with a specific travel account I set up that serves two purposes. The first of which allows me to easily track my trip spending to ensure it is in line with my designated budget and secondly, to safeguard my regular day-to-day bank accounts. If something happens to my travel cards, my other accounts are not compromised.

> *Six of us were robbed while on vacation. As we were walking along the beach after dark, a group of youths swarmed us and took all our valuables. Credit and bank cards, ID and all the jewelry we had on our person. Now we only carry the minimum with us and leave alternate credit cards and spare ID in the room safe.*
>
> *Bob - Canada*

Verify whether your destination has widespread use of credit or bank cards. If not, you may have to determine whether you can obtain local currency or another currency that is widely accepted. For example, in some countries, US currency is widely accepted in lieu of local currency. If you use your phone for communication, itinerary or document proof (travel, insurance, confirmation of medical needs/vaccinations etc.) or as your camera, your phone becomes one of your essential items. Remember, any electronic devices will require charging so bring your charging cords and power converters (if appropriate).

A quick note that if you do use your phone for taking pictures or short trip videos, you should think about buying and bringing a portable charger so you can ensure you have sufficient power on your shore excursions.

Binoculars

I always bring binoculars on a cruise, but I know that not everyone shares my belief that they are an essential item. I like to sit on my cabin balcony and examine passing ships, landmarks, stars or visible ocean/sea creatures. Binoculars allow me to do so with closer visibility than with the naked eye or an enlargement on my phone. That means my binoculars are always on a magnetic hook, hanging at the ready, by the balcony door.

On a cruise in January 2023, my husband and I were in Cabo San Lucas and following a few hours of walking exploration on shore, we decided to stop for a drink. The little outdoor bar was crowded, and shortly after being seated, a couple asked to share our table. We soon learned that they too were on a self guided shore excursion. While we were sailing with the *Norwegian Cruise Line*, they were sailing with the *Princess Cruise Line*. I asked them if their ship had left Los Angeles on January 6th and they confirmed that it had. I told them that I had watched their ship set sail and then return to port to have someone removed from their ship.

When I mentioned that I had noticed the return of their ship and the opening of the water level doors, the man expressed surprise that I had been able to see that from our location. I revealed that I had taken my binoculars in hand to see what was going on as it was unusual to have a ship return to port just after sailing. I was able to provide them with details as to what I had seen.

The man was astounded that someone would bring binoculars with them on a cruise. He could not see the point. I understand that not everyone owns binoculars and that the added weight and room they take in a suitcase might put some people off, but for me, they add value to the trip. Therefore, I suggest you make your own decision as to whether you will find them of use or not.

Pro-tip on the binoculars: We have been on some cruises where there were binoculars in the cabin. Check before you leave to see if your ship supplies binoculars.

Luggage Scale

In these days of the weight of luggage being an issue with airlines, I recommend that people invest in a small luggage scale. This will help you weigh and distribute the weight of clothing between bags. On a recent trip we arrived at the airport to see several people with open suitcases trying to rearrange items in their respective bags to meet the weight requirements. Having a luggage scale will allow you to weigh your bag before you head to the airport.

Lightweight Luggage

I seldom win anything, but I once won a set of designer leather luggage. Oh, how I loved the look and feel of that luggage and the fact that I had won something that I never would have bought, made it special. However, the large bag weighed over 16 pounds (7.5 kilograms), empty. It was double the empty weight of my usual similar sized bag. As much as the luggage delighted me, I continued to use my standard super lightweight luggage. Every available pound counts when travelling.

Clips or Clothes Pins

A lady we met on a cruise told me she always brings clips to hold her towel or other items, onto her balcony chair. She has a preference for back-to-back cruises so she may do a hand wash of items and clip them to dry outside on the balcony. She was also the person who told me to mix fabric softener and water into a little spray bottle to spray out the wrinkles in items that have been hand washed. She was right, it works!

Bug Spray and Sunblock

Always a must for those hot, sunny port stops. The ship will probably offer these items for sale but you will find yourself paying more.

Over the Door Shoe Rack

Attaching over the bathroom door, these are handy if there is a lack of counter space in your bathroom or vanity area. These are generally made of lightweight plastic and the shoe compartments make great storage spots for a large assortment of items you might bring. The one I use is clear plastic so I can see what is in each compartment.

Power Strip/Power Converters

There can be a lack of electrical outlets on some of the older ships. A power strip will add additional power sources. You can buy power cords that also have USB ports which will also be of use to you on the older ships if you need to charge a number of electronic devices. Check with the cruise line first to ensure they allow the use of these power strips onboard the ship on which you are sailing.

A power converter will allow you to use both the 110V and the 220V plugins you will find in your cabin. They can essentially double your power sources.

Umbrella

Many cruise ships do supply umbrellas but there is usually only one per cabin. Consequently, I always pack a small collapsible one that opens up to a full-size umbrella.

Arrive on Departure Day or Earlier

Our homeowner's association negotiated a special deal on a last minute three-night cruise and we booked. Since we live a few hours drive to the cruise terminal, we decided to drive down that day rather then take the bus that had been arranged by the association. We were told it was better to arrive in the afternoon for check-in because everyone gets there between 10am and 1pm. We were aiming for a 1pm arrival but got caught in a major traffic jam. Then we found the parking lot was quite a distance from the check-in location and it took us over an hour to get the shuttle to take us there. By the time we finally arrived, the cut off time to check-in had passed. We missed the cruise since it would have cost more then we had paid for the whole trip to meet up with the ship at the first port stop.

John - USA

When to arrive at the cruise port of departure is always a subject of discussion, particularly among those of us who do not live anywhere near a port. It is especially tricky if you are travelling in the winter or during times when there is a probability that adverse weather conditions might be a factor. You must decide when and how you want to arrive.

Let's first examine a same day arrival in a port city. You can drive, fly, walk or take some type of other ground vehicle transportation (taxi, bus, shuttle, drop off by family or friend, ride sharing program etc.). Your choice of transportation will depend on what is available to you and what you believe will best suit your needs. What method you choose to get to the port is less important than your arrival time. Cruises have an embarkation cutoff time. Know it and make sure you are there before it rolls around.

Drive

If you drive, you should be aware of the distance and estimated travel time. A rule of thumb is to take whatever time you think you need and double it. I personally like to triple it if I am driving a route involving over an hour on a highway because an accident can easily delay you several hours. Consider other possible traffic issues such as route closures and construction zones.

Ensure you are aware of the available parking facilities and have an alternate if the location is full. Factor in the cost associated with leaving your vehicle in the parking facility and how you then get to the cruise check-in point once you leave your vehicle.

If you are being dropped off by a taxi, shuttle or bus, make sure your transportation leaves early enough to navigate any traffic delays.

As for walking, if you are close enough to walk, you are probably already living in the port city or staying nearby. Therefore, you are not faced with a decision as to when to arrive at the city of departure because you are already there.

Fly

Cruises tend to leave in the late afternoon on any given day which means that people have the choice of arriving at the port city the same day as their scheduled cruise departure. If you read the comments on any cruising website, you will see from entries that this has not always worked out well.

As mentioned, there are those of us who do not live near a port and getting to one usually involves a drive of several days or flying. When booking flight(s) to the departure port, if you are thinking of same day travel, you must ask yourself what the associated risks are as they relate to the air travel. If it involves more than one flight, the risk of delays or problems increases.

I am going to start with a little story about my experience and tell you how my laissez-faire attitude towards port city arrival day changed.

Prior to the time of the coronavirus disease shutting down a lot of vacations and the subsequent transportation problems that have befallen the travel industries, I had a certain tolerance for risk. I was OK flying in the same day as our cruise departed. I was also fine flying through some notoriously busy airports to make connections to get me to my destination port. If a seat sale had me flying on four discounted flights around the globe to get me to the ship's point of departure, I was also OK with it. Once at the departure city, I had also been known to land, collect my luggage and throw in a quick local tour before heading to the ship. If a ship set sail at 5pm, I was aiming for a 4pm port arrival.

My husband Dan has a low risk tolerance and likes to arrive two to three days before our cruise is scheduled to depart just in case there is a problem. He also plans air travel that has him taking the most direct flights, through airports with good reputations for timely aircraft movement and using air carriers that have top marks for on-schedule service. To heck with the cost, he books for success. I have a certain empathy for him, since we have missed flights, flight connections and we both have memories of certain panicked drives to airports.

I am cognizant that during the unpredictable Canadian winters, snowstorms always lurk on the horizon. In the middle of summer, when booking that February, Caribbean cruise, snow is not normally the first thing that comes to mind, but Dan plans for it. When I book a flight, I always envision blue skies, clear runways and sober flight crews. Dan has a mental image of massive traffic hold-ups, airport shutdowns, aircraft delays, aircrew illness and perhaps a nuclear war or two. He is ready for any possible flight delay while I exude optimism.

On a 2019 sailing, Dan insisted we depart two days in advance of the cruise. We were headed for Fort Lauderdale and the timing of our trans-Atlantic cruise was late April. In my mind, April is the spring month known for warmer temperatures, rain and few weather travel delays. I wanted to fly the day of our cruise departure, but Dan insisted on a two-day buffer. I tried to compromise saying that surely the day before would suffice but he dug in his heels. He eventually wore me down and consequently two days before our cruise, we boarded the aircraft ready for departure. Spring was late arriving that year and as we headed for the airport, I found it a bit chilly and rain was in the forecast but I had no worries, we were headed south and into some lovely weather. We were also travelling in business class so I was looking forward to a bit of in-flight pampering. As we boarded our flight on time, I mentioned to Dan that clearly his fears of travel delays in April were groundless.

Shortly thereafter, an unexpected ice storm hit and we sat on the plane waiting. As time passed and the ice fell, Dan felt vindicated. Flying in April was NOT the worry-free travel I had forecasted. More time passed and we sat there held hostage to the cruel whim of mother nature. At one point the aircraft was pushed back and we headed to the de-icing station. Due to the sudden storm, there was a delay at that point and then we were finally taxied to the runway where another delay occurred as air traffic control worked to clear the back log. As we sat there, more ice pellets began to fall which necessitated another trip to the de-icing station. Eventually the flight was able to take off and we were finally airborne. Needless to say, our departure was late.

Once we arrived at our destination, our priority tagged luggage did not appear and we waited for the bulk of the hold baggage to be deplaned. We ended up waiting until the last of the bags had been off-loaded and sure enough, the last piece of luggage to arrive from our flight was one of ours. But our second bag was missing and as such, we had to go to the luggage claim office to report that we had a missing bag. That meant we missed our complementary hotel transfer. As we filled out the missing baggage form, I was getting frustrated with this rather unpleasant run of bad luck. Dan, however, was looking cheerier as time moved on. Delayed flight and a missing bag were all indicators that arriving the same day is NOT a good idea and he was quite happy that he was being proven right at every turn.

Our trip to the hotel was also delayed as our back-up transportation – the multi hotel shuttle bus, was nowhere to be seen. Not only had we missed the direct transfer, but the group hotel shuttle had also departed. We walked to the taxi queue and where previously there had been a long line up of available vehicles, now there was an empty roadway. No taxis were to be seen. Even the taxi dispatcher/controller had disappeared. Yes, this day was not going as planned. We eventually found another hotel shuttle and were treated to a long wait as the bus made its way to various hotels to drop off guests. Naturally our hotel was one of the last stops.

We arrived around 9:30pm, "hangry" and one bag short.

Later, the next day, (which was the day before the cruise), we heard from friends who had just flown in, that the weather conditions in Ottawa had been similar to those we had experienced at the time of our departure. Their flight had been significantly delayed. Their comment that their flight delay had led to a very anxious day for them, resulted in another smug look in my direction from Dan.

While our friends had been delayed, we, having arrived late the night before, had enjoyed a relaxing day in sunny conditions. Late in the day, we were informed that our missing bag had been located and it was subsequently delivered to our hotel room. Dan pointed out that had this been the departure day of the cruise, the wayward bag would have missed the boat as it was delivered to our hotel after 5pm. I am convinced that hidden behind his cheery disposition was a man basking in self-righteousness.

The day of the cruise, the weather in Ottawa had worsened and Dan, who was gleefully tracking Ottawa's weather, informed me that multiple flights departing that city had been delayed or cancelled. Had we waited until that morning to fly; we would not have made the cruise. Had we departed the day before the cruise, we might possibly be missing a bag. His position regarding the merits of flying to the cruise port early had been justified.

129

I have accepted that my same day flights are a thing of the past. Armed with proof of what disasters can arise and given the current post covid lockdown transportation issues that arise, Dan insists on expanding every trip by a minimum of a few days to account for any unforeseen event. I now agree with him.

Work Boots and Baggage Delays

On one cruise I met a fellow who was sporting steel toed work boots, shorts with the cruise line logo and a t-shirt advertising one of our port stops. In a conversation with him, I learned that he worked in the oil industry on a twenty-eight-day rotational shift. He booked his holiday to begin the day after he got off shift with the rationale that he would get home, pack, and he and his wife would catch an evening flight to the port city. That plan would result in them arriving the day before their cruise left.

Unfortunately, inclement weather delayed his departure from the work site. His wife packed a bag for him and left on the trip according to their original departure schedule with the belief that he would soon follow. Thinking that her husband was going to be able to get home to collect his bag, she left it at their house. Apparently their airline tickets had a limit of one checked bag per person and she was unwilling to incur an additional baggage charge by bringing it with her. She believed that he would collect it before joining her. Unfortunately, the weather delay resulted in him missing several flights and he had to hurriedly make alternate travel plans that had him arriving at the port the day of the ship's sailing. He confessed to becoming increasingly worried that he would miss the sailing. He arrived a mere 30 minutes before the ship's departure without having made it home to collect his vacation bag. He was still in his work clothes.

Upon arrival in their cabin, he learned that his wife had not intermingled the clothing between their bags and there was nothing for him to wear. The cruise line, sympathetic to his plight, had given him some items from their store and a free tuxedo rental to tide him over but they did not have any footwear in his size so he was forced to wear his work boots.

At every port he was hopeful that THIS was the port where his bag, which they optimistically had a neighbour ship to their first port of call, would catch up to them but to the best of my knowledge it never did.

These two stories are examples of delays, and I can fill this book with success stories of people travelling long distances to arrive in port on the day of their cruise. I merely want people to think about the possibility of delays and determine what would best suit their travel needs and risk levels: Same day arrival or not - You decide.

Embarkation Joys and Woes

I have been here since 8am sober, hungry and my ass is tired from sitting. When I can finally board, stand back, I am moving to the buffet at the speed of light.

(Woman sitting beside me in the embarkation tent waiting to board the ship.)

Congratulations, you have finally made it to embarkation day. Your cruise is about to begin, and your travel adventure has started. You are in for a world of fun. I want to make sure that you have the necessary information to make this day easier and as smooth as possible. In support of that goal, I am going to provide you with some dos and don'ts to ease your embarkation process.

The above quote is from a woman sitting beside me in an embarkation waiting area. She had a 2pm boarding time but had arrived much earlier and was despondent over not being able to board the cruise ship early. Additionally, her excess booze and clothes iron had been confiscated from her carry-on luggage. Clearly her day was not going as planned. I will be touching on excess alcohol and prohibited items in the next chapter so for the purpose of addressing embarkation, I will focus on getting to the cruise port and easing the boarding processes.

Getting to the Cruise Terminal/Port

This sounds like a fairly simple process. You arrive at your departure city and make your way to the cruise terminal. However, not all ports are as straight forward as it might seem. For example, cruise ships do not dock in Rome. Civitavecchia is the port servicing the city of Rome and it lies about 37 miles north of Rome. That means that getting to the port requires a bit of thought before hand. In one of my articles about Rome as a port stop, I address various ways to get to the port so I will not duplicate that information in this book and I cannot cover all ports. Suffice to say you should always know where your departure port is located and know how you are going to get there.

Next, make sure you are aware of which terminal your cruise ship is using to board your cruise. A busy port will have a number of terminals. Take the popular cruise port of Fort Lauderdale. It has nine terminals serving different cruise lines. Fortunately, the terminal information will be available to you beforehand from your cruise line/travel agent and easily checked. Additionally, common transportation means (such as taxis, buses, hotel shuttles etc.), will often know which cruise line is served by which terminal.

At some ports, you can easily spot, and walk to your cruise ship. We did this at one port wherein we observed our ship docking that morning while on an early walk and later we simply directed our taxi driver to the ship, knowing the check-in facility had to be nearby.

Ascertain in advance of your departure date, whether you can actually walk to your ship as ports tend to be secured areas where people may, or may not, be able to walk to the terminal check-in point. I will direct your attention once again to Rome's port of Civitavecchia where you can get yourself to the port entrance gate but have to take a shuttle bus from that point.

Most importantly, know the name of your ship and the cruise line. I know this sounds like basic information everyone will have but as evidenced by the following story, not every couple invests the same amount of time and effort into trip planning and detail.

> *My wife and I were vacationing in the USA and for our return home, we were taking a trans-Atlantic cruise that started in Florida. We were staying outside of the port city with another couple and the four of us had booked a private car hire to take us to the ship.*
>
> *We had enjoyed a night out the previous evening and our morning was a bit hectic as we had slept in and were running late. We had to rush to get packed up in time to meet our pre-arranged car and driver. We had prepaid our accommodation, so checkout had already been taken care of and we simply hurried out of our room to the front entrance where our friends and the driver were waiting for us.*

About 20 minutes into the ride to the ship, my wife and I realized that we had left our passports and money in the hotel room safe. Shit! A quick phone call to the hotel confirmed that our room had yet to be cleaned and a member of staff then went to the room and took possession of our items to hold for us. My wife and I already felt guilty that we had been late and made the other couple wait, so rather than all of us go back, it was decided that I would be the one to return while my wife and the other couple continued to the ship. Our driver arranged for another car to meet me at a certain point and take me back to the hotel.

The return to the hotel was quick and by the time I was back on track, I figured I was about two and a half hours behind the others. There was no danger of me missing the ship as I had lots of time. As we entered the city and headed towards the port, this new driver asked me what terminal he was taking me to. That is when I drew a blank. I had no idea. I could not even remember the name of the ship. My wife was the one who had made all the cruise arrangements with my input on destination and ports. We had been on three previous cruises, all with different cruise lines. The driver was making various suggestions, but they all sounded familiar.

My wife and I had only brought one cell phone since we would normally be together and we wanted to avoid roaming charges. I had that phone so I could not call my wife. I tried our friends but could not reach them (I later learned that they had their phones turned off as they use some kind of internet enabled phone program when travelling and that had a different telephone number). While I wracked my brain trying to remember the cruise line, my driver tried to reach the first driver to find out where he had dropped the other three off. Finally, in desperation I called my in-laws in Glasgow as they had a copy of our itinerary and could give me the information. As I was on the phone with my mother-in-law, my driver reached the original driver and learned where he had dropped my wife and friends off. Problem solved. Everyone but me found the incident quite comical but I was not so amused.

The next time we were leaving on a cruise, I put my jacket on and found a note in the pocket. Opening it up I found my wife had written: Hello, My name is Brendon. If I am lost, please deliver me to (name of ship). I suspect the story of my forgetting the name of the ship will live in family history for decades to come.

Brendon - Scotland

Embarkation can be a Breeze

I have gone through horrific boardings but not to despair, I have also been part of boarding processes that were so seamless and fast that they still stand out as a pleasant and quick experience. For example, we once boarded a cruise ship in Southampton, England wherein the boarding process was so quick and pleasant that we are still shaking our heads in wonder. The entire experience was a surprise because the day had not started out so smoothly.

It was 2018 and we were booked on a Mediterranean cruise. We had stayed at a historic hotel in the town, and soon discovered that a number of our fellow passengers had the same idea. When we made our way to the front desk to check-out, we found ourselves in a crush of people, all intent on accomplishing the same task, at the same time, and headed to the same ship. The two desk clerks were swamped, and the check-out process slowed to a crawl when one customer demanded a discount because of an issue with her pillow. Her complaint engaged one of the desk clerks for a full 25 minutes. That reduced the available staff members to one and he valiantly did his best to process everyone as quickly as possible. Early checkout had not been an option and as I stood there waiting, I made a mental note to ensure the next hotel we stayed at the night before a cruise, had online (TV or App), options or offered night before check-out service.

Finally, it was our turn to check-out and the clerk accomplished this task quickly and efficiently. But the next problem quickly presented itself as we, and many others, had a problem getting transportation to the port. Walking was not an option and ride sharing programs were fully booked. I had read in my pre-cruise research that taxis to the cruise ship terminal were easy and inexpensive. Believing that information to be accurate, I had booked no hotel to port transportation in advance. Unfortunately, taxis were at a premium so although we had planned on arriving at the ship around 12:30, we actually arrived later than intended. We expected huge crowds at the port and by this time we were hungry. Our 6am breakfast seemed a distant past and the prospect of food on the ship, seemed a long way off.

Upon arrival, we saw that a large number of people were there to check-in. Our worst nightmare. To make matters worse, my husband's luggage had been damaged in transport when we shared a taxi with another couple and the car boot (trunk), had taken out one of the wheels on his large suitcase. Consequently, his suitcase was determined to veer off in any direction but the one we wanted. We moved towards the check-in point expecting a significant amount of wait time.

But much to our surprise and delight, our check-in at the port was quick and easy. Our large luggage was checked-in, our cruise passes issued, and we were treated like royalty. Not only were we checked-in quickly, but we were also processed through security in record time. Upon boarding, we found our cabin was ready and that our large pieces of luggage had preceded us onboard and were waiting for us in our cabin. Now THAT was a first for us.

What made our embarkation process so easy? In part it was the professionalism and expertise of those working for the cruise line, but we can also take credit for easing the process. We had completed check-in on-line several weeks in advance. We had the necessary documentation/identification ready for inspection and we ensured that we did not have any prohibited items in our luggage such as an iron or a clothes steamer. We also had the allowable amount of wine in our carry-on for easy inspection. In short, we had read the cruise line instructions and reviewed the advice offered by fellow cruisers about the boarding process. We were well prepared.

Some quick tips to make your embarkation day painless are as follows:

1. Complete as much documentation as possible online in advance of the cruise;
2. Know where you have to go and the distance from your starting point (be it the airport, highway, train station, hotel or other accommodation);
3. Know how you are going to get to the cruise ship terminal;
4. Consider possible traffic problems you might encounter;
5. Have your travel documents ready upon arrival at check-in;
6. Have required medical/vaccination forms ready;
7. Have your proof of service/employment documentation such as Military, Fire, Police service etc. ready for inspection, if required;

8. Allow the porters or cruise agents to take your large luggage for delivery to your cabin; and

9. Be prepared for security screening.

On the very first cruise they ever took, my mother-in-law (M-I-L) had heard about people being turned away for not having proper identification. To be on the safe side she brought everything. Birth certificates, passports, driver's licenses, marriage records, library cards etc. When asked for ID she started to pull everything out. At one point the representative told her that what she had already produced was more than enough but she persisted in bringing out all the documents she had brought. Finally when M-I-L had finished, the rep said with a straight face: "Sorry, we can't accept you without your middle school pictures." Everyone laughed except M-I-L who always explains when telling this story, that she was about to call someone to get those pictures until she realized they were joking with her. She still laughs about it.

Morris - USA

Security and the Smugglers

Before we leave for our cruise, we take two empty bottles of wine, fill them with vodka and add a little food colouring. We then cork the bottles and shrink wrap the cork. Just before security, we give the bottles a good shake to make sure the colouring has not separated. It looks like we are bringing the allowable two bottles of wine per couple onto the ship. (Name Withheld)

Security

Some people are highly skilled in bringing booze and other contraband items onto cruise ships. They might be considered acceptable "smugglers" by some passengers but cruise lines don't agree. Before getting on a ship, you will have to pass through security screening. This security process is very much like the screening you would usually undergo at an airport screening point. It normally consists of passing through a walk-through metal detector and having your carry-on items pass through x-ray machines (some screening processes may also have electronic vapour detectors). The x-raying process may be followed by a hand search which can be triggered by something observed in your carry-on bag, or simply a random selection.

Security is looking for various items such as weapons or other contraband. When giving talks about cruising, I am often asked to provide examples of what would be considered contraband. Frankly there are numerous items I can name, but I will start with the most common: Alcohol. If you ask people about their opinion on bringing extra alcohol on to the ship, you are sure to get a variety of responses. Many seem to think that smuggling booze onboard is an acceptable and expected activity. I offer no opinion other than to say, every cruise line has a policy regarding alcohol and I recommend people follow those policies.

Thinking that cruise line personnel do not know about various items for sale to help people smuggle booze into sporting venues or in this case, onboard a ship, is unrealistic. Security personnel also scour the internet to look for such items. Beverage binoculars, sunscreen tubes, coffee mugs with booze compartments and the rather inventive bras with special liquid refreshment areas. Security have seen it all. A favourite standby is the old mouthwash bottle filled with an alcoholic beverage tinted green or blue with food dye.

As seen in the offering at the start of this chapter by a cruiser, another common trick is putting alcohol (gin for example), in a wine bottle and corking and sealing the bottle. If you engage in making your own wine, you have the tools to do this and the chance of the cruise line taking the seal off and uncorking the bottle to verify the contents are slim. But cruise lines do look at the wine bottles sporting screw caps. On a cruise departing Fort Lauderdale, I had a bottle of wine in my carry-on bag. I was expecting it to be examined by hand but as it was within my allowable limit (one bottle of wine), I was not concerned when security wanted to open my bag and have a look. The screener asked to see the bottle and upon inspection, sent me over to a security desk where another agent closely inspected the cap. When I questioned the purpose of this secondary look, the security agent told me that he was looking for signs the bottle had already been opened. Since it was clearly still sealed, I was soon sent on my way.

Cruise lines are very clear as to what can and cannot be brought onboard one of their ships. Usually, you are allowed a bottle of wine for each adult, but allowances can vary according to the cruise line. If caught with alcohol not approved, or above the allowable limit, the best that can happen is the beverage is confiscated and returned at the end of the cruise. The worst is that the beverage is confiscated and not returned. Although I have not heard of people being denied boarding for excess alcohol, it technically is a breach. It is important to remember that a cruise ship has the right to deny boarding for serious policy breaches.

If you are underage, you cannot bring alcohol onboard even if you are going to/or returning from, a port stop in a country that has a drinking age that meets your current years. The nineteen-year-old son of a friend of ours had his bottle of rum confiscated because he was under twenty-one. He bought it legally in port and thought that he would be allowed to keep it while in the territorial waters of that country. He was wrong.

Sometimes bringing the booze onboard is done at a port stop or during a shore excursion and alcohol purchased on those occasion can also be taken away as all persons returning to the ship must pass through security as soon as they board.

I offer myself as an example. On one stop in Croatia, I had visited the countryside and bought an odd-shaped, small bottle of what, according to my translation app, was walnut wine. The only reservation I had about buying the liquid is that I bought it from a roadside stand and it was clearly homemade. I debated whether it was wise to buy home-made booze. I overcame my reservations, paid and promptly put the little bottle in my purse, thinking nothing further about the matter.

When I returned to the ship, I submitted my purse for a security check and it underwent an x-ray examination. The bottle showed up on the x-ray, was subsequently physically examined by security and I was asked what type of liquid was in the bottle. I told them what I believed it to be and the bottle was "seized". I was informed that it would be returned to me at the end of the cruise which was fine with me. Since I planned on taking it home, I had no concerns about access during the rest of the cruise and if the bottle was not returned, I was not going to worry about 10 ounces of wine that cost me about $2.

The night before the end of the cruise, there was a knock on the door and I was given my little bottle back. I guess if I had wanted to, I could have opened it at that time and drank it, but the intent when buying it, was to take it home and I was grateful I had it in time to properly pack it into my checked baggage so it would not be seized at the airport in my carry-on. Later, when telling this story, a woman told me she had also bought home-made wine on a port stop. She explained that when asked what the liquid was, she told them *"vinegar"* and was allowed to take the bottle to her cabin. In her case, she also took her purchase home.

I have found that on cruises where beverage packages were all included, the security personnel were quite lenient about allowing beverages to be brought onboard. My husband bought some Limoncello in Italy and was allowed to take it to our cabin once security verified that he had the beverage package.

As evidenced by the examples I have given, security screening will identify alcohol, but lest you think that only alcohol is seized, you should be aware that any excess liquid can be seized as the man carrying a case of bottled water found out.

I can provide other examples of contraband items such as irons. Deemed to be fire hazards, irons are routinely seized as are handheld steamers and restraints such as hand cuffs. Additionally, anything considered to be a weapon, such as guns, large knives or pepper sprays etc. are not allowed. If you are in doubt over an item, contact the cruise line or your travel agent and ask.

Good Vibrations

Vivian from Canada related the tale of having her carry-on bag checked at security. Here is her story:

> *I was going through security screening to get onto the cruise ship when my carry-on bag was flagged for a hand search. I was surprised because my husband was right behind me and he was carrying the two bottles of wine we were allowed. I could not think of what in my bag had triggered the hand search.*
>
> *The girl doing the search was fairly young and I think she was not that experienced in her job. With a look of puzzlement, she rooted through my bag and eventually pulled out my vibrator. It was clear from her expression that she did not know what it was and she was examining it from every angle. One of the nearby screeners saw her and he had a quiet word in her ear. She turned bright red and dropped the vibrator on the floor. It made a noise when it hit the floor and she shrieked a bit so everyone in the screening area peered over at us. We all kind of looked at the vibrator laying on the floor and she looked like she was going to cry. It was clear she did not want to touch it again. The more experienced screener picked it up, handed it to me and asked me to "Ensure it was not broken" as I could "Make a claim for any damage".*

I turned it on at the same time as he was saying we could go somewhere private to check for damage. Too late, it was already vibrating and the audience this situation had attracted were either horrified or delighted with its ability to function. We were hurriedly cleared through the remaining security process and we were soon on our way to the ship.

***

We were in a line up to pass through security and in front of us was a family of five. Security was interested in one of the bags and asked permission to open one of them and have a look at something that had caught their eye. One of the kids had packed a pet snake. It was a big one too. I am not sure what happened to the snake or the family as they were all taken aside and then into a private room. From what I could see, the parents were pretty annoyed with the kid who looked like he was about 9 or 10.

Peter and Kellie

Is My Cabin Ready?

Don't expect your cabin to be ready if you board the ship early. Use the time to explore, have a meal, meet up with friends, lounge with a drink or engage in some fun activity that tells you your cruising adventure has begun.

On the first few cruises I enjoyed, I boarded the ships late and close to the time of sailing, so my cabins had been ready upon arrival. After I had a few cruises under my belt, I started to arrive and board earlier and came to learn that cabin availability upon boarding is not always the case. If you arrive early, most cruise ships will allow you to board and encourage you to tour the ship and partake of the buffet (or food in other available restaurants that are open). However, your cabin may not be ready, or accessible, until a certain time. That is why in my chapter entitled Embarkation Joys and Woes, I recommended that you check your large bag(s) with the cruise line when checking-in and have them delivered directly to your cabin. If your cabin is not ready, you do not want to be wandering around the ship trying to navigate busy common areas with large pieces of luggage.

As much as I advocate checking in your large pieces of luggage, I strongly endorse retaining your carry-on piece even though those too can be checked in. I learned this lesson on a Mediterranean cruise in 2007. Upon arrival at the check-in point at the port, one of

148

the porters took my large suitcase and then motioned for me to give up my carry-on bag. I was reluctant to hand it over, but another member of staff encouraged me to allow them to take it to the cabin. Against my better judgement, I agreed and allowed the porter to take the carry-on as well as my large suitcase leaving me with nothing but my small purse to carry. I came to regret this decision. Yes, I was able to wander the ship, unencumbered by any luggage, but my bags were not delivered to the cabin until later that evening. By 8pm, I had been able to access the cabin for hours and yet no luggage appeared. That meant I was unable to change for dinner and items in my carry-on luggage, that I would have liked to access, had to wait until the bag was delivered. Consequently, I always like to retain possession of my carry-on bag. Of course, this only works if the piece you consider your "carry-on" is in fact a bag that would meet most airline definitions of what constitutes a carry-on baggage. If you have done a lot of travelling, you will have seen the oversize bags that people try to pass off as a carry-on. You need to also make sure that your carry-on bag has what you need until your large bag(s) are delivered. Read On:

> *When you asked for stories about funny incidents relating to packing when taking a cruising holiday, I decided to share what two tired, baby parents packed in their carry-on for a cruise.*

> *My wife and I were what I would have described as efficient packers. We used to be able to pretty much pack*

everything we would need for a trip, in our carry-on bags but that changed when we had twin boys. We decided before we had children that we would continue to cruise and that our children would be a part of our regular cruising vacations. Nothing much was going to change. I look back at our naive optimism and shudder at our lack of awareness as to what being baby parents entailed. What were we thinking? Suddenly, strollers, diaper bags (filled to the brim with assorted baby paraphernalia), and other baby items became the norm. Free arms became a thing of the past when making our way onto a plane or ship.

Our return to cruising came about when the boys were just shy of their first birthday. Foolishly, we decided to travel with them when the babies were the most active and required the most baby stuff. As we were getting on the ship, we were each carrying a child and large baby bags. We were also dragging the bulky double stroller. Normally the boys would be in the stroller, but both decided to scream at the top of their lungs when we tried to put them back into it after passing through security. There we were, carrying two really unhappy babies, their bags and now the stroller. We had spent a lot of time preparing the bags for the boys and little time thinking about what we personally would need immediate access to once on the ship. We had kept one of our carry-on bags with us after check-in which we thought would fill our needs until our large bags were delivered. While I had the stroller, my wife was wheeling that carry-on bag. We were extremely grateful that our cabin was immediately available to us.

Upon accessing our cabin, we discovered that we had done a great job of packing for the boys and a really piss poor job of packing for us. Our one and only "adult" carry-on had shoes. Nothing but shoes. We had to wait for the delivery of our luggage to the cabin before we could change. That took several hours. While the boys had everything they could possibly need, we were still in our travel clothing that were wrinkled, sweaty and sporting a whiff of baby vomit.

Jason - USA

Cabin Availability

I have experienced cabin availability differently on various ships and I can say with a degree of certainty that not all ships have the same policy regarding cabin accessibility. I have been able to access my cruise ship cabin upon arrival on the ship just after check-in (for me about eleven in the morning), and as late as four o'clock on late afternoon sailings. Morning departures tend to have a tighter window for boarding and cabin availability.

I recommend that you plan to enjoy a meal and a wander around the ship and if you are able to access your cabin earlier than expected, then you can enjoy the privacy it will afford you. If you are not able to access your cabin, make good use of the time in numerous ways, such as booking specialty dinners or looking for specials in the spas. This is also a good time to take photos of the ship and areas that are not yet busy or crowded.

I have friends who hit the gym and others who change and relax by the pool. There is a lot you can do while waiting for your cabin to be ready so go explore the options. Your vacation has started!

When we were in our 30's a bunch of us booked a Caribbean cruise. We boarded early and after helping ourselves to the buffet and drinks, we decided to walk around and check everything out.

Our friend Jason decided to go swimming but his suit was in his suitcase and he could not access it nor his cabin.

Jason decided to go swimming anyway and went into the pool in his underwear. Some other people saw him and they too went in wearing only their underwear. I guess they thought it was normal. I think the ship's crew were pretty surprised to see about 15 people all in their underwear in the pool.

Finding Your Way Around the Ship

My roommate from college and his partner were meeting us onboard a Caribbean cruise. On departure day we wandered around the ship for hours looking for them while they did the same thing. Our generic "Meet you at the bar." proved to be harder to do than we thought. We went from bar to bar, while they did the same. We kept missing each other.

Jerimiah – Location Unknown

Ships come in all sizes and unless you are on a smaller sized vessel, there are bound to be numerous bars, a variety of restaurants and a plethora of gathering points. You will want to prearrange where and when you are meeting friends which, is important when on a large ship.

I am usually familiar with the layout of a ship before I board and as the number of cruises I take increases, the more I become familiar with the deck plans of certain ships, or a particular class of ships. There are people who memorize the deck plans of the ships they are sailing on and without any apparent thought, can name on which deck a particular bar or restaurant can be found.

These people impress me as they not only do their homework, but they have also accumulated a large amount of really good information about the ship. Unlike some, they don't tend to wander around like lost souls.

My husband is not an advance research type of individual when it comes to a ship. Within minutes of boarding, he generally finds out where the buffet is located and considers that a job well done. Everything else, for him, is a mission of discovery undertaken over the length of the cruise. By the end of the cruise, he will have found the various venues, nooks, crannies and other points of interest. He will know where most of the bars and restaurants are located, and he will always have checked out every onboard shop. This is all accomplished by the old-fashioned method of physically walking around the ship. Aka: Ship Exploration.

How does one find their way around a ship? There are numerous methods with the first being to look at a diagram of the ship on the app. Almost all major cruise lines have an app that you can download onto your phone or tablet. This app will deal with your booking but also provide you with a significant amount of useful information. In addition to daily activity guides and reservations (such as specialty dining reservations), there will be a ship's layout detailing what can be found on which deck. Whether you are looking for the pool, medical facility or the spa, the app will have that information for you. This is great if you are adept as using apps or are happy to carry your phone with you throughout the day. I still print out a ship deck plan and put it up on the wall of our cabin so we can look at it and easily find whatever venue we are looking for at any given time. It is useful as a quick reference point. Was the specialty restaurant we liked on deck 4 or 5? Where is the martini bar located etc., the deck plan acts as a quick reference without the need to consult the app.

When you get off the elevators there is almost always a diagram of the ship detailing what can be found on which deck. Also look for the indicators telling you where you are on the ship as there are usually more than one set of elevator banks or stairways and there are times you may get turned around and be a little uncertain if you are headed towards the aft or forward.

On a recent cruise, we often used interactive screens found in common areas. Not only were we able to quickly find out where the venue we were searching for was located, we were able to make dinner and theater reservations and check daily menus. These screens have other, useful functions, but I am listing the ones we frequently used and found most helpful. The ability to quickly change or make reservations was great. Previously we had only used the screens for locating venues as I had become accustomed to using the phone app for those functions. The interactive screens are another useful, onboard tool if you don't have your phone handy.

In summary, cruise ships are large and I often use embarkation day to wander the ship getting to know the venues and offerings. I also use the time to photograph some of the ship's specific locations when they are sparsely populated. As noted in the previous chapter, embarkation day will often afford you the opportunity to get a great photo of the pool area with nary a sunbather or swimmer in sight. Additionally, not all restaurants are open. Take the opportunity to photograph those or examine their menus.

First day specials can often be on offer and may afford you savings. You will be asked if you want to make specialty dining or spa reservations. Such first day offerings can be at a reduced price. On our last sailing, a first day special dining reservation was offered at a 30% discount.

We always eat in a specialty restaurant our first night of the cruise. These places are usually not busy which means that the pace is more relaxed and the staff very attentive. The prices are often heavily discounted so if someone wants to try out a specialty restaurant, the first night of a cruise is the best and least expensive time to do so.

Bridget - Canada

The Muster Drill

If you are writing a book about cruising, ask what's with the people who don't complete the muster drill and hold everything up when the crew have to chase them down and get them to do the drill?

Gloria - USA

The *International Convention for the Safety of Life at Sea* (known by the acronym of SOLAS – 1974 version), is a maritime treaty that is the enabling authority dictating that a passenger safety drill must be conducted by a ship within 24 hours of initial port of departure (basically at the start of the cruise). The *International Maritime Organization* oversees the treaties and compliance. Essentially, the muster drills (also known as safety drills or lifeboat drills etc.), are mandatory.

Most cruise lines host the drill before each ship's departure at the start of the cruise. The primary reasons are twofold:

1. To ensure the ship's crew are familiar with their roles and responsibilities during an emergency; and
2. To ensure passengers are familiar with what they are to do and where they are to go in case of an emergency and to recognize the alarm systems.

Muster drills have changed over the years. Once upon a time, passengers would be required to take their lifejackets from their cabins and report to their muster stations. I recall being shown how to put on my life jacket and standing in an assigned line by our lifeboat with various other passengers similarly sporting their floatation devices. We all received our instructions on the proper handling of emergency situations and how, once at our assigned stations, we would board the lifeboats.

Over time the process morphed and for a number of years we all gathered at a central point to watch a video presentation with a reminder to check the back of our cabin door for our muster point location. Being married to a firefighter for decades, I always checked the location of my assigned meeting or muster point and made sure that I was aware of the various routes I could take to get to that station. My theory is that I would rather find it when I had plenty of time and was relaxed, than later in a hurry.

Recently, cruise lines have used their apps to provide instructions. On a cruise I took in the fall of 2022, we had to watch the online presentation and then report to the gathering point for a crew member to scan our sea pass and confirm that we had viewed the safety presentation. Our crew member was quite diligent and quizzed us as to the alarm signal for proceeding to the meeting point and other safety issues. Apparently, we passed and were allowed to return to our cabin and continue to unpack.

On a subsequent cruise in 2023, we could review, online, the safety drill a few days before boarding and confirm that we had watched the drill. I thought that was a fairly quick and easy process but once onboard, prior to sailing, we still had to go to our muster station and have our pass scanned as a confirmation that we had attended and were cognizant of the safety protocols.

On every cruise there are usually one or two who fail to show up for, or participate in, the muster drill. Ship personnel will track them down and lead them through the process. Ship Captains will ensure that all passengers have participated in the drill and most cruise lines issue warnings that failure to comply can mean removal from the ship.

My wife and I are from Los Angeles and were booked on a Mediterranean cruise out of Italy. Because of work commitments, we did not leave until the day before our cruise and arrived in Italy the morning of our cruise departure. This was a big trip for us, and we were excited. We did not sleep on the overnight plane ride.

We arrived in Rome and caught a train to the port. By the time we got on our ship, we were exhausted. We had lunch and a few drinks while we waited for our cabin to be ready. Within minutes of being able to enter our cabin, we were asleep.

We missed the safety boat drill and I guess we slept through the knocking on our door by the crew trying to find us. We were woken by our room attendant, who was physically in our room with a person from security. They explained the situation and walked with us down to the muster point. They were really nice and apologized for having to come into our cabin and waking us up. As for us, we were a little embarrassed to be escorted down but we now know just how seriously they take those boat drills

Ken – USA

***

When we were young we took cruises with our parents who would make us put on our life jackets to go to the muster stations. It was normal to do that back then. Recently we went on a family cruise with spouses to celebrate my parents 50th anniversary. Mom made us all go back to our cabins and get our life jackets and put them on before us all going down together for the drill. The ten of us were the only ones on the entire ship wearing life jackets. My two teens were mortified. Rather than be embarrassed, my mother assured them that in case of an accident, we, at least, would be saved. As for everyone else she said, they were screwed.

Gord - USA

Tipping on a Ship

My husband Dan is a tipper and carries an assortment of US dollar ones, fives, tens and twenties with him to tip any staff member he feels deserves recognition. It does not matter if I tell him that tips have already been included or that we will tip at the conclusion of the cruise, he liberally hands out daily tips which makes him popular with the staff and unpopular with some of his fellow cruisers.

Tipping onboard a ship is known by many names; Gratuities, Service Gratuities, Crew Appreciation, Crew Incentive, Hotel and Dining Service Charges, Staff Service Charges etc. No matter what you call it, it amounts to the same thing, some form of staff appreciation. If you ask people about their opinion regarding tipping on a cruise, you are bound to get a myriad of comments. Some in favour, others against.

Some cruise lines, automatically include the gratuities into their cruise fares and advertise that those gratuities are always included in the fare. Other cruise lines may include gratuities as part of a bonus booking offer so although they are including the gratuities in their sign-up offer, it is not a routine practice to include the tips.

In many cases, the gratuity will appear as a separate item and be automatically added to your onboard account, supposedly for your convenience. That is why it is important, when booking a cruise, to pay attention to whether gratuities are included or not and to

161

understand how and when they are expected to be paid. The cruising websites have a number of stories of people who went to settle their onboard accounts only to find the hefty addition of the gratuities. It should also be noted that different category cabins, may result in differing rates. If you are staying in a suite, expect to pay more in gratuities per day.

Optional or Not

You may ask yourself why I have included information about the gratuities in an area of the book that follows my addressing check-in and boarding. Stay with me on this, there is a method to my order of business.

If gratuities are optional on a cruise, you can go to the customer/guest/client services desks and request that they be removed if you object to paying the gratuities or want to have them paid on a more personal level, directly to the staff members you want to recognize. This can be done on the day of embarkation or in some cases, a day or two before the conclusion of the cruise. Check with your cruise line to determine as to when you can make the request.

IF the gratuities are not optional and cannot be removed, please consider them as part of your cruise fare. In those cases, I always pay them in advance of the cruise.

Cruise lines will indicate that gratuities are shared among all the staff, including those who may not be in contact with the guests. The kitchen workers, those toiling in the laundry etc. We are told that gratuities are distributed to all the workers, not just those we see. I have been given differing information as to whether this is accurate. I have not completed any in-depth research into the veracity of this information and the handful of staff members I spoke with on different cruises, offered contradicting information as to whether they received the money or not. One employee, a dealer who worked in the ship's casino laughed when I asked him. *"The only tips I have seen are the ones personally handed to me by guests."* Our head waiter on another cruise told me that the gratuities were included in the wages. Unable to speak authoritatively on the subject, I simply provide the information I have been given and let you, the reader, decide.

When in Doubt: Ask

As mentioned at the start of this chapter, my husband is a "tipper" and he will often ask what someone (such as the waiter or room attendant), prefers with respect to how they are tipped. On one cruise, our cabin steward told us that we did not need to tip him, but if we did, a daily tip would be appreciated as opposed to being tipped at the end of the cruise. I understand his rationale, a daily tip meant he was seeing, on a daily basis, what you think of his work. It also meant he was getting his tips. It is not uncommon for some people to simply leave without tipping or to promise to tip and then depart the ship without giving one.

On another cruise, Dan left money every day for our cabin steward.

About mid cruise, I returned to the cabin early and ran into the steward's assistant in the hallway. He took a moment to thank us for the tips as clearly the room steward was sharing the money with him. I was happy to learn that this was occurring, but it did make me think of those who we don't see on a face-to-face basis and how gratuities factor into their shipboard wages.

Tipping the Bartender

One of the most common pieces of advice that people will give you re tipping on a cruise ship, is to tip the bartenders when you first get on the ship to ensure great service. I personally find that the bartenders and bar staff on cruise ships will always give great service however, I am married to the consummate tipper and so by the time I arrive at the bar, my husband has already made their acquaintance, so I lack objective data. I can however relate one story about differential treatment.

On one cruise, Dan had been at a particular bar for daily trivia while I attended various lectures or other events. A few days into the cruise, I showed up for the first time for the start of what was progressive trivia. I arrived before Dan as we were meeting up following attendance at separate activities. Two other couples soon joined me. The five of us had trouble getting the waiter's attention. One particular waiter seemed set on ignoring our table, and the other tables immediately around us. This changed as soon as Dan joined us. The waiter rushed past several tables with customers waving to get his attention and quickly made his way to Dan's side.

He was most anxious to please. This pattern continued throughout the cruise. I could speculate it was Dan's sunny disposition that was the attraction, but I am fairly confident that the frequency of Dan's tipping on the days and events prior, that had made him an attractive customer.

Tippers versus Non-Tippers

We have been on trips where gratuities were automatically integrated into the cost of the cruise. Because gratuities are already included, fellow cruisers may take you to task if they see you giving cash directly to a member of the crew. Sometimes referred to as "extra" tipping", there are people believe it encourages a double standard of service and an expectation by staff that everyone should engage in additional tipping.

In his youth, my husband was working as a bartender to help with his university costs and the tips he received went a long way to supporting himself. Consequently, you will never convince him that tipping is not a good idea. However, I am conversant that in various countries, tipping is not the norm and in some cases, is considered vulgar.

My recommendation is to make your own decision as to what you want to do. If gratuities are included in your cruise, then the issue is moot. If gratuities are optional, make your own informed decision.

Behind Every Smile There is a Story

On a Panama Canal cruise in January 2023, our cabin attendant was quite excited that he was going on holidays at the end of our cruise. He had not seen his wife and children in person in eight months. He was so full of enthusiasm about his upcoming break that we soon knew all about his family, their ages, likes etc. He even shared pictures with us and it was rather nice to get to know him a bit.

We know people who become friendly with the staff onboard the ships. Whether it is the bartenders, the dealer in the casino or the person making that morning omelet, sometimes connections are made and retained after a cruise. A friend of ours is the consummate connector with people he meets on the ship. By the end of a cruise, he often knows the home countries of various staff members and a little about their families. When the tsunami struck Indonesia on December 26, 2004, he contacted various crew members he had met, to see if they, or their families, were alright. For him, part of the cruising experience is making connections and learning a bit about the people behind the smiles. Ships have crews that represent multiple countries and if the staff are not busy and have a moment to chat, I always ask people to tell me a little bit about their home country. Some of my trips have been influenced by information I have received from crew members sharing stories or data about their homelands.

On one cruise, the small group I was with had fallen into the daily habit of meeting in a particular bar for drinks and as a result, became familiar with a certain member of the bar staff. Towards the end of the two-week cruise, we were chatting with this staff member and we learned that her contract was ending. She was returning to her home country and it was clear she had missed her family and was anxious to see them.

I asked her what had precipitated her decision to join the cruise line; Was it a desire to travel, meet people etc.? She told us that she had been trapped in an abusive relationship and she joined the cruise line as a means of escape. It gave her a job, a place to live and got her away from a bad situation. She had been working various contracts for a couple of years and felt in a secure enough place to return home. Listening to her story, reinforced that behind every smiling face, lies a story. I try to remember that when considering gratuities.

Making Friends Onboard

Cruise ships are usually places where a stranger might engage you in friendly conversation at various events and you strike up a friendship.

You have booked your cruise and boarded the ship. If your cabin is unavailable, you might just start your cruising experience with a visit to the buffet or bar. Suddenly, in mid bite, the people at the next table start talking to you like old friends. If you have never taken a cruise before, this might seem to be strange behaviour. Relax, this happens on cruises all the time.

I can regale you with stories about people I have met on cruises and who remain friends to this very day. I can also point you to various websites where cruising friendships are often the topic of conversations. People meet, have common interests and stay in touch after the cruise. They subsequently plan trips together and meet up on future cruises.

I am not sure whether it is the friendly atmosphere, the confined areas within a ship or just the whole vacation vibe that makes people more friendly, I just know that it seems easier to meet people on a ship.

Following the cessation of cruising (due to the covid pandemic), and the subsequent start up again, people were more cautious about joining tables or socializing at close quarters. However, with the advent of the vaccines, more people are feeling comfortable about cruising and about meeting people. Don't be afraid to start up a conversation. You may find yourself a lifelong friend.

If you are single or a solo traveller, your cruise ship might have singles tables, or a solo traveller meet and greet. Additionally, there may also be daily or ongoing activities and events geared towards singles.

I met my husband on a 14 day cruise. I was divorced and on a trip with a group of friends and he was on the trip with his brother. We met at a solo traveller event. It was not love at first sight; it was more like we kept running into each other at these solo events and got to know a little bit more about each other every day. He tells everyone he wore me down until I agreed to have dinner with him. I tell everyone he was like a fungus. He grew on me.

Iris - (location unknown)

Be Aware of Your Surroundings

Privacy in your cabin is expected but, on your balcony, or anywhere else on the ship, it is not always a given. Remember, it is possible you will be overlooked or overheard.

If you get chatting with people who are frequent cruisers, you are eventually going to run across someone who will recount a story about seeing something on a balcony or in a public place that was unexpected. I have heard the usual stories about people observed having intercourse on their balcony or in their cabin with the drapes open when the ship is in port. I have also been told of people sitting out on their balconies semi clad or in the nude, not expecting their neighbours to pop their head around the partition to say hi. All I can suggest is that you be aware of your surroundings and know that privacy within your cabin is to be expected if you close the drapes, but everywhere else is not a given.

As mentioned, we often book balcony cabins that are located at the rear of a ship. Called the rear, aft, or sunset cabins, they usually offer great views of the ship's wake. I have already commented on my enjoyment of these cabins but I have learned that the higher the aft cabin, the greater the likelihood that we will hear noise from the bar or restaurant above (as there is usually a bar or restaurant located at the stern, near the top of a ship). If you are just under one of these public locations, heed this warning: "If you can hear others, there is a strong possibility that the others can hear you".

On a westbound Atlantic sailing, I awoke early and went onto the balcony to await the sunrise. As I sat back enjoying the cool, dark solitude and peace of the early dawn, the quiet was broken with the sound of a balcony door opening. There were two women in the cabin beside me who earlier in the cruise had shared information that they had a habit of having morning coffees fortified with a little liquor. I had yet to see or hear them having their special coffees and had surmised that they probably enjoyed their balcony wake-up beverages later in the morning after I had left for breakfast.

On this occasion, they had arisen early, and as they exited their cabin and settled themselves onto their deck chairs, I could hear that they were having what they probably thought was a private conversation. The subject related to one of them suffering from a dry vagina. They were unaware of my presence on my cabin balcony and separated by a large metal balcony divider, I was not visible. They were seemingly oblivious to the possibility of being overheard. Their conversation covered some very intimate details surrounding the problem. I was debating the pros and cons of just quietly returning to my cabin interior when suddenly a voice from the restaurant railing directly above was heard to say, "*Just get some bloody lubricating cream and stop moaning about it."* Two gasps of surprise could be heard from the ladies as they beat a hasty retreat into their cabin. They had learned the lesson that one should never assume that a conversation on a ship's balcony is private. In my opinion, a balcony with a restaurant on the deck directly above should always lead to the conclusion that you will be overheard and possibly overlooked depending on the ship's configuration.

Most bizarre thing I have ever seen.

Fellow in his 70s standing on his head. I get off the elevator and I see this guy (where all the elevator doors are located), with his head on a cushion and his feet up. I went to my room for about 10 minutes and when I came back out, he was still there with security. Did I just see what I saw? Head stand wearing only swimming trunks.

David – USA

***

I once saw an angry woman throw a whole bunch of mens clothing over the balcony and into the sea. I am not sure if it belonged to her husband or a boyfriend but it looked like she threw the lot overboard.

Blake - USA

Hanging With Smart People

The trivia question of the day: How many times can you offer up incorrect answers before your trivia team dumps you?

Pretty much every cruise ship has "Trivia" listed as a daily activity. Both Dan and I enjoy trivia which means during a cruise, we can usually be found attending trivia events. In order to play with some degree of success, I have developed highly honed skills in seeking out teams to join. Specifically, I seek those who are intelligent but not bright enough to avoid me as a teammate. This is very important in progressive trivia as once people realize I'm the weak link, it is too late. I am on their team.

One would think that playing trivia would be straightforward, one either knows the correct answer or not. But I have learned a few things about ship-board trivia and as a result, I realize that it can be a cutthroat activity full of gamesmanship, intrigue and the occasional cheating. Most importantly, I have learned there is trivia strategy and etiquette.

On one of our first cruises, we wandered into an activity entitled "70's music trivia" and collected an answer sheet and a pencil.

Most of the "acoustically good" tables were occupied by groups of six people, as unbeknownst to us, people play in teams. By the time we arrived, teams had already been formed and skill sets evaluated. Naïve as to the strategic aspect of the game and the team model of play, we parked ourselves at a little table for two by the entrance and struggled to hear the music being played. The concept in that trivia game was to listen to a few lines of a song and then write down the name of the song and the artist(s) who sang the version being played.

This is perhaps the worst type of trivia for me since I never remember song titles or the names of artists. Fortunately for me, I was sitting with a music savant, my husband Dan, who easily named each song and artist. For the most part, my involvement was limited to mutely sitting and observing Dan writing the correct answers onto the paper. There was only one offering that he was unsure of and happily it was one of the three songs I know so I gave him the correct title. Unfortunately for me I did so by actually speaking. Yes, speaking out-loud. A trivia no-no and my faux pas did not go unnoticed.

"*Shush*" the woman at the next table hissed at me. Surprised, I looked at her wondering what I had done. Seeing my shocked look she said, '*If you know the answer write it down, don't give it to the world.*" The others at her table nodded thereby reinforcing her words. Duly chastised, I determined that if in the rare event, that I knew another correct answer, I would jot it down on a piece of paper and hand it to Dan. I promptly secured my own pencil and some scrap paper and sat there at the ready. It ended up being an exercise in futility as I never knew another answer so I contented myself with drawing little musical notes and stick people.

Thanks to Dan's knowledge and my one offering, we scored an impressive 25 out of 25. Since the answer sheets were corrected by people at other tables (as no team could correct their own responses), it became apparent to others that Dan was the knowledgeable one in our duo. At the next scheduled music trivia, we arrived early in order to secure a better seat that would allow us to clearly hear the music. Teams with fewer than six people rushed to ask Dan to join their team. Two teams asked if we would mind being "separated". Apparently, they were unwilling to recruit a star player if he came along with someone who was excess baggage. I already knew that when it came to music trivia, I was better suited to merely observe, and as such my feelings were not hurt. This action though, clearly demonstrated to us that trivia was not just the fun activity that the ship's entertainment committee had envisioned. For some, it is a cut-throat competition!

That was the first of what would become numerous shipboard trivia events and although Dan still enjoys the music-themed questions, we generally gravitate to the general knowledge trivia sessions where we both have a sniff at knowing the answer. Having seen the value of team play and combined brain power, we decided that we should try to join a team in advance.

Lesson number one: Join a team.

Before the start of our next cruise, on a cruising related social media site, I saw that an individual was looking for people to team up with for trivia. We were taking the same cruise so I responded that we would love to join her team. Oh, but it was not to be as easy as that. Via a private message we were promptly sent a list of questions essentially designed to determine our skill and knowledge level. Intimidated by the multiple questions neatly sectioned off under various subjects, we opted not to complete the questionnaire. We responded that in hindsight, we were unsure we would be able to make all the trivia sessions and that others would be better suited to fill the vacant positions on her team. Lesson number two had been learned: Avoid highly competitive fanatics.

Since those early days, we have become wiser and more knowledgeable when it comes to cruise ship trivia. We have seen people almost come to blows when it appears someone is using their internet package to find the answers. We have both become adept at writing down our answers to share with our team. One would think that the "shush" from that very first game would have stuck with me but as mentioned, I am not that bright, so it took yet a sterner warning from a woman whose team we joined on a whim when we were enjoying a different cruise. In response to the question regarding the name of Henry VIII's fifth wife, I excitedly spoke the name in a loud whisper. The woman whose team we had joined glared at me. "*Shut the fuck up.*" she said. Startled, I looked at her. *"If you know the answer, fucking write it down."* Yikes! Now THAT was a wake-up call and both Dan and I silently wrote down all answers for the remainder of the game lest we draw her ire. Fortunately, it was NOT a progressive trivia game and we were able to join another team for subsequent play. Lesson number three: Write your proposed answer down so you can share it with your teammates without speaking aloud. That also leads to Lesson number four: Write legibly.

Following the incident with the woman spouting the colourful language, we started to try and chat with prospective teammates in advance of play so we can evaluate their temperament and linguistic predisposition. Lesson number five: If they cannot complete a sentence without use of the "F" word, move on. We later fine-tuned this lesson to include, if they look like a serial killer, or are sporting a t-shirt stating trivia is their life, don't join their team. Since serial killers all look different and rarely advertise, we basically are focused on whether they wear t-shirts that alarm us in any way.

Lesson number six is an easy one but very important: Play with people smarter than you. This can be a bit tricky as we normally assume that most people are smarter than we are. A brief conversation pre-trivia play usually can establish whether they can speak in compound sentences and are friendly, which segues into Lesson number seven: Play with people who are fun. Most cruise ships give out trifling items for wins and even in progressive trivia (wherein your score is cumulative over numerous playing days), the prizes are generally inconsequential. I have yet to see a free cruise being given out to the winning trivia team. As such we are looking to enjoy the experience and yes, make a few friends.

It took us awhile to figure out that enhancing our chances of doing well was contingent on us linking up with smart people. The realization occurred on a trans-Atlantic cruise on the *Royal Caribbean Cruise Line*. We arrived at trivia at the last minute and were forced to sit at the bar. Seated beside us were a father and son team, Richard and Robert. They were from Boston, which was the final destination of our cruise. We soon threw our lot in with them and to our delight, both proved to be most capable players. In fact, we were duly impressed, especially with Robert's knowledge on a vast array of subjects, which we later learned was attributed to his work at the *Museum of Fine Arts*. When he found out we were going to stay in Boston for a week and were planning on visiting the museum, he volunteered to meet us and proved to be a generous and hospitable host. He was an outstanding ambassador of the museum. But his prowess in general knowledge trivia left its mark. Aha! A eureka moment. If we play with someone smart, we do better in trivia and acquire knowledge regarding various topics.

Learning from our experience with Richard and Robert, our next cruise, on the *Cunard* line, found us linking up with two couples from England. Gail, Tim, Mary and Gordon were generous enough to ask us to join them to form a team of six for one of the earlier general trivia games. Fortunately for us, we managed to answer a question or two, so they were kind enough to invite us to join them for additional trivia sessions. Little did they know; my superpower is the ability to offer the wrong answer with a high degree of believability. By the time they came to realize my knowledge and skill level was minimal, it was too late. We were a semi-permanent fixture on their team. The four of them were very good players so our score benefitted greatly from their skill and knowledge. The message learned from our previous cruise, was reinforced on this voyage: Play with people who know things. Lots of things.

Prior to the covid crisis, we came off a *Celebrity* cruise having once again lured people onto our team by pasting looks of quasi-intelligence onto our faces and appearing as if we had encyclopedic knowledge of just about everything. If no one offered a place on their team, we had a "Plan B". That involved hoarding the last four chairs, so people had to sit with us.

The innocent victims on that cruise were four people from Florida in the USA. Two of them, Georgie and Joe, being chemists, were a trivia player's dream as their knowledge of the periodic table of the elements allowed them to answer all those pesky "chemical/metal symbol" questions that always pop up. No longer would we have to rely on my stock answer of "iron". We actually had people who would know the answer. They also came with knowledge of a vast array of topics. To our absolute delight, they were fun people who were quick to forgive when I talked them out of the correct answer. *"No, no, Latin is NOT the official language of the Vatican, it is Italian"*. I

179

could provide more examples of a host of wrong answers I offered up, but they quickly learned to just write the correct answer down on the response sheet while giving the impression that they agreed with me. The joy of playing with people who are nice AND bright, is that they don't remind you of your errors and still greet you with a smile when you show up for trivia. As such I repeat Lesson seven: Play with people who are fun because it is vital that you enjoy the people on your team.

Post-covid cruising offered up some challenges as we did not know whether or not we wanted to play in a crowded room and specifically, whether we wanted to join with other people. Fortunately, we took a chance on a cruise from Vancouver to Hawaii and met a brilliant couple from Northern Ireland whose company was so enjoyable that we will be cruising with them again in the near future. That experience was followed up with two more cruises and new trivia teams. We met two sisters, Brandi and Amber, on a *Norwegian* cruise who were trivia impressive. We simply sat in awe of their encyclopedic knowledge and in one particular game, the focus was on a certain TV show. I thought I would be fairly good in that category but their ability to give the correct response to questions concerning the most obscure show details, demonstrated that they were in a trivia class far beyond me.

We will continue to play trivia and we will employ our seven lessons. Whether we win or come in last, we have learned that the real prize is the friendships you make.

Sometimes Shit Happens

Who among us has not had something go wrong? Life hands us surprises and shocks and cruise line events mirror life.

To be perfectly fair to everyone, I don't want to present a completely rosy picture about cruising because clearly, that would be inaccurate. Things can, and do, go wrong on a cruise. When I talk about things going wrong, I am making the distinction between disasters and times when things simply go badly. Let me clarify. When speaking with people about disasters that befall cruise ships, most people will bring up two incidents: the Titanic (April 1912) and the Costa Concordia (January 2012). Occurring almost 100 years apart, these two maritime disasters are indeed tragically memorable. The fact that these two incidents, separated by so much time, come to mind, is a testament to just how safe cruising is in these modern times. When turning our attention to when things go wrong on a cruise ship, the examples I am given are numerous and varied. I am often provided with stories of bad weather, malfunctioning toilets and onboard illness. In other words, no death occurred, and events onboard took an unexpected turn. In this chapter I will focus on times when things go badly, otherwise known as a time when shit happens.

If you read stories about cruising, you will know that although cruise lines have huge numbers of sailings per year that proceed smoothly and without incident, there are times when things do not go 100% according to plan. Take for example, the fire on the *Carnival Freedom*. The ship was docked in the Grand Turks on May 26, 2022, when it experienced a fire on the starboard wing of its funnel. A fire on a ship is generally great cause for concern but not so much in this case. There were no reported injuries and the proliferation of cameras at the ready, ensured that the event was well documented by those onshore and onboard. What struck me when watching a lot of those videos, is the detached interest of some of those watching the fire. There did not seem to be a lot of concern about a fire on the ship. I suspect that the fact that the ship was docked at the time and that the fire occurred in the daytime, were probably contributing factors to people remaining calm.

I mentioned that unexpected bad weather can adversely affect cruise lines and I have a lot of sympathy for cruise lines in this regard. No cruise line can predict the unexpected as those on the *Viking Sky* learned in March of 2019. The ship was sailing along the Norwegian coast when it lost power in bad weather. Sailing in the midst of waves exceeding 26 feet, it is reported that the ship began to take on water and list. A mayday call was issued. An evacuation of the passengers started and there are some great news footage videos of the incident as well as online clips of furniture sliding about on the wind tossed ship. Luckily the weather improved, and the ship, with the remaining passengers, was able to make it to port with the aid of tugboats.

Speaking of the Norwegian coastal weather, the *Norwegian Spirit* sailing in September of that same year (2019), also ran into problematic weather when on a two-week Scandinavian sailing. Four port stops had to be skipped and heavy fog made the majestic views almost impossible to see. Missed port stops happen from time to time and usually equate to some annoyed cruisers. Four missed port stops on a single sailing is quite dramatic and clearly memorable for those passengers.

As mentioned in the opening paragraph of this chapter, there are a number of complaints about toilets that do not function properly. I am going to take a brief moment to comment on how toilets work onboard a ship. Cruise ships, although surrounded by water, use very little in their sanitation processes and generally, as in the case of aircraft, use a suction system. There is a little bit of water in the toilet bowl and when the toilet is flushed, the bowl contents are sucked down into the sanitation system. All large cruise ships have an internal sanitation process plant/systems to address onboard waste.

Because of their internal waste disposal systems, when toilets do not work properly, cruise lines have the infrastructure in place to address the problem. No need to return to port, they usually have the mechanisms and experts in place to make the repairs.

When presented with stories about toilets not flushing (or otherwise not functioning properly), I have always been told that the problem was quickly fixed or the cruisers were moved to another cabin. Consequently, I provide the information about the possibility of toilets not working properly, and couple it with the advice that cruise lines always seem to expeditiously address that type of problem IF there is no loss of power on the ship. I have to confess that the number of stories about toilets not functioning properly has impacted on the title of this chapter. Take for example, the February 2013 incident involving the *Carnival Triumph*. A fire onboard resulted in a loss of power, which in turn resulted in problems with the waste disposal system. Nicknamed the "poop cruise", passengers had a number of graphic stories about what happens when waste disposal systems fail to operate as intended.

Problems are not always mechanical or weather related and can present themselves as unforeseen surprises to the passengers as those on the *Crystal Symphony* learned in January of 2022.

In 2021, cruising had mostly been on hold due to fears of the spread of the covid virus so by January of 2022, cruisers were starting to return to their favourite lines and resuming travel. The *Crystal Symphony*, which was scheduled to dock in Miami, was diverted to the Bahamas to avoid a possible seizure of the ship due to unpaid fuel charges. The unexpected diversion to the Bahamas delayed the return of the passengers to the US by a day and instead of sailing into Miami, people were ferried to Fort Lauderdale and returned from that point.

When requesting stories about unexpected occurrences impacting cruises, I received a number of offerings encompassing complaints detailing cabin dissatisfaction to a plethora of what I consider minor complaints (soot on deck chairs, flat soda, running out of ice cream etc.). For this chapter, I have tried to focus on major incidents that adversely affected a cruise or resulted in major changes to a cruise itinerary.

For example, Bev and Ed from Canada had booked three back-to-back cruises on the *Cunard Line Queen Mary 2* when the ship ran into mechanical difficulties in April 2023. The first of their three cruises was cancelled by the cruise line before they were able to board for the first leg of their journey from North America to England. Fortunately, the ship was quickly repaired and the cruise line arranged their flights to England to catch the second leg of their sailings.

What happens when one out of two of a ship's stabilizers stop working? The following story came to me from Doug and Karen, also from Canada. They were sharing information on what happened to them on a cruise to the Galapagos Islands on a small ship that had a stabilizer stop working.

> *Well, when the ship you are on only holds 90 passengers, movement is more noticeable than on the larger ships. You already feel the motion of the*

ship but with functioning stabilizers, things are generally fairly steady. However, when one of the ship's stabilizers stops functioning, things go for a wild ride.

Meal service was an adventure with dinner plates and cutlery dancing all over the table and often headed towards our laps. Diners had to grab and hold onto their plates, while the crew moved quickly to catch items such as coffee pots from sliding around. Whatever we were drinking sloshed around in half-filled glasses or cups. Staff were on the run a lot!

In our cabin, drawers would slide open and then closed. To cut down on the slamming noise, our resourceful cabin steward provided ropes, elastics and bungee cords to help keep the drawers and closets closed. It was necessary to ensure that all loose objects were stored away. Of all our cruises, we never had a cabin look so decluttered!

Sleeping became an adventure as the bed pitched and rolled. I was certainly getting an aerobic workout trying to stay in it. My back was tight and sore because I used those muscles all night long in order to stay in a bed that rocked like a cradle. My husband's muscles were fine because his side of the *bed was against the wall and he wasn't concerned about rolling out of bed.*

The cruise was memorable and quite the adventure.

The Things You Hear at the Bar

We don't normally hang around bars, but on cruises, we may stop by a bar after a shore excursion or for a pre dinner drink. Bars on ships are often great sources of entertainment. You never know what you are going to hear.

The man looked at us sadly stating that he had lost another sea pass card following a night in the bar. "*I don't know how it happens*" he lamented. "*One minute I am having another drink at the bar and the next thing I know I am wandering around the ship looking for my sea pass.*" He shook his head despondently, pondering the mystery of the lost passes and opining on the fact he was now on a first name basis with the staff at Customer Service and security. When asked how often he had misplaced his card, he gloomily stated he had lost count after three but was confident that he was on a path to some kind of shipboard record. "*If I lose one more, I am sure they will staple the next one to my forehead.*" he offered before returning to his beer to contemplate the mysteries of the disappearing sea passes. You meet all kinds of people at the bars on a ship and I have often thought about writing a book based solely on interviews with bartenders.

I am sure the stories about things they have seen and heard onboard would be fascinating. After all, unlike the local pubs/bars where there are regulars, ship bars have a gathering of people from different backgrounds, geographical locals and political ideology. Add alcohol to the mix and the combination makes for some interesting conversations.

One bartender told us about a passenger who kept telling joke after joke. He went on for over an hour. He said that everyone at the bar was entertained and thought the fellow was hilarious. When someone asked him if he was a comedian by trade, the fellow said that he was a mortician and therefore always appreciative when he had a "live audience" to hear his jokes.

Cougar Zelda

In the chapter entitled *Starting to Cruise*, I spoke of the woman we nicknamed Zelda who was on the hunt for husband number four. At age 67, with her flaming red hair and bedazzling wardrobe, Zelda hung around the martini bar and within a short period of time knew most of the people who had become 'regulars'.

A veteran of numerous cruises, she had many a tale to tell and I was never sure whether they were in fact true or the product of an entertaining and talented storyteller.

One of her most amusing stories revolved around her doing a disco dance on the bar of a ship during the 70's when cruise ships were a little more formal and bar dancing was not an approved ship activity.

In truth, I don't think it is an approved activity these days either, but I digress. Apparently, Zelda met her third husband that night. She "felt" the music and got up on the bar to do a dance and "mesmerized" the crowd. Not only did she entertain her fellow passengers, but one in particular thought the incident was hilarious. She told us that any man who enjoyed a good laugh and "*unbridled fun*," was worthy of her and she focused her attention on him. This man, who was a few years younger than her, was destined to become husband number three all because he liked her "bar dance". With a wink and a laugh, Zelda told us that husband three's wife at the time, was not as impressed with her moves as he was. She informed us that he passed away about two years after they married, and my friend and I hold the opinion that she might have simply worn him out. She was a bundle of energy and I imagine also quite a handful.

Another of her stories involved a couple who were sitting at a bar with her. She said they had arrived around six in the evening and stayed at the bar when she went to dine. She returned to the bar around eight to find them still in their same seats but now they were "*sniping at each other*". By nine that evening, they were arguing, and their quarrel suddenly turned physical. Other passengers separated them. Security, which had been called by the bartender, arrived and the husband was led away. According to Zelda, the wife suddenly objected to the removal of her husband and she aggressively

190

jumped onto the back of one of the security guards. The wife had to be physically dragged off the guard's back by the bartender and some of the ship's staff who had also responded to the call for security at the bar. *"That was one hell of a battle,"* Zelda offered up. Shocked, I agreed with her and asked if the couple were removed from the ship. *"Oh no"* she said. *"They were back the next day and the whole thing was repeated again. I think by the third night they were told they would no longer be served if they got into another fight but I heard they just changed bars."*

That story always struck me as a bit of a tall tale but unless I run into Zelda again, I will never know. I look for her when I go to a bar on a cruise. I imagine she is on husband 20 by now and still sporting her fiery red hair and big laugh.

Over the years, I repeated this story to various ship personnel on different sailings and I was surprised when told that couples physically fighting is not an uncommon occurrence, nor is it unusual for security or staff to be assaulted when trying to separate couples.

The Runners

When you leave the ship to go ashore on a port stop, always make note of the time you must be back onboard. Ships have a departure time, and they will leave you behind if necessary to maintain their schedule. I recommend you be back onboard one hour before departure time (or the ship designated return time,) or take up jogging in preparation for the panic run experience.

In 2011 my cousin Linda, her husband Leo and my husband Dan decided a Mediterranean cruise was just the ticket for a fun vacation. They chose the western Mediterranean as a destination since the ship had stops in a number of locations that were highly desirable. I had already been on a similar voyage to essentially the same stops a few years before, but they convinced me that another cruise would be a great idea. They were correct, it was a fun filled vacation with a lot of laughs and some interesting sightseeing. We threw in some pre and post cruise touring and a great time was had by all.

Having had a blast on that cruise vacation, we decided to do it all again and invited family and friends to join us. Following some pre-cruise touring for part of the group, we all met in Rome and on the 26th of September 2013, we left on an eastern Mediterranean cruise. The cruise was fairly port-intensive so at the start of the trip we were busy with tours we had self-organized. By day eight, when we docked in Rhodes, we had no structured tour planned and everyone had the option of walking from the ship into the center of the old town. The touring pace would be set by each individual, and they would also decide what they wanted to see or do. Staying on the ship was an option as well for those who just wanted to kick back and enjoy a little pampering. For others, a trip to the beach was the perfect down time.

Dan and I decided to walk into the old town as there were several things we wanted to see. A UNESCO World Cultural Heritage site, the medieval town is exceptional and there is so much to see. The walled city, once a stronghold of the Order of Knights of the Hospital of Saint John of Jerusalem, offered up everything from fabulous historical views to modern day shopping. We walked, talked and shopped for about five hours. I say "talked" because we kept running into people from our group or fellow cruisers as we made our way through the cobbled streets.

Weather wise, we were treated to blue skies, warm temperatures and a cooling breeze from the ocean which made the day perfect for sightseeing. We were soon lost in the cultural and historical offerings at hand and eventually we decided we should make our way back to the ship. By the time we started to return, it was around 4:00 p.m. and the ship was due to depart at 6 p.m. for our next destination. We had dinner reservations for 7 p.m. so we had plenty of time to get back to the ship, shower and change for dinner with a little time left over for a sail away drink on our balcony.

As we retraced our steps, we happened upon an open public area that was partially bordered by several restaurants, many of which had outdoor seating. Once again, we encountered people we knew. Two of our friends, Violet and Marianna, were having drinks at one of the restaurants. Basking in the sunshine of the day, they had a table that was strategically placed to overlook the square and provided them with an excellent vantage point for people watching. We stopped and chatted with them for a few minutes and compared notes on purchases made and deals that had been found. As tempting as it was, we declined their offer to join them for a drink as we wanted to get back to the ship and shower before dinner.

We were back on the ship by 4:45pm and were soon showered, changed and sipping wine on the balcony. Family members were in the cabin next to ours and we had opened our balcony divider to form one large outdoor space. They soon joined us, and the four of us proceeded to watch the late arrivals return. Everyone should have been back onboard by this time but there are always people who are a little late and forced to hurry in order to reach the gangplank before it is pulled away. Watching these runners make the dash to the ship had become a bit of entertainment for our group. Two cabins to my left were my cousins Wanda and Deb who were also ensconced on their balcony and set to enjoy the show.

As we watched people hurrying to return, we saw that the wind had picked up, so late comers were now facing a considerable head wind when dashing to the ship. As time quickly passed, the wind significantly increased. People were now bent forward, fighting the strong gusts that threatened to push them one step back for every two steps forward. One tiny, slim woman, appeared to only make it back with the help of two of her companions who had a firm grip on each of her arms and half lifted/dragged her to the ship.

Sheltered from the wind, we sat back in comfort and enjoyed our drinks while watching people fight distance and strong wind gusts in their fight to reboard on time.

Finally, we noticed the crew start to pull away one of the two gangplanks and dismantle the awning around the only remaining gangplank. Clearly departure was imminent. Now THIS is the point where it really gets interesting for the watchers because anyone who is not onboard is dangerously close to *"missing the boat"*. It is a bit of a sport to observe people run to get onto the ship as the crew prepare for port departure. Consequently, there are always people on their cabin balconies at departure time specifically to watch the leave-taking process. Just when it seemed like the last gangplank was about to be stowed and the buoy lines unhooked, we spotted two runners.

Dan noted that these two had certainly left things to the last minute and were in danger of missing the ship. It was not a simple matter of just running a straight line directly to the point where we were berthed. There was a security point and a bit of a staggered L shaped routing to get to the ship so we could see runners from quite a distance before they were actually close to arriving at the gangplank.

There was something familiar about the two people running towards our ship. I picked up the binoculars we had brought and zoomed in on the figures. Much to my surprise, it was Violet and Marianna. Running with their purchases clutched in their hands and bouncing off their sides with every step they took, they were in full flight mode. Their faces clearly showed their concern and the stress of having zero time before the ship left. They were also fighting that strong head wind that was making the task on hand that much harder.

I could hear shouts of encouragement from people on the ship who were watching from their balconies or the upper deck common areas. *'Hurry girls, hurry'* screamed people from various vantage points. *'Violet, Marianna, run like the wind'*, I heard my cousin Wanda yell. *'Run, girls, run'*, shouted my mother. I added my voice of encouragement to the others. Then I heard more shouts as another runner appeared at the port entrance gate and was also engaged in the sprint of terror.

The concern we had for our friends was alleviated when it was clear the staff at the last remaining gangplank were going to wait for the runners but it put the question into my head as to whether or not ships actually will leave passengers when they are late back to the ship. When talking to Violet and Marianna later, they confirmed that they had simply lost track of time. They had sat enjoying the ambiance of the historic location and the chance to embrace the moment. How often are you in Rhodes, sitting at a table in a cobbled medieval square? How frequently do you get to bask in beautiful Mediterranean weather, while people watching? Too many times people rush off a ship, dash from site to site and then hurry back to the ship without taking the time to really appreciate where they are.

Violet and Marianna are two friends who usually take a moment to enjoy the experience of a locale. Rarely does this "stop and appreciate where you are" attitude cause them grief. On this occasion, they had no excuse for being late since they did not have too much to drink or get waylaid by any person or event. They simply failed to notice that time had quickly passed, leaving them in a precarious position with respect to a timely return to the ship.

When we returned home from that voyage, I did some research into whether ships do or do not leave people stranded at ports. Obviously, I had previously heard accounts of this happening, but I was looking for direct evidence. I was not interested in hearsay stories or internet postings that may or may not be true. My research determined that the answer is yes, ships will leave passengers behind and have, on occasion, left passengers who are on a shipboard organized shore excursion behind. However, it is important to note that cruise lines will wait as long as possible (and what is possible varies with the company, itinerary and the port).

Cruise lines seem to have differing policies with respect to what action they take if it appears that a passenger has not returned from a shore excursion. It often starts with paging the missing passenger to see if they have already boarded. It may also involve sending staff to that individual's cabin to determine if they are there or to establish whether passports have been left in their cabin safe etc. The universal position of the cruise lines is that if you miss the ship, and it is not as a result of a cruise line booked activity, you are responsible for rejoining the ship and the associated costs for doing so.

I found my research into understanding how and why people missed their ships interesting and there certainly were a lot of good and bad reasons people had failed to make it back onboard. One story I was told in person, while on a cruise, involved a family with a disabled daughter. The daughter had suffered a catastrophic brain injury in an accident and was wheel chair bound. When on a Mediterranean cruise and returning from a self organized shore excursion, they were delayed in getting the wheel chair with their daughter, out of the accessible cab and they missed the ship. It cost them considerable money and two different cab rides to be taken to the next port to catch up with the ship.

Some people claim to be habitually late and show pride in arriving mere seconds before the ship sails. However, in the case of Violet and Marianna, I am certain that they will never be part of that group.

Naked Dave

Did you ever have a dream where you're naked and everyone else is not? Well, something like that happened to me except it was not a dream.

Dave - Canada

Every cruise gives us memories and we come away with moments to cherish, tales to tell and laughter to share. One cruise was no different although the laugh enjoyed is at the expense of a good friend, who has given me permission to share his story.

Dan and I had booked the inaugural passenger trans-Atlantic repositioning cruise of the Celebrity Edge departing near the end of April in 2019. We were soon joined by several friends who also booked the cruise. Various travel plans were made, shore excursions discussed, and we all looked forward to the trip with great anticipation. One of the members of the group is a fellow named Dave.

Dave and his wife Claire are seasoned travellers who have wandered the world on both land and cruise holidays. To say they are knowledgeable travelers would be an understatement, so we never expected to hear that Dave had a shipboard incident that would leave us all giggling. A very bad night indeed. What happened we enquired?

Dave sadly shook his head, heaved a big sigh and said that his eyesight is not what it used to be and that had caused him great grief the previous night.

It seems that sometime during the wee hours, Dave had to use the toilet and not wanting to wake his wife, he stealthily got out of bed and quietly made his way towards the cabin's bathroom. The blinds in the cabins on this new ship, make the rooms extremely dark and Dave's room was no exception. Knowing that the cabin's bathroom had a night light, he looked for any faint shimmer of light to get his bearings and lead him to his destination. He sleepily saw some faint light showing through what appeared to be a door frame and felt his way to it.

He was determined to be quiet and do nothing to wake Claire up, so upon arriving at the faint light, he felt for and found a door handle. Quickly he pulled the door open and stepped into what he thought was the bathroom. As soon as he stepped out, he realized his error. The door he had just walked through led not to the bathroom but the hallway. The realization hit him at the same time as he heard the door click shut behind him, effectively locking him out.

Normally that would not be so bad, however Dave sleeps in the nude so he was now naked and standing in the ship's corridor. Compounding the issue was the sound of another cabin door opening and the voice of a woman thanking her friends for inviting her for a drink in their cabin. Dave could hear their farewells: "*Good night, see you tomorrow*" and knew that it might only be a matter of seconds before he was discovered.

Naked and in imminent danger of being seen, Dave pressed himself against the door and tried to alert Claire to his dire situation. *"Claire, Claire"* he whispered in as loud a voice as he could manage without drawing attention to himself. There was no response. He tried again with the same result. Trying to make himself as small as possible, he started gently knocking on the door. *"Claire, Claire, open the door"* he whispered with some urgency. Finally, with more force he banged on the door and with greater emphasis said *"Claire, Claire, OPEN-THE-FUCKING-DOOR"*.

Upon waking, Claire looked around. She could not see Dave but she could hear his voice. She went to the bathroom and opened the door. No Dave. However, she could clearly hear him and the desperation in his voice. *"Where are you?"* she asked. *"I am in the hallway, open the door"* he responded with even greater urgency.

Claire opened the door and her naked husband rushed past her. *"What were you doing naked in the hall?"* she asked as she shut the cabin door. Dave, relieved to be inside the cabin without threat of arrest for being a "streaker", explained to her what happened.

The next morning Dave shared his story with us and commented *"You don't know how relieved I was that the woman turned in the other direction when she left her friend's cabin"*. We all wondered if she had indeed turned in Dave's direction, seen his naked butt and then choose to walk in the other direction. After all, Dave had been too busy pressing himself against the door and trying to get Claire to let him in, to look at the woman to determine if she was headed his way.

Claire, the master of the understatement said "It is a good thing I heard him and opened the door. I think they have a dress code on this ship". Dave simply responded, "It would have been much ado about such a little thing".

The rest of us now refer to him as "Naked Dave".

Pirates – Arrgh Matey

Our family was booked on an eastern Africa cruise that would take us through the Suez Canal. My father-in-law read a book about piracy incidents in the Gulf of Aden and Somali Sea and became quite concerned that we were going to be in imminent peril if we took the cruise. Thankfully he attended a talk about cruising and that issue was covered. He was told he was in greater danger of pirates stealing his passwords in the free wi-fi zones on ships or at port stops than by armed bandits in speed boats.

Benjamin

In this chapter, I address only the possibility of pirate activity at sea and not terrorism against cruising passengers. As such, I do not deal with the 1985 incident involving the *Achille Lauro* and the attack by four terrorists. That incident will be covered in my next book.

A pirate is described as a person who commits an act of robbery by ship or in a coastal area. Piracy is deemed to have occurred when an act is committed in international waters for personal gain. Modern day pirates look for valuables such as money, cargo or ransom potential.

Are there pirates in this day and age? Yes there are but the risks to passengers on a large cruise ship are negligible. Let's look at the general criteria for attacking a ship:

1. Availability / proximity to the pirate home base;
2. Ease in attacking;
3. Valuable cargo/persons/personal items;
4. Ransom potential;
5. Chances of boarding success;
6. Armed deterrence by security personnel;
7. Determination of quick reward versus holding for ransom;
8. Prospect of retaliation by external forces;
9. Probability of capture; and
10. Likelihood of punishment.

Areas of Pirate Activity

Cruise ships do sail in areas where there has been pirate activity such as off the east coast of Africa, north-west coast of South America and Asia. However, cruise ship companies engage in threat and risk assessments when determining routes and areas of potential danger. Cruise lines work to ensure that their ships cruise away from problematic coastal waters and implement measures to be both proactive and reactive to the possibility of jeopardy and changing threat conditions. Similar to dealing with evolving weather conditions that might pose a danger, cruise lines will continuously monitor for evolving threats.

Ease in Attacking

Logistically, it is too difficult to capture a large cruise ship and corral all the crew and passengers into a manageable area. A cargo or container ship would be easier and be a more controllable target. Additionally, there are trained security personnel onboard cruises and the sheer size of the ships render them difficult targets.

Valuable Cargo, Persons and Ransom Potential

Clearly a cruise ship will have persons with money and valuables. It will also have cash onboard for casino payouts and other items. Such a vessel certainly would be considered a high value target for ransom. However, realistically and logistically, it is too difficult to capture a large cruise ship, round up and contain all the crew and passengers and then find a spot to "hide" the ship while waiting for a ransom to be paid.

Chances of Boarding Success

Cruise lines avoid high risk areas by ensuring their routes are as safe as possible. Cruise ships also may impose blackout conditions to restrict deck movement in areas of elevated risk and have their security and other staff on alert for any menace, suspicious or concerning behaviour associated with boats or persons in the area.

Security experts advise that there are two methods of committing piracy against a large ship. The first is to forcibly board the ship, the second is to employ modern weapons, such as a rocket launcher, that threatens structural damage to the ship if the ship's captain does not allow boarding. Neither have happened in modern day cruising.

There have been a few occasions where pirates in speed boats have harassed cruise liners but they have been unsuccessful. To put your mind at ease, there has never been a successful pirate attack on a modern cruise ship. That is not to say you won't find the odd pirate onboard ship. Read on.

> *We were on a ship during Halloween and there were a lot of the American passengers dressed as pirates. There were hundreds of eye patches being worn that evening and a proliferation of pirate jokes. Arrrrr Matey!*
>
> *Brodie – United Kingdom*

WI Fi Pirates

I am not an expert on internet security, nor do I pretend to have a great deal of knowledge on the subject. A lot of websites have security systems in place to combat malware and viruses so there is less of a risk than there has been in the past. However, a little caution when using public wi-fi is in order. A public wi-fi connection can be compromised. Draft your e-mails in advance of connecting so you limit your time connected to the internet.

Free port wi-fi may be attractive and sailings that include free wi-fi onboard may make you feel in touch but be cyber communication smart. Be aware that cyber-pirates love to visit unsecured networks and steal sensitive information. This could include passwords and financial information.

Internet or digital piracy, is the illegal copying and subsequent use of copyrighted material obtained from the Internet or a digital source. When giving talks about cruising, I usually field a question or two about digital piracy. Specifically, the subject of photographs comes up in relation to pictures that people may post on their social media pages or blog writing/online journaling platforms. It is important to remember, when posting material on an Internet site, that, unless access is restricted, you are most likely posting to a public forum. Your images and/or writing, unless annotated as an image owned by, or copyrighted to you, may be considered publicly available material for use by others.

Theft on a Cruise Ship

As with public spaces everywhere, thefts can and do occur on a ship. As tempting as it may be to have your phone or wallet with you at all times, don't leave them unattended. The same for expensive items. On one cruise, a man told me he had his i-pad stolen when he left it on a chair. He went to the toilet and then to get a drink. He thought that leaving the i-pad on his chair would be an effective way to save his seat. When I asked him how long he had been away, he said about 15 to 20 minutes.

When you are going to an event on the ship, think about what you will need and bring the minimum.

A pro tip on saving a chair in event you are just stepping away for a few minutes, bring a magazine, book or old piece of clothing to leave at your seat. Do not leave valuable items. Whenever possible, have one person remain at your seat/table. One of the people we know tried leaving their drinks on the table as a way of showing the table was occupied but found upon their return that a waiter had collected the drinks while they were gone and cleaned the table.

Lanyards & Retractable ID Holders

You will need to carry your key card and having a holder of some form will be useful if you don't have pockets. Do not leave your card unattended on a table or chair.

Some people use a lanyard with a plastic cabin card holder that will also hold a little cash for tips. Others carry retractable room key holders or clip on plastic pouches to carry their passes. I prefer a plastic, clip on, retractable zip ID holder that is waterproof. I can put a little cash in it, maybe a tissue or two and my cabin card. It will clip onto whatever I am wearing. Try and ensure you keep your valuables with you or locked up in your cabin safe.

We were on the pool deck when the couple occupying the deck chairs next to us asked us to look after their things while they went swimming. They left their cell phones, watches and wallet laid out on their chairs. We had never met them and had not even been talking to them. Their request just came out of the blue but we thought, OK, we will keep an eye on things. An hour later they were still in the pool and hanging out with their friends. We finally got tired of being their security guards and my friend went over to them and told them we were leaving and they should find someone else to guard their stuff. Then they seemed pissed off.

Janie

Excursion Challenges

My husband and I live near a beach and my sister, and her partner live in the Northwest. We see the beach daily. On a recent Caribbean cruise, they wanted to go to the beaches at each port while we wanted to visit places of cultural interest. After the second port we decided that the only way to keep the peace was by each couple doing our own thing at each stop.

Joan- USA

The upside of taking a cruise is that the ship will deliver you to a port and you are able to leave the ship to tour. Cruise lines plan their itineraries with popular destinations in mind. They are not about to take you to a location where there is nothing of interest to see and do (unless it is a private island for a beach day). Consequently, you will generally arrive at a port and be spoiled for choice. What are you going to do? What do you want to see?

For some, it might be an easy choice. They may have always wanted to see something specific at, or nearby, a port stop. For example, a friend always dreamed of seeing the statue of David by Michelangelo so when her cruise ship stopped in Livorno, she took one of the many available trains to Florence to see the statue. She did not care if she saw anything else at that stop, her destination was fixed. Her travel companions were less certain as to what they wanted to see as the area is rich in choices of possible destinations. Some went to Pisa to see the Leaning Tower while others went to Cinque Terre or joined her in Florence. They all declared that they could have spent a week in the area and not seen everything that they wanted to see.

That scenario leads me to the downside of port stops at locations that offer up a plethora of choices. You generally have one or two days to see as much as possible, so you must be selective and strategic. Sometime those choices are hard.

Consequently, I will circle back to my comments about checking out your port stops and destinations. Deciding what shore excursions to take requires some research and effort on your part and possibly compromise if you are travelling with others. I once was on a port stop in Naples and did a walk off the ship shore excursion. I visited nearby Castel Nuovo to see the artwork and then walked to the old section of the city to look at the architecture. When I returned to the ship, I was speaking with some fellow travellers who had paid for a shore excursion to a winery. They were disappointed with how their day had turned out and asked to see some of the photos I had taken during my walk around. While looking at the photos, they expressed disappointment that they had not engaged in a similar activity. They had failed to do their own research and basically booked the wine tour because an acquaintance had suggested it. They had not realized that they could explore some really interesting places within walking distance of the location where their ship would dock.

Some shore excursions are walk off the ship and walk around the port. Others involve the need to make arrangements for transportation to the nearest town or point of interest. Know what your method of transportation will be in advance. Don't be that person who pays to be taken to a place within easy walking distance.

> *We got off the ship in Puerto Vallarta and there was a line of taxis waiting. We jumped in one and asked the driver to take us to Walmart because we needed to buy some things we had forgotten. The guy drove us across the street. We could easily have walked there in mere minutes.*
>
> *Cathy*

In addition to possibly "getting taken for a ride" when something is within easy walking distance, there is also the concern about finding yourself stranded because you did not arrange and cannot find transportation elsewhere. Read about one couple who were gouged when on an unexpected ride share because they could not find transportation to a nearby town.

> *We took the tender boats to shore only to find there was not a lot to see. We had a choice to walk about 5 miles or wait for hours in a line up to get a local bus.*

There were no taxis so we talked to a couple who had arranged a private car hire and did a ride share with them. We found out later that based on what we were charged, the fee they had us pay was probably the total amount of the car hire. They certainly saw us coming.

(Name Withheld)

Cruise Line Organized Shore Excursion

Ships will always offer shore excursions and there are pros and cons to these. Ship-arranged shore excursions will always take you to the most popular attractions saving you the time and effort of doing research. Additionally, these types of tours are usually packaged deals. They take you from the ship to the site/venue and back again. If you are uncomfortable arranging your own shore excursion, this is the way for you to go. You can sign up for the excursion before or during the cruise. Note, that the most popular excursions may sell out before the cruise, so it is best to book ahead.

The pros are that you will be well looked after and guaranteed to be back at your ship on time or the cruise line will take care of the problems associated with any delay. The guides will always be knowledgeable on their subject and speak the language advertised by the cruise line.

The cons are that these tours are usually more expensive than self-organized tours and, in my experience, they tend to be crowded.

213

You are travelling with strangers who may have differing physical ability levels. I have been on a ship organized tour with people who were using walkers and/or were hearing challenged. On that particular tour, the walking pace of our group was glacial, and the guide kept having to repeat herself because people, many of whom were standing next to her, could not hear. The worst part of that tour was the person who kept asking inane questions. At first, we thought this individual was trying to be funny but by the fourth ludicrous question we realized the individual was serious and really did want to know if people in that country ate "real food".

Self-Organized Shore Excursion

I always suggest that people check out the shore excursions that the cruise line has put together and see if there is anything there that is of interest to them. If there is, my suggestion is that they note the price and start to research whether or not they can arrange to do a similar tour on their own and if so, what the associated cost would be.

I often take the most interesting attractions listed on various ship-organized shore excursions and combine them into a self-organized tour. Cruisers will also look at what local tour companies are offering as shore excursions as those too, will give you a fairly good idea of what an area has on offer. Tailor your shore excursion to meet your specific interests and physical abilities. Be realistic as to what activities can be undertaken or which places can be visited on the excursion. Remember, when deciding on whether to engage in a self-arranged tour, you are responsible for researching and booking your outing. If you are late getting back to the ship, and the ship has departed, you must arrange your own transportation to get yourself to the ship (hopefully at the next port stop). Pay particular attention to the reputation and rating of any transportation or guide you book. Outline your expectations for the tour when booking such as:

1. Meeting point at the port;

2. Pick-up time;

3. Number of passengers to be picked up;

4. Payment method;

5. Are gratuities included;

6. Bottled water (if required);

7. Language of driver/guide;

8. Lunch reservations if required;

9. Who is responsible for the purchase of any venue tickets;

10. Condition of transportation vehicle (air conditioning, wi-fi etc.);

11. Mandatory return to ship time; and

12. Special considerations such as no smoking, no perfume etc.

Be Shore Excursion Smart

When you are on your shore excursion, take note of your excursion vehicle, where it is parked (or will be parked if you are being dropped off), and details about the meeting point and time. I always take a picture with my phone of the vehicle and license plate. I also get the name of the driver and their telephone number in case we have difficulty meeting up or I need to contact them.

Sometimes at certain venues, the drivers will drop you off at the front/ticket entrance and arrange to meet you at a certain spot or pick you up when you are done. That might not be at the same location. You must ensure you know where they will be or how to contact them. I also carry the name of the company I booked through (if not a private driver), so if there are any issues, I can easily contact the company.

Confirm the linguistic capabilities of the driver and/or guide and in what language you expect them to communicate with you while on your booking. I once organized an excursion in Morocco and we specified that we wanted the driver to have proficiency in English. However, the fellow spoke only French. Fortunately, we are able to speak French which meant communication was not an issue but for another group on a different day, it may have been a problem.

In advance of any country visit, I aways have the local police and ambulance numbers on hand (both programed into my phone and in a hard copy for someone else to carry). For example, 911 may be standard in North America but 112 is used in different countries in Europe while other countries use 999.

I also make a list of my country's embassy contact information and ensure everyone in my party has that number. I check for local rules and customs that might impact on my visit. Most importantly, I have the contact information for the port, cruise line and ship.

We asked our 18 year old son to research some beaches for us to visit on our shore excursions. He must have searched only for topless or nude beaches. My wife was not amused.

Lucas - USA

A Shore Excursion Tale

When a monkey jumps on your head, remain calm, take out your rubber snake and wave it in the monkey's face. The monkey will quickly move away. It works every time.

Groomed by a Monkey

I have encountered wild monkeys on numerous occasions and in different countries. Although many people think of them as cute little creatures, I hold a different opinion. They are hair pulling thieves and hooligans who are one move away from being total jerks. If they have not already stolen something from you, they are in the process of plotting their crime spree.

Lest you think me overly harsh, let me relate a few incidents that led me to my current position on the beasts. Once, while in India, we asked to be taken to Galta Ji which is an ancient Hindu Pilgrimage site about 10 km from the city of Jaipur. We said we wanted to see monkeys and this temple complex is known for having an abundance of monkeys hanging about. At that time, I still thought monkeys were cute and their little shenanigans were just adorable. Our driver, apparently only hearing the part about us wanting to see monkeys, took us to another temple that had a large number of primates but there was no nearby parking lot. Consequently, we had to leave the van unguarded on the side of the road and walk up a long, U-shaped hill. On the way up to the temple, we passed a large number of monkeys. Oh, how delightful. I took loads of photos and while we were all admiring and feeding these little cuties, some of their cronies were taking the windshield wiper blades off our van and damaging the mirrors. There was nothing endearing about their wanton vandalism.

Another time in Bali, a long-tailed macaque stole my travel journal. I had been sitting on the ground floor balcony connected to my hotel room and updating the journal. At the same time, I was having my lunch and enjoying a cool drink. The little thief jumped down from the overhead pergola, startling me. The beast promptly stole the journal out of my hands. He may have been aiming for the half sandwich I was also holding but he got the book instead and fled. Over the railing he went, and I followed him in hot pursuit. In the heat of the midday sun, it was an unequal contest as he was acclimatized to running in sweltering temperatures while I was not. He was also more agile and apparently immune to the verbal abuse I spewed and the aspersions I cast on his heritage. While I was in the midst of the big chase, his cronies promptly stole the rest of the food on my balcony table and one of them drank my drink. I never did get my travel journal back so if anyone finds it, please return it to me. I doubt the robber was literate so no chance he shared the contents with his partners in crime.

I could give more examples, but I think I made my point. Monkeys are not to be trusted. With this in mind, we had a port stop in Gibraltar and I was determined to travel up the mountain to see the caves. But I was well aware that going up the mountain meant that I would probably come into contact with a primate or two. Gibraltar is known for its Gibraltar Apes who hang out at the scenic lookout points. These apes are in reality, tailless Barbary Macaques and there were plenty of them to see.

I was informed by our guide and by way of various signage, that the apes are fed by the state and should not be given food by tourists. I had already decided that I would not be carrying any foodstuff with me so the government's warning about feeding was just a reinforcement of my position. Those beasts would not be fed by me.

I had also heard that certain food, such as chocolate, was bad for them as it is reported to make them more aggressive. As such, I relieved my husband of his granola and chocolate bar before we left the ship and once by the caves, I avoided standing near anyone eating or having food in sight. Apparently, not all visitors were aware that eating in front of the apes was a poor idea. Certainly no one told the apes that they should focus on the fruit that was sitting on the ground waiting for them, as they seemed to think that better food was in the offing from the tourists arriving on scene.

Having seen what monkeys can do when we were in India and my past experience with aggressive little monkey thieves, I was prepared to face the apes that I knew would be awaiting at various stops. I deliberately did not have earrings, necklace(s), or any jewellery adorning my person, nor did I have a plastic bag in hand which I had heard would also attract the little fiends. Apparently, they harboured the misconception that plastic bags held monkey treasures and would grab them.

I did not walk anywhere near the apes and avoided passing underneath trees or wires where they were visible. I was on high alert. Nevertheless, I let my guard down and while I was taking a video of a few monkeys with babies, a rather aggressive male hit me from behind. The first inclination I had that I was the newest monkey perch was the sensation of having something heavy land on my head and then the feeling of feet on my shoulders. Once safely perched on my shoulder, he decided to give me a good grooming and started going through my hair and digging into my scalp.

Startled at having something jump on me, I let out a yelp of surprise. I remained calm but I was not enjoying the experience as much as those who were capturing videos of the incident were. I was not worried about the ape biting me but I was concerned about lice or fleas becoming unwanted visitors on my person. My unwelcome guest was quite content to groom me until people tried to shoo him off me and then he grabbed onto my hair as that was the best way to retain his position. The more people tried to get him off me, the tighter his grip on my hair. It was only when our taxi driver waved a fake rubber snake in his face, that he abandoned his perch in favour of a more appreciative hostess. He left with clumps of my hair in his hands and a look that bespoke of his distain at my lack of appreciation for his spa skills. After all, had I booked a scalp cleaning and massage on the ship, it would have surely cost me.

My close encounter with the Gibraltar Ape was all well and good but I was quite happy to get back into the taxi bus and head to the Great Siege Tunnels. I kept asking Dan to check me for signs of lice which ensured that other people in the shared taxi gave me a wide berth.

The lesson of how to scare off a Gibraltar Ape was not lost on me and I made a note to bring fake rubber snakes with me whenever I enter an area inhabited by monkeys or apes. In fact, I just travel with one permanently, you never know when you might need one.

Crowds in Port

Postcard sent from Dubrovnik, Croatia:

> *Our ship was surrounded by large cruise liners who discharged their passengers at regular intervals. Our time in port was spent fighting the crowds and cursing the bad luck that brought us here on a day when over 14,000 other cruisers arrived.*

I laugh when people tell me that they take smaller ships as there will be fewer people in port. As evidenced by my postcard, our ship had arrived in Dubrovnik on a day when a large number of other cruise liners were either docked or tendered. The walled city was teeming with visitors making the streets busy and the shops crowded. Although the theory that a smaller ship will have fewer people onboard and therefore have less people getting off at port stops sounds reasonable, the reality can be very different.

Check your port stops in advance of your cruise to see what other ships might be visiting that day. There are numerous websites that will provide information on ships in various ports but for me, the quickest and most accurate way, is to simply visit the port website to see if it has a listing of the ships that will be in port on your arrival date. For example, in advance of a fall cruise in 2022, I looked up the port of Vancouver for the upcoming sailing and learned that there would be two cruise liners docked at the port. Both were departing at 4pm which meant that the cruise line terminal area would have heavy passenger traffic between 11am and 3pm. Looking at a map of the terminal, I was able to ascertain as to the best route into the building and whether traffic was likely to be congested on the access road and taxi drop-off locations.

Knowing how busy a port is going to be will help you make smart choices regarding your shore excursions. Can you buy tickets to certain places, such as a museum, in advance? If you are booking a private car hire or tour, you will need to book early to get a good price and a reliable driver. Some types of shore excursions have a limited number of tours in a day so you may need to book in advance. For example, at a port stop in Halifax, we thought a walk-off shore excursion would suit us as the port is fairly easy to navigate and most things that we wanted to see could be accessed on foot. My husband wanted to visit a specific brewery which we were going to walk to after we had toured the Halifax Citadel. Unfortunately, we learned that the brewery tours were completely booked and a few other locations on our list were also fully booked. We should have arranged our tickets in advance.

Knowing how busy a port will be will also allow you to plan your shore activities in advance, based on what the most popular attractions might be. You will want to get to those attractions as soon as possible to avoid the crowds, or late in the day after the bulk of the other tourists have finished. One example that always comes to mind is the Vatican Museum in Rome. The Sistine Chapel is always busy in the summer and by mid to end day it is packed. Always buy your ticket in advance and get to the museum as soon as you possibly can. Remember, your cruise ship will be docking in Civitavecchia, over an hour away, so plan your transportation to get you to the museum, which opens at 9am, as quickly as possible. If there are five other ships in port, you need to ensure your transportation to Rome is planned, booked and your destination fixed otherwise you will find yourself in long lineups and missing 50% of the places you want to see.

Knowing how busy a port will be will also help you decide how much time you will need to return to the ship. For example, the road from Monaco to Villefranche in normal circumstances is a fairly short drive of around 14 minutes but when a number of cruise ships are in port, the road is heavily travelled and traffic slows to a crawl. If you are anxious about making your ship's departure time, you will have to ensure you plan for delays.

Crowds in port also create some everyday issues outside of the obvious transportation and site visit problems already outlined. ATMs around the port and in high traffic areas can run out of cash. Restaurants and bars can be busy and service slow. When in an area where bargaining is part of the sales culture, vendors are less inclined to haggle when they have a large number of other potential customers as evidenced by the following story.

> *We were in a bazaar in Morocco and I was negotiating for a puzzle box. We were almost at the price I wanted to pay when a tour bus from one of the high-end cruise ships pulled up and discharged all its passengers. I could see more buses approaching. The seller immediately lost interest in negotiating with me as he sensed fresh meat had just arrived. I moved further into the market to get to vendors before the newly arrived hoard. I soon learned that there are no bargains to be had when the market is packed with tourists many of whom just pay whatever is asked rather than bargain.*
>
> *Anne-Marie – Canada*

This Port is for You - Shore Excursions Continued

Never make a decision regarding a shore excursion solely based on the recommendations of others. Engage in a little research.

We had completed a shore excursion at a certain port and arrived back at the ship a few hours before departure time. Since our excursion had started early in the morning and involved a lot of walking on a very hot day, we decided refreshments were in order prior to heading to our cabin to wash and change.

On that particular ship, there was a bar not far from the embarkation entrance point. People returning from various day trips were streaming by us and we soon spotted friends of ours. *"Did you have a good shore excursion?"* my husband asked.

"Worst port stop ever." was the reply. The couple joined us for about ten minutes and expounded on the horrors of their day. They hated the city, they found the reported city highlights to be average and in their opinion, there was little of interest to be seen. After a quick drink they were soon on their way and as we were preparing to go to our cabin, another couple we knew arrived back at the ship and

stopped by to chat.

In response to my question as to how they enjoyed their day, they gushed that it was the best stop of the entire cruise. Two decidedly different critiques of the same place. Upon further discussion, we learned that they had done the same thing as the first two people, so it was not a matter of visiting different places or partaking of differing activities. The four people had done exactly the same thing and visited the same historical sites yet their take on what they had seen and done were polar opposites.

I wish I could tell you that this was unusual, but it is in fact, often the norm. My husband disliked a certain port stop in Greece while my niece Sarah, touted it as the best stop of our Mediterranean cruise.

I was provided with similar information from a reader who was commenting on my travel website. This reader told me that on a Baltic Sea cruise, she, and one of her close friends, disagreed on whether a certain stop was excellent or simply average. Her friend can't wait to make a return visit and flooded her social media pages with photos of the town while the other had little good to say about the same location. This reader told me that if she is on a cruise that stops there again, she won't bother to get off the ship.

When looking at things to see in any port, do a little research and learn what there is on offer. There are some ports where choices are easy and there are multiple things to do and see. For example, Barcelona offers up a number of what I call the "sites with sights" meaning the locations are places that are sure to have something people want to see.

Follow these simple guidelines:

1. What do you know about the port?
2. What is at the port that interests you?
3. Are there famous points that you want to see?
4. Consider your budget and marry up your activities with the amount of money you can realistically spend.
5. Do you need to pre-book/arrange transportation?
6. Can you pre purchase tickets to activities or locations such as museums?
7. How are you going to get to the places you want to see (not all ships dock at, or in, the middle of a city (i.e.: the Rome port is 37 miles/60 kilometres away from the city).
8. The port might be located in a different city from the one advertised. An example would be the city of Livorno. Often referred to as the Florence stop, cruisers will find that Florence is about 60 miles/96 kilometres away.
9. Don't book a shore excursion unless it has points of interest for you.
10. Check out the physical activity levels associated with shore excursions and choose something suitable for your physical abilities.
11. Dress appropriately for the location and the weather.

12. Allow yourself enough time to do the activity and tour the place you want to see.

13. Choose your shore excursion travel companions to ensure you are aligned with what you want to see and do if arranging a private tour.

14. Verify that the place you want to visit is open on the day your ship will dock. For example, there are places that are closed on Sundays or markets that only operate on certain days of the week.

15. Are there port warnings that you should be aware of that will require certain precautions.

16. Do you anticipate that there will be communication issues (language barriers).

Dressing for the Port and the Activity

While on a stop in Mexico my husband and I had no option but to take an organized bus tour to the Mayan ruins at Chichen Itza. On the return trip I over-heard a conversation between two people.

Person One: *Did you see the slutty dressed woman?*

Person Two: Oh my God, yes," was the response. *Everybody saw her.*

I am not a fan of name calling or being catty about an individual's clothing choices, but I confess to knowing instantly who they were talking about. On the trip was a very attractive woman who had chosen to wear a very short, fully skirted dress and platform style sandals. She had great difficulty walking over the sand and rocky ground and constantly looked like she was about to topple over. As wobbly as her gait was due to the unsuitability of her footwear, the most noticeable part of her outfit was the full skirt which would catch in the wind and fly up around her waist to expose her thong. She spent considerable time clutching at the dress, trying to hold it down. A truly difficult task given that the hem of the dress ended about two inches below her bottom.

She did not have a lot of material to work with, so it was a futile task. Needless to say, she drew a lot of attention. I could tell from her expression that the interest was unwelcome and it was not appreciated by her male companion.

At that time, we could still climb the pyramid and although she had several problems with the skirt flying up, the woman opted to climb the pyramid. The steep, narrow steps are best climbed on all fours, which she did. Her bottom exposed to everyone below and once at the top of the pyramid, the dress swirled around her waist leaving everything below exposed. I could hear the clicks of cameras and I am sure there are a number of photos of her taken by people who had no idea who she was and were simply photographing her because of her exposure.

Walking back towards the bus when it was time to leave, she turned her ankle on the uneven ground and with no support in the platform sandals, she fell, skinning her leg. Luckily, I had some antiseptic wipes to help clean her abrasions, but I am sure she was quite bruised and sore for days afterward.

She is not the only one I have seen who failed to wear appropriate clothing for the shore excursion they had undertaken. There are religious sites that may have dress codes attached. For example, when in Rome, many people want to visit St. Peter's Basilica and are surprised when they learn that there is a dress code and sleeveless tops and above the knee shorts don't make the cut. Going to visit the USS Arizona Memorial at Pearl Harbor? You will need to wear shoes, shorts and a shirt as no bathing suits or bare chests are allowed. Large bags/backpacks are also prohibited in many locations. I always recommend that people check for dress codes or clothing restrictions in advance of visiting any planned site to ensure that you are wearing, or have available to wear, appropriate clothing. I confirm in advance of each visit even if I have been there before as things can change.

I also suggest you think about what clothing is the most suitable for the shore excursion. Not only am I talking about the obvious clothing to walk, climb, swim etc., I am also talking about appropriate dress for the environment (both weather and social). Ensuring that the clothing you are wearing is warm or cool enough for the weather is only one component of a travel equation. Make sure your clothing is suitable for the social environment. Around a port, the local people may be used to seeing different dress styles and someone wearing shorts might not be out of the norm. But if you're headed to an area away from a port, ask yourself whether the standard of dress is different? Should you undertake to wear more conservative garb to avoid offending local standards or breaking local dress codes. It is simple to check before you leave to see if there are clothing/dress suggestions for visitors to specific countries. In Canada for example, I always check with the Canadian government travel advice and advisories site. Most countries have such websites, so I suggest you visit the web page(s) operated by your country's government and read the advisories specific to your nationality and warnings relating to the countries you intend on visiting.

https://travel.gc.ca/travelling/advisories

Scams, Perks and Gouging Jerks

When travelling, be aware that everyone you meet is not always honest and all businesses do not operate with integrity.

My friend was leaving on a cruise that would stop in northern Africa. She was very excited over the opportunity to shop in the souks and since I had recently travelled to North Africa, she wanted to chat about what she could expect.

In anticipation of her engaging in a buying spree while on holiday, she was on a pre cruise diet. Consequently, we met for lunch consisting of garden salads and mineral water and I shared my recent travel experience with her. I included information on the bargaining techniques I had used, and what I perceived to be the dos and don'ts of shopping in market environments. I included travel warnings and reminded her to be alert for the possibility of items being switched when put into the shopping bags. One thing we specifically spoke of, was the availability of designer dresses which were on her radar of items to buy and the reason for her diet. I told her to be mindful of her purse if she decided to try on any clothing.

My friend set off on her trip and from time to time I would see postings on her social media accounts about her trip and how much fun she was having at the different port stops. Then her accounts went quiet. No more photos or updates, only silence. That is not necessarily a bad thing because cruises can be busy with plenty of activities to occupy one's time. There is also the matter of internet access on a ship. If you don't have an internet package, and do not want to buy time, then you will have to wait for access to free wi-fi or a return home to catch up on your social media or personal communication..

Upon her return we met up for a meal of pasta and wine. I was anxious to hear about her trip. How was the cruise? How did she enjoy the port stops? Did she get any good deals or buy anything of interest? As a travel writer, I always quiz people on all aspects of their trips, and I feel that I generally learn a little something from everyone.

According to my friend, the cruise had been going well, and she bought a few things early on in her vacation. However, she was being frugal with her money thinking that the best deals would be found in the souks. With great anticipation, she was determined to scour the market stalls for bargains. Being a shopper by nature and a lover of "deals", it was her intent to do the bulk of her buying in the markets. She was ready when the ship finally docked at the much-anticipated port stop in Africa.

She told me that she approached the first market with a sense of excitement. The atmosphere was lively, and the sights, sounds and smells were everything she had envisioned. As she made her way

Sleeping in a Life Jacket

around the various stalls, she was bombarded with offers of purses, pashminas, carvings, spices, and other assorted goods. Finally, she spotted a row of stalls that had clothing, specifically formal wear. She had found her shopping nirvana.

Silk, chiffon, sequined and feathered evening dresses beckoned her, and a number of stalls offered a varied selection. Going through the mixture of choices at several booths, she was delighted to find the styles on offer were contemporary and the quality satisfactory. Spoiled by choice and actively pursued by vendors, she finally zeroed in on a black and gold sequined evening gown. It looked to be the right size and the style was one that she thought might suit her, but she hesitated.

The merchant was over the top in his praise of her selection and offered to drop the price from the modest $450USD he had quoted. She said that she could not afford that price and was not sure of the style choice. She was a little worried that it was too revealing for her taste. He suggested the price could be dropped if she was at all concerned about the cost. As she held the dress up against her and peered in the full-length mirror, he lowered the price to $400, then $350, and even lower to $300. She then tried the dress on over her clothes and thought it looked Ok but the line was impacted by her clothing and so she did not have a clear picture of what the dress actually looked like on her. The merchant, seeing her indecision, dropped the price dramatically and mentioned that for a mere

$80USD, this creation could be hers IF she bought it right then and there.

My friend vacillated as there were other dresses that she liked in the surrounding stalls, but she would be in the same position of not seeing exactly how any dress would fit if she could only see it over her clothing or held against her body. She asked if there was any place she could try the dress on and was led to a curtained area that was apparently used by the customers of several vendors. A little leery about the privacy, she asked one of the women accompanying her to stand guard as she tried the dress on. She removed her top and pants and since the dress had a fitted bra, she removed her bra and placed them on a little stool. There was no mirror in this curtained area so in order to see how the dress looked on her, she had to go back to the vendor's stall. At the last minute she remembered to take her purse. Accompanied by the friend who had acted as a guard, she went to the mirror so she could now see the overall look. Upon closer examination, she determined that the dress was far too figure-hugging and low cut for her taste. Back to the curtained area she went only to discover the clothes she had left on the stool were now gone. She looked everywhere, lifting the stool, pushing aside curtains, even conducting a search of every stall that was near the curtained section.

She called her friends and they all embarked of a search of the area. Even the vendor joined in on the search, but her clothes were no where to be found. My friend said she suspected that the merchant had an accomplice who took her clothes but since he was always in the presence of her friends who had remained at his stall, and he spoke to no one else, she could prove nothing. Other nearby vendors were happy to help by offering their evening wear for sale but they no longer seemed willing to negotiate prices.

There was nothing left to do but to buy some clothes to wear and my friend was not going to buy formal wear to replace her casual clothing. Clearly, she had to find stalls that sold casual clothing. However, the merchant did not want his fine evening gown to be worn around the market while she searched for items to buy from some other merchant. In fact, he did not even want her to continue wearing the gown as it was hot and he was worried about sweat or damage to the garment. He demanded she either buy the dress or take it off. She sent two of her friends off to buy some alternate clothing and told the vendor to wait for their return. But he wanted her out of the dress immediately and was unwilling to wait. Security was called but their presence failed to resolve the issue. She was told her clothing had disappeared because she "abandoned it" in a common area. As for the vendor's position, he was within his rights to demand immediate payment or return of the dress as she had already been wearing it longer than 30 minutes.

Angry and suspicious of the vendor, my friend handed over $80USD. Not enough money said the vendor. Apparently, the sale price only applied to the dress if bought before she tried it on. He claimed that she had now sweated in it and the dress was not in the shape it was when she was first shown it. In his opinion, she should be paying him the original price of $450USD BUT because he was sympathetic to her plight and sad that she had lost her clothing through no fault of his, she need only pay $300USD. Livid, she protested and supported by her equally indignant friends, they appealed to the security personnel who had remained at the scene. Security indicated that there was no deviation from their initial ruling. The merchant was in the right. The garment was not hers; she had not bought it and therefore he had the right to demand it back. He also had given her a substantial discount on his originally stated asking price so she should be grateful.

Not even the prospect of the imminent return of her friends with other clothing was enough to stall the demand for immediate payment and simply returning the garment was no longer an option. Paying the requested $300 amount, my friend left the souk in her newly purchased evening gown. Refusing to look at anything else she stormed out of the market and made her way back to the ship. She vowed that not a penny more of her money would be spent in that country. She told me that she got a few strange looks as she stomped angrily to the ship looking absurdly over dressed and by her own admission, quite sparkly. Undoubtedly there were some amused looks from fellow passengers and crew members who all suspected that there was a story behind her return in formal wear.

To add insult to the situation, the clothing her friends had quickly bought for her were also non-returnable even though they had not been worn.

Unlike some who blow off troubling incidents that occur when travelling, my friend said the theft put a damper on her holiday and to this day, she still laments the loss of her favourite bra.

I don't want people to get the impression that shopping in the souks, or any market for that matter, is dangerous and thefts rampant. I could fill these pages with stories of fun filled shopping trips in North Africa and other areas of the world. But it is critical that people be aware of potential problems and do a little research before leaving on a trip. Vigilance and awareness are the keys.

Even the most seasoned travellers make errors in judgement when travelling and thereby fall prey to scams.

We were on an Eastern Mediterranean cruise with a stop in Malta. We got off the ship at the port of Valletta and walked into old town. We spent a fabulous day exploring, doing a little shopping and enjoying our encounters with the locals. We had a delightful, leisurely lunch at one of the old town restaurants. Upon arrival back at the ship, we ran into some people we had met on the cruise who had a less than positive experience. They had fallen prey to an old, pricing trick. They stopped at an open-air restaurant for a drink and were offered the special beverage of the day which appeared to be some type of Sangria like inspired beverage that came in a large pitcher. They agreed to order the drink but failed to ask the price. The sun was shining, the weather perfect and they were thoroughly enjoying themselves. When asked if they wanted the special appetizer tray, they said yes. No one asked the price. The appetizer tray consisted of bread, some herbed oil drizzled on the plate and a few olives. The contents of the tray were enjoyable but there was nothing substantial or worthy of rave reviews. When they were ready to leave, they found that the pitcher and the appetizer tray were priced in at a whopping €275 euros. Because they had ordered a "special" that was not listed on a menu, the landlord could set the price at whatever he wanted. Protesting the amount proved unsuccessful and they had no choice but to pay. By comparison, at a restaurant just up the same street, my husband and I had a bottle of wine, appetizers, bread and two main courses for €48 euros.

the business Dan had named. They chatted amicably as they walked to the store which still had the tie in the window. Unfortunately, the place was closed, and the good Samaritan seemed genuinely disappointed that Dan had missed his opportunity to buy the desired item.

The man suggested they get a drink at a nearby tavern and Dan agreed. Once in the tavern, they each ordered a beer. An older woman approached them both and the fellow obviously knew her. He engaged her in conversation and told her what they had been looking for in case she knew of a shop that sold ties of a similar nature. The woman started to recommend some stores and made suggestions as to what would be a good price. Dan had offered to pay for the two beers and when his companion suggested they buy the woman a drink for being so helpful, Dan agreed. She ordered a glass of champagne. When the bill came, the two beers and one small glass of champagne came to an astounding €100 euros. Dan knew he had been suckered but protested anyway. All to no avail. He was told the champagne was very expensive and that he had to pay the full amount or the two large fellows who had suddenly made an appearance at the bar would have a chat with him. Knowing how the scam worked didn't make it any more palatable and calling the police would have resulted in an unlikely ruling in his favour. He paid the amount, but his love of Greece was sorely tested by the incident.

***

These stories serve as a reminder to pay attention to your personal items and to always ask for a printed menu or price list in any bar or restaurant. I also recommend the following:

- Ask the price of something before you buy or order it;
- Make sure you know what currency they are giving the price in;
- Ask them to write the price down (I carry a little pad for that);
- Never show how much money you have (aka: never flash the cash);
- Pay attention to the money you get as change (amount and quality);
- Try to keep possession of your credit card. Have the vendor bring the payment processing machine to you or you can accompany them to the point of sale;
- Always cover the keypad when entering your PIN number;
- Visit/use ATMs in public, well lit areas;
- Try to always use ATMs associated with a bank;
- Look at the card readers at ATMs. If it looks different, move on; and
- Check your credit card and/or bank balances when travelling.

Injury on a Shore Excursion

We had docked in Sydney, Australia in October 2022 and I was walking around Angel Place where there is an artist's display of bird cages suspended above the lane. I failed to look where I was walking and tripped on a broken curb. I ended up in the emergency department of the Sydney Hospital getting stitches. Having warned people for years about being attentive to where they are walking, I became my own cliché of an inattentive and careless tourist.

As evidenced by the above commentary relating to a vacation mishap, injuries can and do occur when off the ship. When people ask what happens when such events take place, my response is always tied to the nature of the injury. If it is serious, obviously the individual is taken for/should seek, immediate medical treatment. If it is minor, the person normally continues, a little worse for the wear, with their shore excursion. This chapter is designed to give you some general pointers about enjoying shore excursions and to talk about injuries and/or health issues that occur when on vacation.

When I give talks about travelling, I tell people to be realistic about their physical capabilities and pay attention to where they are walking. Although this sounds like basic common-sense advice, it always bears repeating as I can attest for failing to heed my own guidance.

I Fell Down

Falls are the most common occurrences since people are often walking on uneven surfaces or not paying attention to where they are walking. When it comes to falls, I have heard various reasons as to why someone fell but the most commonplace refrain is "*I was not looking at where I was going*".

People also fall when they try to engage in activities that they normally may not do, such as ascending steep inclines. When cruise lines organize shore excursions, they will often indicate the level of effort required by the participants and annotate what one can expect. Phrases such as "uneven pavement" or "entails steep uphill walking" give warnings as to what can be expected. People should be attentive to these warnings and be realistic about their physical capabilities.

If you injure yourself, assess if you need medical attention and be honest about your needs. Don't be afraid to seek professional medical attention if you require it. Granted, you may be visiting a certain site for the first time and you are only there for a day, which often means you don't want to miss a minute of your time there. However, your health must always come first. Health concerns/injuries can range from those that can be addressed back at the ship, to those requiring immediate medical attention.

On one trip in Sardinia, we were visiting the site of a nuraghe ruin when a member of our little group fell. He sustained cuts and scrapes to his hands and knees but shrugged the fall off claiming that his biggest injury was to his pride. Despite his protestations, his knee kept bleeding and our best efforts to stem the flow of blood were not successful. A trip to the ship's medical facility was in order as soon as we arrived back in port and a few stitches solved the problem. Our friend told us the ship's doctor informed him that it was not uncommon for people to return to the ship from a shore excursion with a few bumps and scrapes.

Here are a few pro tips:

1. Look at where you are walking;
2. Scan the path in front of you for possible hazards;
3. Don't check your phone or camera when walking;
4. Watch for doors that can swing open;
5. Watch for people/vehicles at possible collision points;
6. Use available handrails (stairs, pathways and tunnels);
7. Wear suitable footwear;
8. Place the full length of your foot on steps;
9. If climbing, maintain three points of contact; and
10. Don't drink or eat from visibly unclean sources.

Physical Awareness

When on shore excursions, people may also succumb to heat, dehydration, or other physical ailments. Be aware of how you are feeling and signs that something may be physically wrong.

I will speak firstly about heat and dehydration. Two common problems that make an appearance on shore excursions, particularly in areas when you might experience high or extreme heat. Some common symptoms of heat stroke are:

- headache;
- nausea and/or vomiting;
- flushed appearance;
- cramps;
- muscle weakness;
- rapid breathing / rapid heartbeat; and
- confusion / disorientation.

Dehydration can be quite serious and in addition to including some of the preceding symptoms, can lead to shock, weak pulse and low blood pressure. It can also lead in extreme cases to death. If you are going on a shore excursion, make sure you have access to water and take the weather conditions into consideration when determining the appropriate apparel as this cruiser learned:

We were on a shore excursion to Pompeii in the middle of July. It was stinking hot and the heat from the sun was bouncing off the stones and made it feel like we were walking in a furnace. There was not a tree in sight. I had dressed in shorts and a sleeveless top to keep cool. I had not thought about the effects of the direct sun on my skin because I had put on sunscreen before we left the ship and I felt that it would offer me enough protection. I quickly sweated the sunscreen away. I am a ginger and I was soon burnt to a crisp and I felt like I was going to throw up. The tour guide finally gave me his umbrella to act as a form of shade. My boyfriend had to hold it over me as he helped me back to the tour bus.

Colleen – UK

Don't Procrastinate – Get Help

Next, I want to address the need to be aware of general health issues that might be exacerbated by your activities. If you are experiencing signs of a heart attack or stroke, you need to get help straightaway. Unless the ship is the closest form of medical facility, do not wait, seek help immediately from the closest local facility.

If at this point you are shaking your head at this advice and wondering who would not seek immediate help for a medical incident, you should be aware that denial of a problem is a frequent occurrence with heart attacks. People are in the midst of enjoying a shore excursion and they start to feel unwell. They don't want other people to be alarmed, they also don't want to acknowledge that there might be something seriously wrong. Unfortunately, people do suffer from heart attacks or strokes on shore excursions, and it is important to be aware of the possibility and be prepared to take appropriate action.

One woman recounted a situation that she experienced. They had been on a private shore excursion and there were 8 people in their group. One man, who she described as very fit and seemingly in the best of health, suddenly became a little confused. The woman told me that she would not have thought anything of it and the man's wife did not appear overly alarmed and laughed at his apparent *"fuzzy brain"*. However, another couple on the tour started to ask him questions and then started to ask him to do things such as lift his arms. Apparently, they had medical training and recognized the signs of a stroke. An ambulance was called, and the man was taken to a hospital where he was admitted.

In cases where an individual is taken to the hospital and will not be continuing on the cruise, the cruise lines are known to be very accommodating and particularly helpful. I have heard of incidents where the cruise line either packed, or helped pack, the cabin contents and delivered them to the individual or travel companion at the location requested. Cruise lines have also arranged for a member of staff or local representative, to assist the injured/ill person and/or their companion. There are tasks that cruise line personnel have done to aid those who must leave the cruise for various health reasons including help with contacting family members, facilitating medical transfers and providing information on local health care facilities and accommodation. If something happens while on a shore excursion, regardless as to whether it is a ship organized excursion or a private one, let the cruise line know as soon as possible.

Accidents Happen on Any Type of Holiday

I had a travel agent tell me that it was not a good idea to write about accidents that can happen on shore excursions. The idea behind the suggestion was that people should be presented with the rosier side of cruising and no mention of things that could go wrong should make its way into a book designed to encourage cruising. I disagree. I believe that transparency is the key to being informative. I also pointed out that things can go wrong on any vacation, whether it is a trip to visit family or a voyage around the world.

I use an example of a colleague who went on a long-anticipated safari in Africa. A vehicle he was travelling in was involved in an accident and he was badly injured. His three-week holiday turned into two months of hospitalization and subsequent six-month recovery.

Here is another example of a vacation mishap that had nothing to do with cruising:

> In January 2022 we arrived in Moorea after a night's flight from USA. On our first evening we walked to a nearby restaurant from our hotel.
>
> It was still daylight when we returned to our hotel at which point, we discovered that we had left our room key at the restaurant. Gary volunteered to retrieve the key while I waited in the hotel lobby. By this time, it was dark outside and there

were no streetlights, no sidewalks, and only the narrow, two-lane road. Gary jogged by the edge of the road toward the restaurant. At one point a car was coming towards him and the vehicle's lights shone directly in his eyes, affecting his night vision. He moved to the side and fell into a 5 1/2-foot-deep concrete "ditch". There were no barriers nor markers indicating the presence of the ditch and it had not been visible to him. While lying there, Gary could not see what else might be in the ditch with him and he realized that no one would be able to see him from the road. He managed to roll out of the ditch which left him lying in the wild grass. Fortunately, Gary's fall had been illuminated in the headlights of an oncoming car and the driver turned around to check on Gary. He then drove Gary back to the hotel.

Gary's legs were skinned and had been scraped by the concrete as he fell. We cleaned his wounds and made ice bags for his broken lower right leg/ankle. Gary is a Podiatrist and can easily recognize a broken bone when he sees one. I am a registered nurse and I had brought a big first aid kit with betadine soap, bandages, aces, antibiotic ointment, gauze pads, oral antibiotics and *advil/acetaminophen, and large zip lock bags: All were used.*

The next morning the hotel staff took Gary to the only clinic on the island and the clinic doctor examined Gary. There was a language issue as the doctor spoke French and little English. There was no x-ray machine on the island and the nearest island that had an x-ray machine did not have anyone available to read the x-ray image to confirm the diagnosis and determine if there was indeed a broken bone or sprain. The doctor prescribed an air cast and issued a prescription for a tetanus injection to be obtained at the local pharmacy. I gave Gary his tetanus shot and attended to cleaning his wounds.

The hotel found a pair of crutches for Gary so he could hobble about without using his right foot. He could not raise or use his left arm which meant only one crutch could be used.

When Gary returned home, x-rays showed that he had sustained a broken left humerus mid arm, and a left broken ball of the shoulder joint (smashed into so many small pieces that it could not be wired surgically back together). Gary wore a shoulder and arm sling for two months so the shoulder and left upper arm could heal.

With time and lots of physical therapy, Gary has returned to the active life he enjoys: scuba diving, snow skiing, sailboat racing and doing triathlons. That said, he no longer runs in the dark in a place without streetlights and sidewalks.

Paulette & Gary–USA

Formal or Informal

Hey Gail, If you are going to write about formal wear, tell your readers I have a black and gold sequined evening gown, approximately size 10/12. Worn once. Paid $300 USD but willing to take best offer for it.

Petra - Canada

If you want to see some strong opinions about cruise ship attire, ask whether formal wear is still the standard for dinner on a ship. On various cruising sites, many a war of words have been fought over what is, and is not, appropriate dinner wear. Even among my own friends, people have formidable opinions on what is appropriate attire.

One of my friends, refuses to wear a tie when on a cruise and the best he will do, is a sports jacket for dinner. On the other hand, my husband loves formal nights and any cruise without at least three such nights is less likely to make his short list of cruise choices.

There are three basic deterrents associated with formal nights and they are the cost of formal clothing, the amount of room formal clothing takes in luggage and lastly, general comfort. As a result of these issues, some cruise lines have deviated from formal nights and have now elected to promote a less formal option that allows people to choose what they want to wear. Consequently, those nights are a far cry from anything remotely formal. Personally, I find the optics of a room filled with mixed clothing choices detracts from the elegance of a formal evening, but I understand and respect the clothing choices of my fellow cruisers. I will address the three deterrents in order.

The Cost of Formal Clothing

Not everyone has a tuxedo at the ready and ball gowns can monopolize a significant amount of space in a suitcase. Consequently, people have become creative. My friends have amazed and entertained me with all manner of formal and semi-formal clothing options. I find that women usually have a number of dresses to wear or will mix and match a black skirt or pants with different tops, while men might stick with one suit combined with different shirt and tie options to change up their looks. There have been some creative choices and I salute those who dare to be different.

Brenda and the Repurposed Wedding Dress

Times have changed and short of weddings and special events, people don't have the same number of occasions to wear formal outfits as those of 50 years ago. It could be that Dan and I are just in the wrong social group but the best we manage in a year is maybe four or five social events requiring formal wear and even then, semi-formal seems more the norm. When is the last time you have been invited to a ball? Before anyone starts sending me e-mails about ballroom dancing, I will be addressing the subject of ballroom dancing themed cruises shortly. But for now, the point I want to make is that normally, people don't tend to have a lot of formal wear and it can be expensive.

On one cruise, we were waiting at the martini bar for our friend Brenda and her husband to meet us for a pre-dinner drink. It was a designated formal night, and I was in a long black skirt, with silk blouse and a sequined dinner jacket. My outfit was a special nod to my highly developed mix and match formal cruise wear skills that allow me to vary my look with tops and jewelry changes but not subject me to packing challenges. Suddenly there was Brenda resplendent in a deep purple ball gown with layers of tulle and lace. Impressive and sweeping, this dress caught the eye of everyone, and a hush fell over the bar.

"My goodness Brenda, you look amazing" I gushed. Now this was truly a dress that was something out of a 1950s movie.

"It's my wedding dress" said Brenda. "I spent $3500 and only wore it once so I figured I would get it dyed and wear it as a formal ball gown".

The idea was as impressive as the dress. It also explained why she had a huge garment bag as her carry-on when we were flying to the port city. Clearly this type of action is not suited to all wedding dress styles, but her dress had made the transition very nicely. She told me after the cruise that if she had to dye it again, she would choose black so she could change up the look with

257

different jewelry and wraps in different colours. As it stood though, she wore that dress for every formal night and received massive compliments on her impressive ball gown. I always felt underdressed and frumpy next to her when she wore that outfit, but I imagine that pretty much everyone sitting next to such a special creation would have felt the same.

The Name is *"Bond"*

We were leaving on a Cunard cruise and my husband Dan was in his usual pre cruise mode of deciding what to pack and secretly buying new things to take along. As previously mentioned, he is a shopper and in addition to assorted items such as swords, shields and medieval armour, he is not averse to buying more clothing. Although I normally would not question him spending money on things that he wants, he had previously stated that he did not need any more clothing and had specifically commented *"If you see me buying any more clothing, you can make me return it because I don't need anything"*. Since his walk-in closet was full and he had completely filled the closet in the spare bedroom, I was up for the task of being the purchase police.

One day, shortly before the cruise, he arrived home with a garment bag and several bags containing shirt boxes. Observing him entering the house, I challenged him on his purchases.

"I bought a new tuxedo jacket for the trip," he said.

"You already have a tuxedo and a combination of shirts and bow ties," I responded.

"Not like this," he replied and showed me his purchase of a creamy white tuxedo jacket.

"It's just like James Bond wore," he said, clearly proud of this purchase. A rather animated discussion took place about the merits of this newest clothing acquisition but in the end, he kept the jacket and wore it on the cruise. On the second formal night he donned the outfit and when one of the other dinner guests made a comment about him looking very *"Bond like"* he shot me a look of triumph. Clearly the desired appearance had been achieved and he was in his glory.

Lest you think that you need to buy all new clothing for a cruise, please note that this is unnecessary. If you have a suit, you can bring the one suit and change the look up with different ties and accessories, or, wear the same suit and tie. Nothing says you need to wear a different look every formal or dressy night. The same holds true for dresses or pant suits. Changing up jewelry also provides a different look as does the addition of long gloves.

Long gloves, once the mainstay of the formal evening, became less of a necessary item in the 1960's but still are worn at some formal events and give an elegant and classy look to an outfit. Just remember, if you wear gloves, take them off when seated for dinner as they are never worn when eating. Also remember that the only jewelry worn on the outside of a glove, is a bracelet. Do not wear any rings over the gloves.

Before making any decision to buy new clothing, take a look at what you have in your closet, or what you have access to by way of friends or family, and determine whether you need to buy anything new to wear.

> *My friend and I are plus sized ladies and we find that clothing for us is often priced higher with semi formal selections being limited to "mother of the bride" type outfits. We now will borrow from each others wardrobe when cruising. This way we don't have to always buy new outfits.*
>
> *(Name Withheld)*

Room In Your Luggage

I have cruising friends, Linda and Chris, who live in Northern Ireland and who are the masters of the cruise pack. Linda once posted a picture of two medium sized suitcases that were at the door ready for their next morning departure. I was astounded. Who leaves for approximately two months with that limited amount of luggage? I thought I had mastered the art of comprehensive cruise packing but I bow to the skill that Linda and Chris exhibit. On back-to-back cruises, they had suitable clothing for every event, always looked well turned out and stylish. Clearly one does not have to have a large amount of luggage to carry all the necessary clothing.

Cruisers simply have to exercise selective choices and smart packing.

Yes, formal and semi formal outfits can take up room in your luggage, but as mentioned, mixing and matching accessories can change up a look. Ensuring that you have one pair of shoes to go with all your dressy outfits will also save on space. You don't need more than one small evening purse and even that is optional. Although I like to carry an evening purse to hold my phone, cruise card, tissue and a comb, many can't be bothered. As long as a person has their cabin access card/pass they feel that they don't need anything more.

To help plan out evening wear, look at the length of your cruise and the number of formal evenings that your cruise will have. Your cruise line will tell you in advance of the cruise, the number of formal evenings and whether there are any special dress events. Decide how you want to dress for those evenings. All cruise ships will have a buffet option for those who do not want to dress beyond their casual norm and some cruise lines offer open choices to people in the main dining room. They allow people to wear whatever they choose.

Once you know how many nights you will require dressier attire; you can start to plan your outfits. If you don't love something, or you don't like the fit, don't bring it. If it is only going to be a wear it once outfit, do you have room for it? If not, jettison it in favour of an outfit that will be suitable for multiple wears.

General Comfort

If an outfit you are considering is uncomfortable, don't bring it. Cruising is fun. You are supposed to be enjoying yourself, not stressing over a more elegant look at the expense of your comfort.

> *I bought a tux and wore it for our once-a-year*
> *cruises. After a decade the tux was tight and the*
> *shirts were chokingly small. After one really*
> *uncomfortable dinner, I told my wife I was going*
> *to the buffet on all the formal dress nights.*
>
> *(Name Withheld)*

Ensure that what you bring is comfortable and you will be happy wearing it for more than five minutes. Pay attention to your footwear as that too, is an area of concern. No one is happy in wobbly heels or shoes that pinch your feet.

As mentioned in the opening paragraph of this chapter, people have strong opinions about formal or dressy attire on a cruise. Read on:

> *I don't like to dress up and I don't want to wear a*
> *monkey suit. My wife loves to get all decked out.*
> *Rather than fight, I bring one suit and a dress shirt.*
> *I will bring a tie but usually don't wear it. I may not*
> *be as formal as many, but I am comfortable and*
> *happy.*
>
> *Peter – Canada*

We only cruise with lines that allow us to wear whatever we want. Who wants to get dressed up when on vacation? It is all about relaxing.

Candice – USA

***

We look forward to formal evenings and can't understand why people won't make an effort to look elegant for a change. It's not like every night is formal night, or that they have to dress up for every meal. We don't want to be sitting beside someone in shorts and a t-shirt at dinner because the cruise line won't enforce a dress code or are sloppy about clothing standards.

Victoria - USA

***

Formal night versus no formal night. You may not want to go there as people are quite opinionated about it all. A real can of worms.
Denny – location unknown

Golf Shirt with Bow Tie Bernard

An acquaintance told me that she has difficulty getting her husband to dress up for any event on a cruise. According to her, he holds the opinion that he has to wear a suit for work and he refuses to wear one on vacation.

263

Since she loves to cruise, she was left with limited options on formal nights when their cruise line of preference enforces dress codes. They could either eat at the buffet, in their cabin or she had to convince Bernard to dress up in some form. The compromise was a golf shirt, with a clip-on bow tie. He would wear a jacket into the dining room but remove it as soon as he was seated. The top button of the golf shirt is unbuttoned, with the clip-on attached at the second button. Technically he is wearing a bow tie but it is not impeding his sense of open collar freedom. She told me that it is not the best option, but it seems to satisfy the cruise line's dress code. She dresses up and he dresses "differently". They are allowed in the dining room, but she said they were once moved to a table out of the way and out of sight. *"You should search the cruising websites"* she said, *"I am sure there are probably comments from people about his weird clothing choices"*. A search of such websites failed to turn up any photos of Bernard.

Connie the Tart

I met a lady named Connie on a cruise who told me that she and her husband missed the first two formal dinners because they brought the wrong bag on the trip. Apparently, their formal wear was in a garment bag in a wardrobe at home. She said, that in advance of their departure date, she had readied their evening attire and placed it all in a garment bag which she then put in a wardrobe in the spare bedroom. Just before leaving on their trip she sent her husband to get the garment bag but failed to specify which wardrobe it was in. Unfortunately, he grabbed the wrong garment bag and as the bag he brought down and placed by the door looked identical to the one she had used to pack their formal clothing, she thought all was well. Neither of them checked the contents until they were unpacking on the ship. What they ended up with was their costumes bag and the closest thing they had to formal wear, were their outfits for a tarts and vicar party. She explained that her husband was willing to wear the vicar suit but she was convinced that her gold lamé mini dress with the battery operated nipple lights would fail to pass muster.

General Observations about Formal Wear

If you find yourself on a cruise where formal wear is expected on certain evenings, here are a few general observations for your consideration.

A t-shirt with a bow tie and suit image stamped on the front of it may be funny but it will not be suitable formal attire on some cruise lines.

You do not have to spend a lot of money to look smart and meet formal wear standards.

Most cruise lines accept semi-formal attire in lieu of formal wear. I often bring mid-calf cocktail dresses and find that they are suitable for formal evenings.

Mix and match different accessories to change the look. A long black dress with different wraps or jewelry will completely change the look of an outfit.

The same holds true for a tuxedo or black suit. One outfit, worn with different colour shirts or bow ties and puffs, put an entirely different look together.

Bring one pair of dressy shoes that will go with all your outfits.

White Tie Versus Black Tie – What is the Difference?

If you want to experience the elegance of a formal evening, and want to make the occasion truly special, here is some additional information that you may find useful.

For men, a white tie event is considered the most formal of dress and is only worn on formal occasions. At the turn of the century, the upper-class society would dress for dinner and white tie was considered the dress de rigueur.

Black tie used to be reserved for semi formal occasions but is now quite common for formal events and dinner parties.

On a cruise, where men are dressing in formal wear, either white or black tie with a tuxedo is acceptable as would be a formal Highland dress (kilt doublet). On cruises where the formal wear is not strictly requested (black tie optional), but suits are requested at a minimum, a business suit would be considered acceptable.

266

Ball Gowns and Semi-Formal Dresses

Ball gowns are full length dresses worn to formal events and balls. They are usually elaborate and considered the most formal of dresses. Although some think of ball gowns as having a fitted bodice and transitioning into a flowing, full skirt, the present-day definition of a ball gown has changed with the times to incorporate traditional dress associated with various cultures.

An A-line dress is a dress that is close fitted at the top and which flares slightly as it falls to the floor giving the appearance of an "A". These can be very elaborate and beaded or plain.

For a white tie event, a woman would wear a ball gown or formal A-line dress.

Semi-formal or cocktail dresses can range from mid-calf to mid thigh dresses and are fancier than everyday business attire. At one time a two-piece outfit would not be considered suitable cocktail attire but now it is. For example, a beaded or decorative jacket combined with palazzo pants would be considered semi-formal wear.

Whether you subscribe to the casual attire cruising crowd, or the groups that enjoy the formal look, plan your attire accordingly and be aware of what is expected in the way of a dress code for dinner.

Costumed or Themed Evenings

Our love of dressing up on cruises is not restricted to only formal nights, we also embrace themed cruise nights such as Mardi Gras, Roaring 20s or 50's rock n roll. Some cruise lines are more likely to have themed nights than others.

Similar to formal nights, people have strong opinions on whether they want to participate or not in themed evenings. But I think it is important to remember that not all costumes require elaborate efforts or special clothing. We were on a *Cunard* Mediterranean cruise and we had brought Mardi Gras masks to wear. Mine was a fairly simple gold coloured eye mask. I brought feathers that I could easily attach the night of the themed dinner which made it a little more intricate and interesting. My husband however had gone all in on his apparel and bought an elaborate devil's mask. He had ordered it online and it arrived a couple of weeks before the cruise. He proudly showed the mask to me along with a mardi gras themed vest to go with his tuxedo. He was quite pleased with his efforts. I was a little skeptical as his mask was not one that could easily be packed in a suitcase.

As we were getting ready to depart on the cruise, a packing dilemma surrounding the mask presented itself. Dan could not pack the mask in his suitcase or carry-on without fear of it getting crushed. To box it up and put it in his luggage, would make it safe for transportation but it would take too much room. How was he going to get this large, intricate mask through two flights (one of which was overseas), a train ride and onto the ship without any damage? His decision was to carry it in a bag which meant a lot of attention was paid to how and where the bag was laid in the overhead luggage bins during transportation.

It arrived safe and sound and he received a lot of compliments on the mask when he wore it for the themed evening. Unfortunately, that meant that he wanted to bring it home again so it could be reused. Once again, he placed it in a bag to carry with him but on the return trip, he had as his carry-on luggage, a number of bags containing treasures he had purchased, and the mask in a separate bag. It was clearly too much carry-on stuff for the airline representative who was checking the amount of carry-on baggage being brought onto the plane. In an effort to reduce the number of bags he was carrying; Dan consolidated the contents of two bags and took the mask out of the third bag and wore the mask on the top of his head. The airline representative looked at him sceptically and asked him about the mask. With a wink at her and a nod in my direction, Dan whispered *"My wife likes it when I wear it. You know…it spices things up."* Laughing conspiratorially, she let him on the plane. The mask made it home in one piece and awaits its next cruise.

> *We like themed evenings on the ships. The cruise lines should do a whole cruise themed to a certain era. Something like a cruise with a theme of the 1920's or 1950's when there was a certain elegance to going out for the evening.*
>
> *Margaret - UK*

Ballroom Dancing

At one time I took public transit to work and being a creature of routine, I ended up on the same train at the same time each morning. I became a nodding acquaintance with a number of people on the commuter train and we would occasionally chat about various things. One fellow, Dave, is a big fan of ballroom dancing. He, and his girlfriend, participate in various ballroom dancing competitions and over several years, shared stories with us, his fellow commuters, about the competitions they had entered.

One morning, Dave saw me and excitedly moved to my side to talk to me about cruising. The previous night their dance instructor had told them about a cruise that was focused on ballroom dancing. Knowing that Dan and I enjoyed cruising, he wanted to know if we had ever taken such a cruise. He had some of the promotional material in hand and it was clear that he and his girlfriend had already decided that they would be taking this cruise.

Over the course of the next few months, he would ask me general questions about cruising but most of his questions related to the theme of ballroom dancing and how the dances and events were held. Unfortunately, I was of limited assistance to him and aside from offering up some suggestions re packing their numerous and elaborate outfits, I had little to offer. I had never taken such a cruise.

Finally, they were off on their holiday and I spent the next few weeks wondering how it all went. Dave returned enthusiastic and thrilled at how the cruise unfolded. Apparently, there were ballroom dancers from various countries, and they had dances and events throughout the cruise. His videos of the events were amazing and led me to sign Dan and I up for dance classes. After ten lessons it was clear that Dan had the skill and rhythm needed to succeed while I had nothing but enthusiasm.

As for Dave and his girlfriend, they subsequently went on more such themed cruises.

Bad Behaviour

Do you know of anyone who has been kicked off a cruise ship for bad behaviour? If so, what did they do?

Kevin – Canada

I received that interesting question in an e-mail. The short answer is "No". I don't know of anyone who has been removed from a cruise ship for bad behaviour. I have followed stories of persons who have been arrested and removed from a ship for criminal actions. I had also been told stories about people who were removed from a ship for health reasons or refused boarding for failing to have the necessary paperwork. But no information about onboard behavioural issues had come to my attention. Consequently, I decided to do a little research.

I began by looking for a definition of what would constitute bad behaviour but not rise to the level of criminal actions. That would eliminate all the instances of drug use, bomb threats, assaults, thefts etc. Additionally, I was not interested in boarding refusals on embarkation day as my focus rested solely on those who had been allowed onto a ship and then removed as a consequence of their actions once the ship had set sail. The cruise lines provide a list of actions that may disqualify someone from sailing with them, or, continuing to sail with them and they are generally criminal or health related. But there is conduct that can result in removal from a ship:

1. Buying or giving a minor a drink that contains alcohol;
2. Being abusive towards staff;
3. Refusing to cooperate with staff direction(s);
4. Reckless Conduct;
5. Disorderly Conduct;
6. Expressing suicidal intentions;
7. Continuous breaking of ship rules; and
8. Engaging in any conduct deemed to be harmful to staff of fellow passengers.

When I asked for stories about when a passenger has been removed from a ship, I received anecdotal information of what people had "heard" about a person being removed from a ship. Without information from someone directly involved, all I can offer up is hearsay and unverified stories.

> One guy was removed from our ship when he kept saying he was going to jump overboard in the middle of the night. Ship security took him several times to the medical facility and the doctors would examine him. He would tell the doctors he was not suicidal but the next day he would be back at it again. By day five they had had enough and he was removed from the ship.

***

I heard about a couple being ejected when they created a big scene about an issue with their cabin. I guess there was a flood or some kind of issue relating to their room and they wanted to be put in another cabin. They were offered a few different cabins but none of them were good enough because they wanted a suite. Staff finally removed them from the ship for being abusive to all the staff they dealt with.

***

A girl was taken off our ship when they suspected her of being stoned all the time. She had track marks up and down her arm and admitted to being a junkie and using but security could not find the source of her drugs and felt she was a danger to herself. I heard that she refused to cooperate with medical.

***

*I was told that someone was taken off our ship because the staff believed that they were not who they were supposed to be. ***

*Author Note: I requested additional details but did not receive any further information.

A search of cruise ship stories generally indicates that passengers, whose conduct affects the comfort, enjoyment, safety or wellbeing of other guests will be the subject of action by the cruise line. The articles indicated that badly behaved passengers can be fined and/or removed from the ship.

The guy was so drunk he was standing beside me when he suddenly threw up on my foot. I said to him "Hey! You just threw up on my foot!" His response was:

"Sorry, I thought it was my foot."

Steve - Canada

Dirty Laundry

On one cruise, as the ship was departing a port stop, my husband announced that it was raining underwear. We were on deck seven and apparently someone from a cabin above had washed underwear and put it on their balcony to dry. As the ship started to move, the breeze caught the items and sent them flying onto balconies below. My husband, who was enjoying a sail away drink on our balcony, was the surprised recipient of monogrammed panties.

As evidenced in the little story above, hand washing laundry and putting it on your cabin balcony to dry, can lead to laundry mishaps. Apparently, this has happened on numerous cruises as we tend to see postings on various cruise ships, that laundry or wet items should not be left on balconies. I have also read articles and heard stories about items flying off balconies and landing on decks, docks or in the water below.

If you are going on a three-to-seven-day cruise, you probably won't bother having laundry done as you can easily bring enough clothes to suit your needs during the cruise. However, on longer cruises, getting your laundry done is pretty much a necessity unless you bring a lot of clothing.

Since I often get asked about laundry on cruise ships, I have decided to devote a chapter to it. The long and short answer about laundry facilities onboard cruise ships is that almost all cruise ships have the ability to do the laundry of their cruisers. If you ask about whether there are self-serve laundry facilities onboard cruise ships, the answer will vary depending on the cruise line. Some cruise lines do offer laundry facilities where guests are able to do laundry on their own. Not into doing laundry when on holiday? No problem, all cruise lines offer laundry services where you pay to have your laundry done by cruise line staff. Those services are considered by some travellers, to be expensive.

I will start with a few comments about lines that have onboard laundry facilities. This is not a comprehensive list, but a sampling of some popular cruise lines. *Carnival*, *Princess* and *Cunard* cruise lines offer self-serve laundry facilities. You can buy laundry detergent and fabric softener on board in the laundry rooms. Use of ironing boards and irons are free. On a longer cruise, it is great to be able to do laundry on a sea day and control the wash and dry temperatures. I first encountered self-serve laundry on the *Cunard Line* and I was delighted that I had the option to do our own laundry. I sent our evening wear out to be dry cleaned but underwear, socks, jeans etc. were all quickly done in the laundry room at my convenience. The laundry room also proved to be an interesting place to meet people.

There are those who avoid doing mundane domestic tasks when enjoying a cruise. Not me. I am fine washing delicates in the sink rather than paying $2 for each piece of underwear. Is it really $2 for underwear you ask? I cannot provide a listing of costs for laundry as they vary from cruise line to cruise line and are subject to change, so I have provided the amount universally charged for underwear as an example and yes, it is $2. The cost charged for underwear probably explains why the person in a cabin above us on that particular cruise, chose to hand wash their underwear and put it in the sunshine to dry. A fresh change of underpants, per person, per couple, for the first week of a cruise, is fourteen pieces which comes to $28 dollars US for the cruise line to wash only your underpants. If you add in other items of clothing, your laundry costs quickly add up. If you do your own laundry in a ship's self serve laundry facility, you could be paying $3 for an entire load of laundry or if you choose to hand wash in your bathroom sink, you are washing those delicates for free. Placing the items in a dryer for a fraction of the price or hanging them up in your cabin bathroom to dry will save you money.

I know people who bring a portable clothesline that they put up in their cabin. They use the line in conjunction with heavy magnet hooks that they have purchased. Some of these hooks can hold up to 150 pounds and they simply put up the hooks and affix the clothesline to them when they do a little wash. They generally wait until their room has been cleaned in the morning and then do their wash. They take the line down before the evening turn down service, so the cabin steward does not have to work around a laundry line. Some people simply do their laundry in the evening and let it dry overnight. Regardless of how they do their laundry, on a cruise of over seven days, they save money on laundry and save space in their suitcases by packing a certain amount of clothing.

If you do intend to hand wash some items, a pro tip from Linda of Northern Ireland, is to avoid wrinkles by bringing a little bottle of fabric conditioner and a small spray bottle. Mix 10ml of the conditioner in the spray bottle with water and you have 'home-made' wrinkle release for any washed item - it works best on cotton clothing. An alternative is to buy a small bottle of a product that will help reduce wrinkles.

Holland America, *Celebrity Cruises* and *Royal Caribbean International* are three cruise lines that do not offer self-serve laundry facilities to their clients, but they do have onboard laundry facilities so you can send your laundry out and have it done for you. As mentioned, there is a cost associated with having the ship's staff do your laundry, washing and (if required), pressing.

On one cruise I sent out some items to the laundry. The next day, I arrived back from a shore excursion to find my clean laundry neatly hung in the closet. Each item carefully covered in a protective plastic covering. Upon closer inspection I realized that I had a few other items as well. I looked at the laundry tag and noticed that the item was a dry-cleaned suit that should have been delivered to a cabin very near ours. I took the dry cleaning to that cabin and knocked. A man opened the door and I said *"Your laundry…" Before* I could finish my sentence, he snatched the laundry from me and said, *"It's about time you got it here"* and slammed the door in my face. Needless to say, I was quite surprised at his actions. About sixty minutes later, we were seated at a table in a specialty restaurant when I noticed this fellow, and his wife were shown to the table next to us. It looked as if he was wearing the suit I had brought to him. Throughout his dinner he kept looking quizzically at me as if wondering where he had seen me before. It was obvious he could not place me.

After we had finished dining, we went back to our cabin for something and ran into him in the hallway. Suddenly it dawned on him *"The dry cleaning!"* he exclaimed. *"Yes"* I said, *"It was accidentally put in our closet with our laundry."* Recalling his earlier actions, he had the grace to look a little embarrassed.

The next day while I was at an afternoon lecture, a waiter delivered a drink to me and stated, *"The gentleman who sent this said to say it was a laundry delivery tip."*

Cruising Pet Peeves

I hate it when a cruise line says I can bring a bottle of wine onboard and then charges me a corkage fee.

Sabrina – Canada

When I asked for information about pet peeves that people have as they relate to cruising, I was inundated with comments about covid restrictions and masking. I have deliberately opted to not weigh in on the masking issue and offer up this list of subjects that really seems to annoy people. Where possible I have used their own words or when the theme is a common one, I have generalized the comments:

1. *Chair hogs. People who put personal items on a chair to hold it for them. They then leave the chairs empty for hours.* This is a reoccurring complaint and relates to chairs around the pool, in the common areas and in the theatre.

2. *People who sit at a table in the buffet restaurant and read, play cards or work on their laptops during busy times.* Tables are often at a premium during the breakfast or lunch hours and are needed for people eating.

3. *People who let their children run wild in restaurants, at the pool or in common areas.*

 Although not a common complaint on all cruise lines, it is a reoccurring theme on a few lines that cater to budget or family travel.

4. *People who touch food in the buffet. Just last week I saw a guy take a bun, look at it and put it back.*

5. *Ultra casual clothing in the dining room. Shorts, flip flops and a T-shirt? Not cool for dinner.*

6. *Drunks. I hate sitting beside loud, obnoxious drunks.*

7. *Being charged for everything. Wi-fi, booze, tips you name it.*

 This is another reoccurring complaint across all cruise lines. As some cruise lines move to all-inclusive type of bookings for a slightly higher price, complaints may be reduced.

8. *The constant upsells. As soon as you board you are asked to upgrade your beverage package or book a day at the spa. They always want you to buy something.*

9. *The art shows. Some cruise lines are worse than others.*

 This is an individual opinion type of complaint. Some people like the art shows and buy pieces of art, while others do not like them. It all depends on the individual.

10. *People walking in or interfering in the walking/jogging lanes.*

 I confess to having inadvertently done this however I try to be more attentive when walking near the track.

11. *Cheaters at trivia. They pretend to be checking messages but are really looking up answers.*

This is also one of my pet peeves. Cheating? Really? There are no major prizes for these events.

12. *People blocking the Promenade by standing there talking. Move out of the way.*

13. *People who abuse the cabin staff.*

14. *The people who try and get into the elevator without letting the people who are already in, get out.*

15. *People who get into the front of the elevator and stop.*

I agree with this one. I understand that you might only be going a couple of floors but at least move to the side so other people can get into the elevator. By getting on and blocking the entrance, you force people have to squeeze past in order to get into the elevator.

16. *People who have loud telephone conversations at mealtimes or anywhere else.*

17. *People who "hog" a viewing platform without letting others have a look.*

18. *People who take up a slot machine chair but are not playing.*

19. *Those who take shore excursions unsuited to their physical abilities. They hold up the entire excursion.*

20. *People who hold up the lines at guest services to obtain information that is available in the daily planner.*

I agree. Read the daily planner as it has a lot of good information on what is going on that day and relating to port stops. It even has the weather!

Starting or Finishing Outside the Official Cruise Dates

We booked a Baltic Sea cruise two years in advance and then eleven weeks before the cruise, we had a family wedding threaten to derail our cruising plans because the wedding was on the day the cruise was to begin. Fortunately, the cruise line allowed us to join the ship at the first port stop. The airfare to get to that port was basically the same as the fare to our original point of departure. We missed two days of the cruise but that was better than missing the whole thing.

Carter - USA

***

Starting or finishing your cruise at a different port than the one on the itinerary, has become a bit of a confusing bundle in these post covid times. Called downlining, people used to be able to join a cruise after the ship they were booked on

had already set sail. They simply joined the cruise at one of the ship's scheduled port stops. This was very convenient for those who wanted to enjoy a specific itinerary or certain ship, but whose schedules did not marry up with that of the ship's departure or finishing date.
Pamela – USA

***

We were booked to attend a wedding on a cruise. Two months before the big event, I got a promotion and the timing of the cruise conflicted with my firm's year-end audit. Participation in this audit was part of my new responsibilities and I could not miss it. I did not make the first four days of the cruise but I was able to get on board at the second port stop and join everybody then. I got to attend the wedding and enjoy the rest of the cruise. The cruise line made joining up with the cruise easy and they even had a representative pick me up at the island airport and take me to the ship.
(Name Withheld)

In these post covid days, the policy of the various cruise lines is not that clear. Some still allow downlining, while others have stopped it.

The reasons are varied and generally tied to local restrictions, testing requirements or other assorted reasons. While some cruise lines prohibit embarking or disembarking at mid cruise ports of call and restrict boarding to the scheduled port of embarkation, others may restrict boarding only at certain port stops along their routing. For example, they may allow embarkation at stop three and four but not two, five or six. It all depends on what their rationale is for refusing or allowing boarding at any given port. The same holds true for disembarkation.

Because this policy may change in the immediate or near future, I will not name the cruise lines that are currently prohibiting this practice as it can easily change before publication of this book. As such, I urge you to check with the cruise line you are thinking of using, to determine what their current policy is regarding this issue. Please note, it is not uncommon for a cruise line to charge a fee for an early departure.

As for why you might leave a cruise early (for reasons other than health or emergency), read on:

You ask about leaving a cruise ship early and we have done that several times because the last port stop was nearer our next destination. On one cruise, our last port stop was Le Havre in France. At the conclusion of the cruise, we were going to visit Guillaume's family in Rouen so it made sense to get off the ship a day early and have family pick us up at Le Havre as opposed to going on to Southampton in England and then having to make our way back to France. After all, the cruise ended the following morning so all we were missing was a dinner and one night's sleep on the ship but we were saving travel time and money.

Leon and Guillaume – Brussels

Lobster Again?

I asked people if they had experienced a "lobster night" on a cruise ship and whether they thought that such nights were a culinary delight of the past. I received some interesting responses.

We were cruising in the Galapagos when part way through the 7-day voyage, lobster became readily available for meals. It turns out that the Government of Ecuador had changed the rules about keeping frozen lobster outside of the harvest season. When the captain asked how he was supposed to know about the change, the answer was that it was announced on the local radio stations. We were offered lobster omelettes, lobster burgers, lobster salads and lobster dinners until the freezer was empty!

Karen and Doug – Canada

***

My story is not really about lobster on a ship but it is a story about how a discussion about lobster led to a friendship.

We live in the middle of the country and we are not used to eating a lot of lobster.

We appreciated the lobster dinners on the cruises. We were on a Panama Canal cruise and sitting at a table of eight in the main dining room. On one of the formal dinners, they served surf and turf and we were really pleased with the meal and the fact that we were getting lobster. One of the couples at our table were from Maine and they kept telling us that the lobster was not that good and the size was really small. We had quite the discussion about what constitutes good lobster and beef.

About three months after the cruise, we got a call from that couple and they were headed our way and asked if they could stop in for a visit. They arrived with a dozen lobsters which they cooked for us. By this time we had forgotten what the lobster on the ship tasted like, but the ones they cooked and served us were huge and tasted great.

A year later we visited them and brought some good midwestern beef for them to enjoy. We have been friends for twelve years and we now cruise together.

Stephen – USA

***

Lobster dinners on cruise ships are things of the past. You generally don't get them anymore in the dining room and only see them on offer in the specialty dining restaurants. On our first cruise they still had lobster night and we had not eaten lobster before. They only served the tail and the lobster meat had been cut so it was partially out of the shell. It was still attached to the shell a bit and when I was trying to remove the meat entirely from the shell it seemed stuck, so I really pulled on it. The meat from the tail flew out of the shell and landed at the feet of our waiter. He didn't say anything about it, he just calmly picked it up and brought me another lobster tail. I noticed that this one had the meat already cut out of the tail. I guess they did not want more flying lobster.

Belinda – Canada

Food allergies

We have only taken the one cruise and the only lobster meal that we saw available was on the menu in a specialty restaurant. If they had offered us lobster, both of us would have turned it down as we have a shellfish allergy.

Christian – Canada

Further to Christian's comments, I would like my readers to note that if you do have food allergies, please advise your wait staff of the allergy as soon as you are seated for a meal. I also advise that you make your food allergy known when you book your cruise as well. If you have a strong reaction to a certain type of food (such as shellfish or peanuts), if you come in close proximity to it, check out the daily menus in case you need to be seated at a table away from other diners or dine in your cabin. In cases of severe food allergies, cruise ships that charge for in cabin meal service can make an exception regarding charges.

Cruise Lines Random Offerings

Reserving Private Rooms and Parties Onboard

You can book a room onboard a ship for a gathering. These private facility bookings might involve a fee or may be provided by the cruise line free of charge, depending on the venue, reason for the gathering and space availability.

I have reserved private rooms for several small events and found the cruise lines to be extremely obliging with respect to making a location available at no charge. Whether it be for a talk, reception, small gathering or even a larger party, you will usually find the cruise ships to be fairly accommodating. I once hosted a scavenger hunt on a cruise and the cruise line allowed us to use a room to anchor the event. Another cruise line allowed us to host a gathering of about 40 friends and coordination was seamless both before I boarded and when on the ship.

I have had people talk to me about the cruise lines offering rooms for cocktail parties or wine and cheese gatherings at no additional cost, not realizing that this is quite common if you are travelling in a large party. If you have put together a group, ask about obtaining a room for your gathering. Chances are you will be able to secure a room at no additional cost. However, in these post covid days, some cruise lines are not encouraging non ship sanctioned activities, so it is best to check in advance.

Touring the Working Part of a Ship

Most ships will offer tours, such as a tour of the bridge or the galleys (kitchens). Some cruise lines will offer a general tour of the ship which will include the engine rooms, bridge and galley. For those who want to see how everything works, these are great excursions. There usually are charges for these types of tours and they must be booked through the ship. Note, if you have a group, it may be possible to have a tour set up and conducted at no charge so if you are a travel agent or group organizer, check to see if this can be done for your party.

On one cruise, I was with a group, and we were offered a tour of the bridge. I had been on previous cruises where the same offer had been made and I had opted out of participating thinking that this was not something of interest to me. This time, I decided that I might as well take the tour to see what the bridge on a big ship looked like and to obtain a few answers to questions about big ship operations that had occurred to me over the years.

I found the tour to be quite interesting and informative. I chided myself for not having taken advantage of this type of tour on previous cruises because there was a lot of information given and so much to take in. We were told about navigation, stabilizers, sanitation, staff education, and a host of other relevant information.

Today, when offered the opportunity to tour any working part of a ship, I always say yes. If I am on a ship that offers a tour that I must pay for, I might also say yes, depending on whether the ship is a new class or build.

Cooking Demonstrations

Most ships will have free instructional presentations related to a number of topics. Dancing, fencing, wine appreciation are a few that immediately come to mind. But the one that often draws cruiser attendance is the cooking or food display demonstrations. I am not a cook but these types of instructional sessions are interesting and filled with tips on food preparation and presentation.

From these free instructional sessions, I have learned how prepare delightful creations that make a table appear inspired and impressive. I can now carve a pumpkin or watermelon with the best of them and I learned that the art of making a tasty meal is not the labour-intensive task I had envisioned. Most importantly I learned that presentation goes a long way to making an impression on your guests.

Ice Sculpting Demonstrations

Growing up in the provinces of Ontario and Quebec (in Canada), I have marveled at the annual ice sculpting that takes place at various winter festivals. No matter how often I see them made, ice sculpting events can grab and hold my attention. Generally, on a ship, you will see a free demonstration of ice sculpting. Fun to watch, you can observe and enjoy some talented creations that are made quickly and efficiently.

Ship Libraries

Some ships, such as those associated with the Cunard line, have outstanding libraries that are impressive. The Norwegian line also offers up ships that have a dedicated library with tables and chairs available for reading. Other cruise lines seem to leave a few shelves bare in a common area and called it a library. On one cruise, I went in search of the "library" only to find a single shelf with two well thumbed books obviously left by other cruisers. The lack of effort on the part of the cruise line was underwhelming.

Libraries are great places to visit to pick up a book if you have run out of reading material or do not want to bring a book or tablet with you on the cruise. In advance of your trip, seek out information as to what kind of library can be found onboard. If the ship has a formal library with a broad selection of books, you will most likely be able to find suitable reading material to keep you entertained.

However, if the ship you are on does not have a dedicated library room/area, and the books on offer are those left by previous travellers, the chances are that the book selection will be slim, or the shelves may be bare when you go in search of reading material. If you are going to obtain a book on the ship, go the first day of the cruise as the chances are that you will have a better selection.

A pro tip with respect to reading material, is to load your tablet or e-reader with a few books to occupy you. That will save you the luggage space and weight of a printed copy of a book. An additional bonus is you can read at night without having the light on.

Although some people suggest loading books on their phone, my personal preference is for a larger device for ease in reading.

We like to participate in all the ship activities.
Everyday there is something fun to do. Over the years
we have tried zip lining and various simulators like golf
and surf but the best activity is always the outdoor
movies under the stars.

Todd - UK

You are Part of the Show

I participated in an onboard talent show and our ship's rep told us we needed to make the end of the show memorable. So me and a few of my buddies decided to drop our drawers at the end of our last song.

It did not go over as well as we had anticipated. I guess we should have worn underwear.

Ken (Location Withheld)

Shows onboard ships can be exceptional, great, mediocre or just not your cup of tea. Some of the best shows I have seen while cruising has been with fellow passengers involved as the entertainment.

I have participated in a few passenger events, such as game shows while my husband, who has considerably more musical talent than I do, has been involved in the game and musical shows along with choirs. All have been enjoyable.

Choir

Several cruise lines offer passenger choir opportunities. Choirs are a volunteer activity that are usually put together for longer cruises. You will find them annotated in the daily activity listing shortly after the start of a cruise. If a passenger is interested in participating in a shipboard choir, they have the opportunity to do so on a voluntary basis and rehearsals take place on sea days. The choir gives a concert towards the end of the cruise with the passengers essentially becoming the entertainment. Quite often these events are beautifully presented, and I have attended a few that were of exceptional quality.

I don't normally refer to one specific cruise line but in this case, I am going to give a hat tip to the Cunard line. I saw a customer choir presentation onboard one of the Cunard ships that was so beautiful it brought me and others to tears. It was an excellent show. The number of participants was large, the song choice excellent and the quality of the singing exceptional. The crew member who orchestrated the choir clearly was skilled in bringing the musical numbers together to create a coordinated and inspired performance.

Singing Competitions

Some cruise lines will offer singing competitions wherein individuals, or groups, can participate in judged events. These can be in different forms with some mirroring television show type competitions and others straight forward competitive singing events.

What they have in common is the participants are cruisers who become the entertainment and are able to showcase their talents.

Group Dance Routines

Much like the choir, this involves joining a collection of other passengers to learn group dancing. Ballroom, belly and other forms of dancing are also group participation activities. These are also events where people sign up, learn a dance or two, practice those dances on sea days and then showcase their ensemble skills at an end of cruise show.

In some cases, ballroom dancing may be offered and guests are able to display their learned skills on the dance floor at any time in the cruise.

Dance Hosts

I have added dance hosts to this section in case individuals want to participate in dance lessons but do not have a partner. Cruise lines will attempt to match up individuals when possible. Some cruise lines will have dance hosts who are individuals available to dance with persons without an available dance partner.

Game Shows

Usually an evening entertainment activity, these mirror television game shows and involve audience members as the participants. They can be a lot of fun, interactive and usually one event instead of a multi day participation commitment.

Normally, this type of activity takes place over an hour which means it is not an onerous time obligation if you participate.

Battle of the Sexes

Quite a few cruise lines will host a battle of the sexes event. Whether it is a pool side activity, held in the theatre, or in one of the other public venues, a battle of the sexes will take place and these are usually well attended. There are too many types of competitions to list them in this book, but you will find them annotated in the daily activity calendar and normally they are of short duration and under an hour in length.

> *My sister and I conquered everyone in a Battle of the Sexes "Almost the Olympics" contest. We were doing an egg toss competition and we managed to first beat our husbands and then all other comers. Neither of us had ever won anything before as we can not be described as "sporty." A picture of us with our medals, was taken and that became the photograph that our parents used in their annual Christmas card. Our 72-year-old Mom said they previously had no bragging photos of us winning in sports so she was going to take what she could get. I am not sure if we should be proud that at age 52 and 50, we can finally say we medaled in something. LOL*
>
> *Bernice – USA*

"Other" Onboard Activities

Card and Board Games – Ship Organized

Most ships will have an area where people can play cards. Check your daily planner to see if there are areas where cards will be played, such as "Bridge at 10am in Meeting Room B on deck 3" etc. Board games may also be available on some ships but I note that these are usually limited. I have played chess on a few cruises.

> *We took a fall trans-Atlantic cruise and there was an active group of Duplicate Bridge players onboard. Usually we are lucky if we get two tables of players but we had eight tables on this cruise and probably would have had more if there had been more tables available. It made for a lot of competitive card games over the course of the five sea days.*
>
> *Douglas – unknown location*

Card and Board Games – Cruiser Organized

Various cruising social media sites have people setting up card and board games onboard certain sailings. If you are interested in such activities, check on social media sites to see if any games are being set up for your cruise. Here is an example of games and activities I have seen set up by people on social media sites for their cruises:

Euchre	Bridge	Contract Bridge
Hearts	Canasta	Cribbage
Hand & Foot	Spades	Pass the Ace

This is not a comprehensive listing, but a sampling of card games I have seen advertised as looking for participants.

Pro Tip on Playing Cards

Look for, or ask staff about, a designated area to play cards. As evidenced by some of the pet peeve comments, people will become quite annoyed with individuals taking up tables to play cards in the common areas during busy times (such as in the buffet area).

Slot Pulls

Cruise line casinos will host slot pulls and I have seen social media groups associated with specific cruise lines, also put together the same type of event. The concept is simple, a group is formed and all contribute an equal amount of money to a pot. On a slot pull I organized, I had everyone pay $5 into the pot but I have seen other amounts advertised (such as $10 or $20). Every person contributes the same amount and that money is put into one slot machine that the slot pull organizer has pre-selected. Everyone gets a certain number of pulls on that machine and the group splits the final amount. Usually, the three people who pull the highest amount will get a little more money as the amount seldom divides equally. Additionally, the casino manager will often donate some items for the slot pull (such as t-shirts or some item with the cruise ship logo).

Cabin Crawls/Tours

These are often organized pre-cruise through various social media sites and are a great way to get to see different cabins on ships. Be warned, if you have mobility issues, this activity may not be for you as it normally involves several decks and a lot of walking along corridors to specific cabins. If you are wheelchair dependant, not all cabins are accessible.

This activity is based on people volunteering to show their cabin to others. There is usually a coordinator who lists the different types of cabins that have been offered for viewing and puts together a route map and small groups. The people, who volunteer to show their cabins are called "hosts" while those who are viewing are called "crawlers".

I have seen crawls organized wherein the first group out consists of the hosts who go to the first cabin and the host of that cabin stays in their cabin to greet the following groups (whatever the number). The rest of the hosts continue to the next cabin where that host drops out and stays at their cabin and so on. The last group of crawlers is always a small one as each host will join that group of crawlers as the last group passes through each cabin.

This is an excellent way to meet people and as mentioned, see various cabins and their layouts. Often hosts will put out drinks, canapés or items from their home country (flag pins etc.).

Poker Runs

Often held in conjunction with other events such as cabin crawls or bar crawls, poker runs consist of people paying a certain amount to participate and then going to a designated spot and choosing a card. That card is then recorded onto a list by the poker run coordinator (or cabin crawl host). If the poker run is held over several days, then a card is drawn at each meeting spot and recorded and after five cards are drawn, the best poker hand wins the money collected. Some poker runs will have one winner while others might have the top three poker hands winning.

Note: If this event is held during a cabin crawl, then five cabins will have the decks of cards and each cabin host will record the card drawn and give the listing to the poker run coordinator at the end of the crawl.

Bar Crawls

I did not participate in this type of event for a number of years as I envisioned that it was just people sitting in a bar and drinking. In 2019, my husband signed us up for a poker run which was being held in conjunction with a bar crawl. I figured we would just go to the bar, draw our cards and then leave. I found a rather interesting group of people from various walks of life and we stayed to talk. The next bar meet up was two days later in a different venue and once again we stayed and chatted for awhile. Although some people were drinking alcohol, others were not. It was more of a social undertaking than a drinking event. As with the other activities I have listed, bar crawls are coordinated by one person who sets up the meet-up itinerary in advance. Usually, these affairs are coordinated ahead of a cruise through social media sites but can also be organized onboard as well.

Flash Mob

I am not sure how these gatherings will transition into a post covid cruising world but these type of events were often organized by the cruise line and listed as a social activity. A flash mob is a group of people who will unexpectedly get together in a public place and start to sing, dance or do both (sing and dance), for the entertainment of others. It usually starts with one person, then a second person joins in and then another etc. until there is a large group doing the same activity. They usually perform one song and then disperse. Cruisers become active participants and practice for the event which will take place towards the latter part of the cruise.

I have also heard of them organized by groups who practice before the cruise and set the flash mob to occur early on in the sailing. One lady told me that her church had organized a cruise that had over 200 congregation members taking the trip. The church choir had planned a flash mob for the morning of the first full day of the cruise as a surprise to their fellow cruisers.

Specific Activities and Specialty Gatherings

Much like the card gatherings, these types of events are usually organized on social media sites before a cruise and center on specific activities to take place on the ship. I have seen knitting groups, book clubs, board game aficionados etc. The concept behind these groups is for like-minded people, who are booked on the same cruise, to meet and pursue their interests.

You asked for information about shipboard activities but not all happenings are organized by the ship or involve action packed adventure. I was researching things to do on an upcoming cruise my husband and I were taking. I have mobility issues and prefer quiet activities while my husband was sure to participate in many of the onboard goings-on. I came across a social media group that had postings about subgroups with various activities for those with differing interests. One of these groups was a posting about a get together for those of us who like to crochet. The idea was that we would meet up and exchange some ideas and tips. Since it was only going to be an hour, I thought I might as well attend and hear what they had to say. If I did not like it, I could just leave. There ended up being six of us and our one hour stretched into two. We all enjoyed our gathering so much that the one meeting expanded into two subsequent meetings. We are still in contact today and exchange patterns and information.

Ruth - USA

*****

I saw in the daily planner that there was a social gathering for people who had served in the military. I debated about going but in the end I finally went. I did not know anyone there but I had some interesting discussions with some of the people I met. It was a lot more fun than I had anticipated and the different ages and backgrounds of people who has served made it well worth the time spent.

Douglas - USA

Weddings Onboard

We got married on a ship and opted for the complete package. We had the stag & hen party, the wedding, the reception and the honeymoon all on one eighteen-day cruise. It was brilliant and I will do the same thing next time around. Don't tell my wife I said that ☺ *Name and location withheld*

Over the years, I have encountered people who were honeymooning on a cruise, but somehow, I was oblivious to the weddings that were taking place on the very ships on which I was cruising. Perhaps if I had seen someone in a bridal dress, I might have clued in. I had naively thought that for the most part, weddings on ships were mostly associated with a bygone era. Imagine my surprise when my mother informed me that my cousin had gotten married on a ship while on a Caribbean cruise.

Later when talking to him about the experience, he confirmed that it was a small, intimate affair that was handled beautifully by the cruise line. Since being enlightened about weddings on cruise ships being very much a modern-day occurrence, I have become better informed.

I have come to learn that getting married on a cruise ship is actually fairly easy and cruise lines offer up special event packages to make the day memorable. They also have wedding planners available to assist in all areas of the planning. To date, I have yet to personally be invited to attend a wedding on a ship but here is hoping it will happen. By way of an update, I have now seen a few wedding parties onboard and I have also seen a few rooms decorated for weddings and observed how elegantly the venue can be put together.

In researching shipboard weddings, I have learned that weddings may or may not be performed by the captain but most often they are performed by an officer authorized to perform marriages. The wedding events can be large or intimate depending on the needs of the couple and size of the group. The ship becomes the one stop shop as the event can be planned, executed and celebrated onboard. Some people have extended open invitations to fellow cruisers to witness their union.

If you have a ship-wedding planned, contact the cruise line to discuss your expectations and needs. You may be able to get a special group rate on the cruise price depending on the number of cabins that will be booked if you put together a group. You can also arrange a colour scheme, pre-order the cake, select your choice of menu and have a discussion as to a preferred location for the wedding. One couple wrote me that they got married on a deck at the aft of a ship at sunset which made for spectacular photos. Another couple wrote that they met on a ship when they worked for a cruise line and opted to get married in one of the private salons.

Weddings on Shore During the Cruise

I met a couple who booked an eastern Mediterranean cruise and arranged their wedding to be held in Santorini, Greece, one of the early port stops on their voyage. They spent the rest of the cruise enjoying various port stops, relaxing sea days and describing their experience as staying at the best all inclusive going. I had not heard of weddings being held at a port stop with the remainder of the cruise used as a honeymoon until they told me about their experience and how well it worked.

Special Events

In addition to weddings, many people decide to celebrate engagements with parties. They may also commemorate special anniversaries or recommitments with vow renewals. These special events can be celebrated on board with the assistance of a cruise line event planner (note the titles may vary according to the cruise line but their role is the same: they help organize the special events of their cruisers).

As with a wedding, cruise line planners are generally predisposed to cater to your needs and endeavour to make the occasion special. Please note that these events should be planned in advance of the cruise, and the size of the party and any special needs discussed earlier rather than later.

Milestone Events

Cruise lines will ask if you are going to be celebrating any special or milestone events while on the cruise. Make sure to annotate your events when booking or in advance of your cruise. Although we have celebrated birthdays, anniversaries and a retirement on a cruise, we did not take advantage of the services of a planner as our celebrations were confined to dinners in a specialty restaurant. Even so, the cruise line generally arranged some little treat to recognize our milestone event.

Help, I am allergic to this Ship

Having found that I seemed to be allergic to the ship, I spent a great deal of time living on the balcony and avoiding closed spaces.

In 2017, Dan and I boarded a west bound trans-Atlantic cruise departing Copenhagen and headed for Boston. As always, I was excited to be cruising and having secured an aft, balcony cabin, I was in heaven. Enjoying our sail-away by standing on the balcony and toasting the start of our adventure, we were oblivious to the problems that were headed my way.

We had just finished a pre cruise trip to Normandy and followed that up with a whirl wind tour of Copenhagen. I had no reason to think that literally sailing off into the sunset would result in any challenge to my health.

Quickly into the cruise we had port stops so we were off the ship a great deal. When we got to enjoy our first sea day, as the day wore on, I noticed that my eyes were red, itchy and puffy. Fearing that I was developing some type of eye infection and having read about people catching the highly contagious pink eye, I went to the medical clinic and was examined by the doctor.

The good news was that I had not caught some infectious disease that would result in me being confined to our cabin. Instead, it looked like I was having a reaction to something to which I was allergic. I was prescribed some medication and off I went thinking the problem had been sorted.

The next three days we were mostly off the ship as we had arrived in Iceland. I felt fine and my eyes cleared as did my breathing. Then we set sail for North America, and it turned into a health disaster for me. Suddenly every time I was in a closed space, particularly when we went to dine, I became congested, and my nose ran like someone had turned on a tap. I was literally and figuratively blowing through tissues at an alarming rate. Our cabin attendant was filling the tissue box twice a day. I was constantly rubbing my eyes and it was soon apparent that I was having an allergic reaction to something. But what?

We never found the cause, but cleaning solvents used onboard, dust and other assorted items came under suspicion. It was bad enough that anytime I went to eat, I became stuffed up but soon it was apparent that I was also suffering the ill effects while in our cabin. The only time the symptoms cleared up was when I went out into the fresh air.

Sleeping on the lounger on our balcony ensured that I was able to breathe and survive the night however, it was a northern Atlantic crossing and it was chilly outside. Dan took pity on me and said we could sleep with the balcony door wide open which meant the room was perpetually cold at night. However, the infusion of fresh air ensured I was able to breathe. Anytime I became too congested, I simply sat outside for an hour or two and everything cleared up. Needless to say, I spent a lot of time engaging in outdoor activities or just reading on our balcony. I now travel with medication to address allergy symptoms should such a problem ever arise again.

Getting sick on a cruise is always a possibility but we all can take steps to mitigate the risk. We must accept that when you have a number of people, originating from different places, and put them in a contained area, the risk of some type of exposure increases. People are bound to arrive from areas where there is an outbreak of flu, cold or some other contagious illness. Particularly during the winter. Statistics show that people enjoying all inclusive resorts run the same risk of contracting an illness as those on a cruise ship and it is always sad when a perfectly great vacation is interrupted if one gets sick.

Everyone always focuses on the restaurants and their cabins, but ships have a huge number of common areas such as the lounges, bars and theaters. Stairway railings, ATM, interactive screens in places like the photoshop or display area. These are all places where the transfer of germs is possible. Factor in fatigue from travel to the ship, or those last-minute pre-cruise preparations, and people arrive excited but with a body system that is tired and out of sync.

The suggestions that you wipe down things in your cabin are excellent, and frequent hand washing or use of sanitizer a great practice. If you feel unwell, go to your cabin and rest. Missing out on activities for one day can prevent missing out on a number of activities for several days.

There is no Shame in Masking

I am not about to enter the rather volatile debate about whether people should or should not mask on a ship. I recommend you follow the directions of the cruise ship and if airborne infections are on the rise and staff ask people to mask in public areas, do it.

Unless mandated by the cruise line, mask wearing is an individual choice. I am fine with wearing a mask and I believe there is no shame in wearing one if you wish. I hold the opinion that people should respect the choices of individuals and refrain from making comments that might be considered incendiary.

> *I had a lung transplant in 2021 and I am sensitive to airborne viruses. I wear a mask when in public spaces. For some reason, people think it is their business to comment on the fact that I mask in public places. I now wear a button that reads "I am a lung transplant recipient! Thank you to all organ donors". That cuts down on mask comments but frankly, I should not have to wear such a button. It is none of their business whether I wear a mask or not.*
>
> *Jim - USA*

In 2022, on a cruise from Vancouver to Oahu, there were elevated incidents of covid on the ship. We were all asked to wear masks in public spaces. Some people chose to ignore the request. One of them, who I was told was quite vocal about not masking, tested positive for covid upon arrival in Oahu. Even though he was supposed to be on back-to-back sailings and had plans to stay on for the next cruise, he had to depart the ship because he had covid and missed the Oahu to Sydney leg.

Dan - Canada

The Travelling Medicine Show

My wife is an operating room nurse and when packing for a trip, she brings everything necessary to treat any medical emergency. I jokingly say that the medical facilities onboard any ship could come to her for supplies. I will put my foot down if she starts to pack a portable x-ray machine.

Paul (no location provided)

On one cruise, following dinner, a group of us were enjoying a post dinner visit when my husband mentioned that he had been having some problems sleeping. Several of the people volunteered their sleep remedies and nonprescription medications that they had brought with them. Everything from over-the-counter drug treatments to herbal remedies were offered. That segued into a discussion on the subject of over-the-counter drugs people had brought with them to treat common ailments or problems that can crop up on a trip. While listening to them, it suddenly occurred to me that contrary to the others in the group, I had embarked on the cruise woefully ill prepared to treat the most common ailments. My mind cast back to the *"allergic to the ship"* cruise and my failure to have allergy medication on hand. I knew I had to make adjustments to my travel preparations and ensure that in the future, I put a little more thought into items I might need. No longer would the four band aids and diarrhea medication be the total sum of my medical supplies. I was going to expand my medicine "chest".

In my defence, knowing that there is a medical facility onboard every cruise ship was reassuring as there would always be a medical professional to prescribe medication if needed. Ships carry a range of basic medication for common ailments and can treat more serious health issues such as heart attacks or certain chronic illnesses. I will address visiting an onboard medical facility a little further in this chapter and for now will focus on over-the-counter medications.

Over-the-Counter Medication

Headaches, muscle soreness, joint pain, etc. are all common ailments that can easily be treated by over-the-counter medication that one might bring from home.

A trip to see the onboard doctor can easily start at over $100USD. Consequently, if you require something as common as a sleeping or headache tablet, it is cheaper to bring your own. You will also have a brand that you have used before and know how you react to it and whether it can be used in conjunction with any prescription medication you may take.

Learning from other People

Some people bring a large amount of medication with them. I once accompanied a friend to her cabin as she wanted to get something for her sore back. She opened a drawer and pulled out an impressive bag filled with every imaginable over the counter remedy. Regardless of the ailment, she appeared to have it covered. *Tylenol, Advil, Aleve, Aspirin* were all well represented and covering a wide range from daytime to nighttime needs. It also focused on all parts of the body (such as the back, knees, sinus etc.). Medicated creams, lotions and potions were at hand, and her onboard medicine chest was the most impressive I had ever seen. She was ready for every possible medical scenario that required over-the-counter medication.

I may not carry such an impressive array of items, but I have learned from her and from hearing about the experiences of others. For example:

> *We were on a cruise when my sciatica started to act up. I did not want to see the ship's doctor as some over the counter pain medication would normally do the trick. Unfortunately, we only had a small travel bottle of our usual pain medication that we kept in our travel bag. When we looked closely at it, we discovered it was half full and the contents had passed the expiry date. So down to the sick bay I went, and they fixed me up. They did not*

*charge me for the over-the-counter medication, but
I had to pay a fee for the visit. Tell your readers to
check the expiry date on their medications before
they leave on their trip.*

Kenny – USA

Pro Tip on Group Travel and Medicines

If you are travelling with a group of close friends or family, rather than everyone bringing a large amount of over-the-counter medication, discuss what you are bringing. Dividing the responsibility for bringing nonprescription medication among yourselves, will reduce the cost of bringing your own little pharmacy and save on suitcase space.

Buying Medications at a Port Stop

You may be able to buy over the counter medication at a port stop. However, it is important to note that not all countries you might visit have the brand of items you are familiar with, and the directions and contents might be written in a language you are unable to read. Translation apps are not always 100% accurate in the interpretation of written directions, possible side effects, or drug interactions. Additionally, some countries have different standards for what constitutes medication requiring a prescription. For example, products with codeine may require a prescription in some countries and be sold over the counter in others.

Prescription Medication

As one reader so succinctly put it:

> *One of our carry-on bags is usually reserved for our medications. We are getting older and we always carry both prescription and over the counter drugs. It used to be that I took Tylenol in the morning if I had partied the night before, now I take it to get my joints moving without a lot of pain. Sad, but just a part of life now.*
>
> *Karen – Canada*

If you take prescription medication, carry it in your carry-on bag/purse and ensure you have it with you at all times until you are in your cabin. Try and keep the medication in the original prescription bottles so it is easily apparent to anyone inspecting the medication, that it is a professionally filled prescription. I always obtain a print-out from my pharmacy of any medication I might be taking just in case the label is worn or not clear. Bring your pharmacy number with you in case you need to contact them. The reason for this is twofold. The first being that I have a quick reference to give the onboard physician a list of my medications in case he/she needs it (so far it has never been necessary). Secondly, if I am travelling to or from a foreign country for the cruise, and my bag is inspected, this will ease my passage through security and/or customs.

Pro Tip on Carrying Prescription Medications

Drugs, particularly generic brands, can have various names and be called something different in another country. If you take prescription medication, have a list of the names the drug may go under. For example, a common anticoagulant is Warfarin which in Canada, can go by the generic name of Coumadin.

Know the Reason You Take a Drug

Know the reason you take certain medications. As people age, or if they have an ongoing health condition, they may take more than one medication daily and forget the specifics of what each drug is supposed to control.

> *My husband, who suffers from a chronic illness, became ill on a cruise and the medical staff were great. They treated him quickly but we did have one blip. They asked about my husband's medications, and he could not remember them all or what they did.*

> *I went to our cabin and brought all the pill bottles to the doctor but some of the drug names were not familiar to the medical staff. The doctor had to look up several of the drugs to see what they were and what symptoms the medicine was treating. Now when we cruise, I have a list of the drugs and what they do.*

Cleo – Canada

Food and Drug Interactions

Pay attention to whether the prescription drug you are taking interacts with any foods you might want to try on the ship. For example, grapefruit can interfere with the effectiveness of some cholesterol medications.

Home Remedies and Other Medical Aids

This is a bit tricky as some people swear by certain home remedies. Baking powder and corn starch as a foot powder may work for foot fungus, but a baggie of this unknown substance can have you tied up in security trying to explain what it is.

Marijuana, Hash Oil and Associated Products

For those who use legal marijuana or hash oil products, you should note that they may be legal in your home country but not acceptable in the country where your cruise might start or end. Many cruise ships do not allow these products onboard even if legal in your home state/province and prescribed by a medical practitioner. This includes weed vape, hash oil or marijuana cartridges.

If you really need to bring them with you, contact your cruise line and obtain their written confirmation that the product is allowed on the cruise you are taking. You will need to do this for every cruise as a written approval for one cruise may not be sufficient for other cruises as the approval might be itinerary dependant.

Visiting the Onboard Medical Facilities

One of the biggest complaints that I have heard relating to visiting a medical facility onboard a ship, is the cost. Usually billed in US funds, a visit can cost several hundred dollars or more. IF you require medical treatment, don't let the prospect of a charge deter you from seeking medical aid. Quick medical intervention can fix an immediate problem and prevent a health issue from getting worse. Once again, I will offer myself as an example.

On back-to-back cruises in September and October 2022, we were in Oahu for two days. Determined to make the most of those days, I did a considerable amount of walking and my step counter registered 23,000 steps on one day and 28,000 the second day. I developed blisters on a middle toe. Blisters are common ailments and I, like so many others, have developed them from time to time over the years. I thought nothing of them as blisters have always healed quickly and completely. They were an inconvenience and I vowed to avoid wearing the culprit sandals for the rest of the trip.

I put some medicated cream on the blisters and covered them with a plaster. The trip continued and by the time we reached the French Polynesian islands, the blisters had broken and the toe was red and angry looking. Thinking that walking in salt water would help, I made sure to walk the beaches and in the water. In the following days, it was clear that the toe was infected and a trip to the medical facility was in order.

I received intravenous antibiotics over two days followed by seven days of an oral medication regiment. The problem was soon fixed, and my toe was fine for the rest of the trip. My treatment came to a total of $1014.40USD which I was able to claim on my medical insurance. The treatment was worth the money as it prevented the infection from getting into the bones of my foot and/or spreading.

Coronavirus Killed Cruising in 2020

For me, 2020 was going to be a busy travel year. I started the year with a three-month house rental on a beach in North Carolina. My intention was to write this book. I was hoping that the peace and quiet of the location would afford me plenty of time to review travel notes and do cruising research. I was positive that the sounds of the ocean would be inspirational. By the end of February, the book was well on its way to completion, and I was looking forward to some upcoming cruises. My husband and I had three cruises planned for that year: a May Baltic Sea cruise, a trans-Atlantic crossing and a late fall western Africa cruise. We had invested a lot of time and money into our upcoming trips, and it was with great anticipation that I spent my free time looking at shore excursions and planning the cruise details.

In January, we had started to hear stories about a new virus that was creating havoc on the well-being of the elderly and those with existing health issues. At first it seemed a distant problem that was adversely affecting people in China but soon we were hearing about the virus sweeping a path through European countries along with dire warnings that seemingly healthy people were becoming quite ill. No longer a threat to only people in high-risk categories, the virus was moving quickly through the weak and healthy with seemingly equal abandon. More and more countries were added to the statistics of having active infectious cases. Suddenly, news of cruise ship passenger infections became front page reading and I began to take greater notice.

The first week of February, there was news about a cruise ship having an outbreak. That resulted in the ship being quarantined in Yokohama, Japan on February 4th. That quarantine last approximately a month. Nine people died as a result of the virus and hundreds of passengers and crew became ill. People were confined to their cabins, which makes me cringe every time I think of those people in inside cabins. Eventually a system was worked out to allow passengers some outside deck access but that "*outside the cabin*" time was severely limited. News of the plight of those passengers made international headlines. Cruise ships in Brisbane and Miami also reported outbreaks leading authorities to question the safety of cruising. The very nature of cruise ships, with high density environments, plenty of group activities and numerous common areas, were perfect environments for transmission.

Governments started to advise against cruising with the initial warnings focused on those high-risk passengers who had weakened immune systems, underlying medical conditions or those enjoying advanced age.

By mid March the cautions became broader, and the warnings were expressing concern relating to any cruise travel. Although not in

Canada at the time, I took note that as of March 11, 2020, the Public Health Agency of Canada (PHAC), had issued its latest travel advisory that included recommendations that Canadians avoid all cruise ship travel. In the United States, the Center for Disease Control (CDC), was issuing similar warnings. Cruise lines were cancelling cruises and their ships were being docked or tendered with only skeleton crews for the immediate future.

It was not only cruise ships that were affected, and I could write an entire book on the dire blow handed to the travel industry as a whole. Airlines cancelled flights, countries closed boarders and holiday goers scrambled to return home. Travel, any kind of travel, became shrouded in uncertainty and a nightmare. Since this book is about cruising, I am focusing on the cruising aspect of the covid shutdowns, but I feel it only fair to point out that the entire travel industry was receiving crushing blow after crushing blow. There were warnings that you may not be able to return home if travel restrictions were imposed by the country you were visiting. Additionally, there was no guarantee that there would be government-organized repatriation flights and warnings that you might be responsible for the cost of repatriation travel were off putting to say the least.

Dedicated cruisers wondered what would happen to their booked cruises and questioned the future of cruising. On March 17th, we left our rented beach home and returned to Canada to await the end of the pandemic. As with everyone else, we watched the news and waited for more information. Our May Baltic Sea cruise was cancelled and rather than take a refund, we opted for a cruise credit knowing that when cruising recommenced, we would want to set sail.

Over the course of the summer, I read thousands of posts filled with speculation about cruising and what would happen. Final payment date for our fall trans-Atlantic arrived and the cruise line we were booked with, looked for final payment. We made full payment even though cruising was still on hold, and I had little expectation that the trip would go forward but as the old saying goes "Hope springs eternal". That being said, I did not bother to book flights because although I was hopeful, I was not about to become reckless and book flights that might lead to refund and/or credit hassles with an airline. About five weeks before we were to leave, that cruise was cancelled. This time I asked for a full refund. Shortly thereafter, I requested a refund for the deposit we had made on our remaining 2020 cruise.

By the first week of September, all our 2020 cruises were cancelled and for the first time in decades, we had no trips planned in the immediate future.

Cruising started to take on life again in 2021 and by June of that year, cruising on a broader scale had begun with cruise lines touting enhanced cleanings, passenger reductions and mandatory masking and vaccinations. Many cruise lines introduced bubble shore excursions which meant that passengers could only take cruise line arranged excursions where sanitation and exposure protections could be controlled. We placed a deposit on a Pacific Ocean cruise (Hawaii to Sydney) and in a fit of optimism, I booked our airline tickets and pre and post cruise hotel stays. That cruise was eventually cancelled by the cruise line and although the cancellation was disheartening, I held the opinion that passenger safety was the most important aspect and as such, I respected the decision to cancel.

As of now, cruising has resumed in most locations, but the sailing/boarding conditions and controls change. Consequently, I cannot list what the requirements are with any degree of certainty. We have recently taken three cruises within a five-month period and I was continuously checking on pre-cruise testing requirements (ship and visited countries).

When taking a cruise in this modern age, cruisers must remain flexible, ready for any itinerary changes due to country restrictions, and be cognizant of health and safety measures. Is cruising safe in these days of covid? The answer is yes, it is as safe as any other vacation that involves shared travel methodology, hotel stays and restaurant dining.

Travel Agents and the Great Covid Cancellation

One person with whom I spoke about a group cruise booking, had the following comments:

> "...the original cruise which was booked for November 2020 with 209 guests confirmed with deposits, had to be cancelled after Covid hit us due to a very grim outlook for the fall of 2020. We then shifted the group to another November 2021, 12-night Caribbean sailing, again on the Celebrity Equinox, only to cancel that one also due to the ongoing pandemic. An incredible mountain of work."

Carole - Canada

When people think of covid striking the cruising industry, they tend to think of the cruise lines. I think of the travel agents (the ones who work directly for cruise lines and the ones working independently or for travel agencies). I have mentioned that I hold high expectations for any travel agent I use. They need to be knowledgeable and competent. I don't expect that they will know everything about every cruise line but they should have a strong base knowledge of most and be willing to research issues and get back to you.

When the pandemic struck, travel agents were swamped with calls about cruises and associated travel. Looking to obtain firsthand information on what travel agents went through, I contacted a few with whom I deal, and I asked about their "covid" cancellation experience.

One agent, Lise, was instrumental in dealing with two of our booked 2020 cruises and the 2021 cruise (which involved a small group of my friends in 5 or 6 cabins). Obviously, I had firsthand experience in how she handled our cancellations but most importantly, I was aware that our booked cruises were a mere drop in the bucket of the number of bookings she had. Consequently, I turned to her to enquire as to her experience as a cruise line specialist who had weathered the great covid cancellations.

Lise was surprisingly upbeat and positive about her entire experience. Yes, she had a lot of cancellations to address and the lack of information as to when cruising would resume made things challenging. Lise had to negotiate refunds, explaining lift and shift options (wherein the same cruise was simply booked for the following year), and how future cruise credits (FCC), worked and how they could be used. There were flight cancellations, pre and post cruise accommodation arrangements and a plethora of other travel related duties to negotiate. As one of Lise's clients during that time, I can attest to her professionalism and positive attitude.

The most challenging for her, was responding to questions as to when cruising would begin again for those trying to determine whether they should obtain a refund or an FCC. The situation was very fluid so it was difficult for Lise to provide advice as to the best option for her customers. Complicating matters were negotiating country shutdowns, air travel restrictions, and the sheer volume of calls, e-mails and text messages. Rather than complain about the mountain of work, Lise simply stated that it was an extraordinary time with exceptional circumstances, and she appreciated the patience and understanding of her customers. No problem was too gruelling and if she did not have an answer, she sought it out.

Contrasting Lise's positive attitude was information received from another travel agent. She described the situation as overwhelming and stressful.

> *There were several days I just broke down in tears especially when I gave out information one day and it changed the next.*

> *...*

> *I booked, rebooked and booked again only to have cruise after cruise cancel. There were people who were gracious and understanding and others who*

*treated me like I created the pandemic. It was not
an easy time.*

Jackie – United Kingdom

I had a fairly lengthy conversation with a travel agent who has since left the business and she provided me with an overview of her experience. She too found the great covid cruise cancellation stressful and a huge amount of work for little return. She described her customers as understanding and lauded their interactions with her as the best experience. But ultimately, she found dealing with an unprecedented industry shutdown was nerve-wracking and taxing.

In addition to talking to travel agents, I scoured various cruising sites to see how people were handling the lack of cruising. Some were positive about the future of cruising and anxious to start sailing again. There was also a fair share of others who were pessimistic and forecasting the demise of the industry. When the cruise lines issued their annual reports, I went through them, trying to determine if any particular line looked like it was about to go under and whether it should be avoided on future bookings. Based on all the information floating around, I did not envy travel agents their jobs and their continued navigation of a dynamic situation.

I received information from different travel agents as to whether they were paid for the work they had completed. Generally, agents receive between 10-16% of the cruise fare and if they book groups, they will receive cabin credits in addition to the percentage. Most of the people to whom I spoke told me that if the cruise had passed the final payment date, that they still received their commission even if the cruise was cancelled and their customers had received refunds. However, if they were doing groups, they did not get the cabin credits, only their monetary percentage.

I salute those travel agents, no matter what title they use, be it cruise specialists, cruising experts, travel representative etc. and commend them for working through a difficult time in the travel industry.

Politics, the Great Divider

When on a cruise ship, if possible, avoid talking politics and religion. Remember, there is NO safe answer.

I managed to get through a large number of vacations, both on land and at sea, without ever hearing a political word. Prior to 2016, the only time anyone ever approached me to ask a remotely political question, was when health care coverage was an issue in the USA. I was participating in a brewery tour in Pottsville, Pennsylvania, and while in the tasting room, a woman asked me about our Canadian health care system. She explained that she was trying to decide whether to stand for, or against, *"socialized health care"* and asked whether I *"liked"* the way the health care system worked in Canada.

All this changed with the USA election in November of 2016. People started to ask my opinion of the president elect. This surprised me since previously, no one, in any country, appeared to care about my political opinion.

By 2017, I noticed an uptick in political discussion onboard ships and on shore excursions. People were asking fellow travellers what they thought of the US president and I quickly learned that there is no safe answer.

Also, for the first time ever, I started to hear comments regarding political affiliation. For example, at one social gathering early in a cruise, Dan made an off-the-cuff remark to a man he was speaking with, that he looked very much like a political anchor Dan had seen on a 24-hour news station. Another man, who had been standing with the two of them, made a sound of disgust, turned on his heel and abruptly walked away. His actions were surprisingly rude. The fellow, to whom my husband had made the comment, laughed and said *"Don't mind him, he thinks you must be Democrats because you watch the channel with that TV anchorman. He doesn't talk to Democrats."* It was our first inclination that there appeared to be some very divisive political issues bubbling beneath the surface. Dan decided to stick to Canadian, British and French television references in the future but soon learned that a reference to the *CBC* could produce strong reactions as well. Hence, he currently avoids all television news references and limits his chats to non politically affiliated streaming services and shows associated with them.

On one cruise, while standing on our mid-ship aft balcony, I noticed that our cruising neighbours to the left and right were outside on their balconies also enjoying the view of the ship's wake. As so often happens on cruises, we struck up a friendly conversation and spoke of such innocuous things as the weather, the future port stops etc.

Then it happened.

"Sorry about our president" said the gentleman on the left.

"What did you say?" asked the one on the right.

"I was just apologizing for our president being such an asshole." said the one on the left.

"He is a great man!" was the indignant comment of the gentleman on the right.

I would like to say that they eventually reached a compromise but that is not the case. A heated discussion ensued, and I tried to follow the conversation looking left and then right and then left and then right depending on who was speaking. Feeling uncomfortable with the way the conversation was going, I quickly decided that it would be more judicious to simply back away from the railing. I quietly made my way inside our cabin.

"What's going on outside?" Dan asked.

"They are arguing about their president." I responded.

Dan went out the balcony door, ostensibly to hear their discussion but the exchange had ended and from that date on, if one was at their balcony railing talking to us and the other came out onto his balcony, either one or the other would immediately turn around and go back inside their cabin. The same with their wives. To my knowledge, they never exchanged another word for the entire cruise.

Unfortunately, this was not the only incident on that cruise or on any subsequent cruise where the name of the president came up in conversation. On one memorable occasion, a woman asked me what I thought of the US president. Thinking it best not to step into that minefield, I said that I was a Canadian and as such I had no opinion as he was *"not my president"*. Clearly that was a trigger statement because she launched into a tirade complete with finger pointing and air quotes about how tired she was of people saying he was not *"their president"*. I waited until she finished and thinking she had missed hearing my nationality, I told her again that I was a Canadian. Then I made an unfortunate mistake. Foolishly, I thought I should describe our system of governance. I told her that Canada did not have a president. *"We have a constitutional monarchy. The crown is represented by the Governor General in Canada, and we have a parliamentary system with a Prime Minister. As such we don't have a president and that is why I said he was not my president"*. Puffing herself up she wagged her finger in my face and said, *"That does not matter, Trump is your president whether you like it or not"*. Feeling that she had put me in my place, she turned and stormed off. I stood there for a moment replaying the conversation in my head trying to see what I had missed. I made a note to myself to never use the term *"Not my president"*.

Lest anyone suffer under the misconception that all political arguments I have heard on cruises revolve around one particular US president, I soon learned that there were strong opinions on his successor.

As seemingly tumultuous as US politics have become, I do not want to be seen as pointing the finger of blame solely on Americans as to their polarized politics. In recent years, I have seen some intense conversations relating to UK, Canadian, French and German politics and I can quote some rather heated comments related to the leadership associated with those countries.

Additionally, following the death of Queen Elizabeth II, I can relate a conversation between a British, Australian and Canadian about the value of the monarchy in modern day governance. The conversation started civil enough but soon descended to bitter recriminations and accusations tied to colonialism.

My advice to anyone on a cruise that is not politically themed/affiliated, is to avoid the subject of politics. You are on vacation and frankly, I have never seen an individual's political ideology be changed through a conversation on a cruise ship. The same advice holds true for the subject of religion. Stick to innocuous subjects and enjoy the pleasure of each other's company.

Book Your Next Cruise While on Your Current Cruise

It was our first cruise and we were travelling with my mother (who is a widow and often travels with us). On our final sea day, we knew it was our last chance to book a future cruise and get a good deal. Since we had a lot of fun, we knew we would all cruise again. Our day was pretty well packed with activities and we really wanted to attend the last of a lecture series we had been following. My mother, who would be going with us on the next cruise, offered to book the cruise while we went to the lecture.

We had talked about some next cruise options and were of a similar mind as to places we all wanted to see. We had a budget and time frame in mind so there were no concerns about her being the one to book the cruise.

Later in the day, when we returned to our cabin, we found my mother on her balcony next door reading her book. She told us we had each saved $500 and got additional onboard credit. She had booked adjoining, balcony cabins with all the same amenities we had on our current cruise. We figured all was well.

It was not until a few months later that we had a look at the cruise documentation and discovered that she had booked us on the exact same ship with the identical itinerary for the following year. When we asked her why, she said it was because she liked the people we were dining with at our table in the main dining room.

Gus and Viola - USA

You are on your cruise and having a great time. You decide that you want to take another cruise. All cruise ships provide their current cruisers with the opportunity to book another cruise while onboard their current sailing. The benefits are usually, reduced price and the attachment of other perks (such as onboard credit or a reduced deposit). It is well worth your time to pay a visit to the designated sales area of the ship where you can examine future cruises and what is on offer as a special incentive for booking onboard. Not ready to book a specific cruise? You can usually buy future cruise credits or certificates, which can be applied towards a cruise in the time to come.

If you are wondering about follow-up questions once you get off the cruise, you can speak directly to an agent of the cruise line, or even your own travel representative. Most ships will notify the travel specialist through whom you booked your current cruise, of the fact you have made a booking onboard. It was explained to me that the premise behind such a disclosure of your information is, that if they had not booked you on the cruise in the first place, the subsequent booking would not have been made. That agent will usually get the commission for your future booking. You can then talk to them about any cruising questions you may have and changes or cancellations you may want to make.

If you have booked through a travel agent that you feel is not deserving of any benefits from a future booking, you can tell the cruise line representative you are dealing with on the ship, that your booking is not to be associated with that travel agent.

Cancelling a Cruise You Booked Onboard

As with all things in life, things change, which means that at the time of booking, ensure you understand what the policy of the cruise line is with regard to changes and cancellations and what type of fare you have been quoted. It is possible that you have been quoted a non-refundable price and as such, your deposit may not be refundable. Make sure to understand what you are getting for your money. I have booked cruises onboard and later cancelled them when I found the timing of the cruise conflicted with a family event or I found a different cruise I liked better.

You can often retain the benefit you received from booking onboard even if you change your cruise itinerary. If we use an example of a $500 price discount combined with a $200 onboard credit on a trans-Atlantic sailing you booked for the following year, and you then decide you don't want to do that trans-Atlantic sailing, you may be able to transfer your cruise benefits ($500 plus the $200 onboard credit), to a different booking if it is with the same cruise line.

Future Cruise Credit Versus Onboard Credit

These two types of credit can be confused but the easiest way to think about them is that you will use your future cruise credit to help pay for a cruise you will take in the future. You will use your onboard credit to pay for items while on, or going on, a cruise. In short, you must be onboard to use the onboard credit or use it in advance to book shore excursions, specialty meals, spa treatments etc.

Using Onboard Credit to Pay for a Future Cruise

To the best of my knowledge, you cannot use your onboard credit as a downpayment for a future cruise, nor can you transfer existing onboard credit to a future cruise.

Future Cruise Credits and Use on a Different Cruise Lines

Can a future cruise credit or certificate be used on different cruise lines? The simple answer to that question is no. Future cruising credits or certificates cannot be used on different cruise lines unless the cruise line is owned by the same parent company and the company has a specific policy that they will accept vouchers from their sister lines.

Death on a Cruise Ship

The worst thing that happen[ed] is that in the middle of the night a crew member fell overboard and was not found, it was very sad.
Shirley – Canada

Shirley's comment had been in response to a question I posed about severe illnesses or deaths that have occurred in association with a cruise. It is not a topic people like to discuss but it is one that crops up in talks I give about cruising. People do not like to think about a tragic occurrence transpiring on what is expected to be an enjoyable occasion but as in life, unexpected and unwelcome events can, and do, occur.

Over dinner on a cruise from Copenhagen to Boston, we were told that there had been a serious medical emergency onboard. It was not until later that evening that we learned that it involved someone we had met on the cruise. His wife had been very active on social media cruising sites and she was an organizer of several independent onboard events. At one such event, a slot pull held that afternoon, we had met her husband and spent time chatting with him. We were told that later that day, he collapsed in their cabin and was being treated in the medical facility. Our hearts went out to him and his wife as we learned that the ship was going to deviate from its intended route to make an emergency stop in St John's, Newfoundland. We knew the medical situation had to be serious if the ship was being diverted from its course and an emergency medical stop added.

The ship tendered in the St. John's harbour and most passengers were on deck to watch the medical transfer take place. The ship stayed in the harbour for a number of hours before resuming the cruise.

A month or two later, the woman chose to provide us with information as to what had happened. Her husband had collapsed in their cabin as they were getting ready for dinner. He was taken to the medical facility where it was determined that he was in a life-threatening condition. A decision was made for the ship to detour to the nearest port having a suitable hospital that could provide the necessary level of care.

The cruise ship personnel offered the woman support in the form of someone to be with her at the medical facility and staff to pack up their personal items in the cabin. The ship's crew arranged for her to speak with her family at home. It was also organized for their daughter to fly to St. John's to be with them.

While tendered, the medical transfer took place and the woman told us that the ship's doctor accompanied them to the hospital to give a full reporting of the diagnosis and treatment. He stayed for several hours at the hospital before returning to the ship and a cruise line support person remained with her after the ship had departed. This unfortunate incident gave us a glimpse into how a cruise ship handles a tragic and sensitive medical issue.

Over the years, I have heard of people dying on vacations and indeed I have attended funerals of people who have passed away when on holidays. It matters little as to whether it was at an all inclusive in Mexico, on a trail walk in Spain or on the beach in Florida, sudden and unexpected deaths can occur. Cruise ships are no different. People who may have health conditions cruise because it is considered a relaxing vacation with options as to whether a person wants to engage in strenuous activities or just relax. There are always people vacationing who have health issues and cruises are no different. People may overindulge in food, drink or physical activities and their bodies may react to a sudden change in lifestyle.

Cruise lines have had to deal with the sudden death of individuals, and they have established protocols for such occurrences. Sad and tragic, such events happen and the need to address the situation in a sympathetic and professional manner is critical.

Murder on a Cruise Ship

Although I talk about sudden deaths due to natural causes, I have also been asked if murders occur on cruise ships and sadly they do, but these are rare. Usually involving persons who are known to each other (often persons who are related), murders on a cruise are investigated as any murder is investigated in a civilized society. However, there are circumstances that can present judicial challenges such as whether a ship is in international or territorial waters.

Some cases might be clear cut in relation to jurisdiction. For example, there is the case of *Kenneth Manzanares*, who in 2017 beat his wife to death while on an Alaskan cruise. He pleaded guilty to killing her in 2020 and was sentenced to 30 years in prison. The case was straight forward as the killer and his victim were Americans, the killing took place in US waters and there were witnesses to the killer's actions. It is my understanding that the witnesses to the beating were all Americans who lived in the US.

But what happens when a murder takes place in international waters? The crime is subject to maritime law which is not as current or clear cut as the criminal laws of many countries. Any investigation is carried out by the cruise line security staff and/or any specialists or investigative agency that the cruise line invites to participate. I have done presentations and talks on cruise line murders and mysteries that delves into the details of such incidents. Although I could speak in detail on this matter, that is not the focus of this book. Just for the record, lest anyone think I pick on cruise lines, I also do talks and presentations on murders and other crimes relating to tourists on land.

If the ship is in the territorial waters of a specific country, it would normally fall under the laws of that country. I have been asked if the FBI, Interpol or RCMP would be able to investigate a murder at sea or within another country's jurisdiction and the answer is "maybe". If at sea, in international waters, the cruise line can ask a specific investigative agency to work with them. Unlike television shows, the logistics would be difficult as the agency would have to have the capacity to deploy resources quickly. Normally their expertise involves a subsequent review and analysis of evidence secured (at the time of the incident), by the security personnel of a cruise line as opposed to on-scene investigation shortly after an occurrence.

As for interceding in an investigation in the territorial waters of another country, the quick answer is that none of those agencies would have the jurisdiction to conduct an investigation. However, if they are invited to join an investigation by the country having jurisdiction, then the answer would be yes. They could provide access to databases, subject matter expertise etc.

If not invited to participate in the investigation, any police agency, not having jurisdiction, is limited in what they can do. They have no official role in the investigation and no standing.

There have been cases where the family members of an individual have requested an investigative agency look at a specific incident, but there must be cooperation by the cruise line and/or country of jurisdiction. Even then, the investigative agency may be limited to reviewing evidence months or years later and their findings would not be legally binding.

Joint Investigations

Given the nature of cruising, it is possible that a police force conducting an investigation into a criminal incident, may seek the aid of one or more investigation agencies located in other countries. This is usually done when there is a need to obtain witness statements/collect evidence from persons who were on the cruise and who have now returned to their home countries.

It may also occur when the country having criminal jurisdiction lacks the resources, infrastructure or expertise to carry out the investigation.

Thankfully murders are exceedingly rare.

Disembarking

Our family had a great cruise and thoroughly enjoyed our time on the ship. Our five-year-old particularly loved the cruise and kept telling us that he did not want to leave. The morning of departure, as we were headed for the gangway, he escaped my grasp. It was crowded and busy and we quickly lost sight of him. It took over two hours to find him.

Bruce - USA

Cruise Luggage Tags

Congratulations, you have taken your first cruise and now the cruise is coming to an end. On your second or third last day, you will most likely be provided with luggage tags which you will be asked to place on your checked baggage. These luggage tags will indicate a colour or number that correlates to your scheduled departure time from the ship. If the time is not suitable to you (for example if you have an early flight and need to get off the ship earlier), go to guest services and obtain luggage tags that will reflect an earlier departure time. The same holds true if you want to leave the ship a bit later. Some ships will ask you to indicate your preferred leaving time in advance but if not, always check your luggage tags to make sure your baggage will be ready for you at the collection point if you need an early exit.

How do you "check" your luggage you ask? You simply tag it and leave it outside your cabin door the night before the cruise ends. But more about this later, as I first want to touch on what you should do before the actual departure day.

Check Your Onboard Account

The day before your cruise concludes. make sure you check your onboard account for accuracy and pick up any purchases you might want to make on the ship. If the day before your cruise ends, you are in a port, then you should check your onboard account the day before. If you have not been checking your onboard account on a daily basis, always give yourself time to review your account near the end of a cruise so you can make any corrections that might be necessary.

Make Purchases

If you have seen something in the shops that you want to purchase, now is the time. This includes buying any photos you may want. I don't consider myself a particularly photogenic individual, but on one cruise, I had a great picture taken at a formal night dinner. It was undoubtedly the best picture taken of me on a cruise ship and I was both surprised and delighted with it. I put off purchasing the photo at the time I first saw it as I thought that there might be other photos that I would want to buy and on that particular cruise, there was some type of special on purchasing photos in bulk (or a certain number of photographs). I convinced myself that buying the photo later, would save me money. The day before the conclusion of the cruise, I had several things to do, including packing, and I forgot about the photo. I did not remember it until the following day when I was off the ship. Once the cruise had ended, there was no way to obtain the photo. It is with regret that I think about my failure to buy that picture the day I first saw it. As such, I always remind people to reserve a certain block of time the day before your cruise ends, to make any purchases you may want. As for me, if there is a photo I want, I buy it the day I see it regardless of whether it is the first or second last day of a cruise.

Items Held by The Cruise Line

If you have any items that are being held by the cruise line, such as alcohol or an item that was appropriated upon embarkation, it is generally delivered to you the night before disembarkation. Make sure this item has been delivered to your cabin and if not, follow up on its whereabouts. Also remember to leave room in your luggage to pack this/these item(s).

Contact Information for New Friends

Exchange information with people you have met onboard and with whom you want to remain in contact. I am delighted to say that we have made good friends onboard various cruises and with whom we are still in touch.

Complete Cruise Comment/Thank You Cards

Make sure you fill out any cruise comment cards or recognize any special staff members you want to bring to the attention of the cruise line. These are called by different names but staff appreciation, crew recognition or star employee cards are some names that may be attached to a cruise line card, wherein you are afforded the opportunity to recognize employees for outstanding performances.

This is also the time that I usually prepare thank you cards and gratuities for staff members such as the cabin attendant, wait staff or a particularly outstanding crew member.

Baggage Collection

Good news, you don't have to carry all your baggage off the ship unless you choose to do so for expediency's sake. You will be asked to put your checked bags outside of your cabin by a certain time the night before your cruise ends. During the night, the ship's staff will collect the bags and take them to the baggage storage area so they can be quickly unloaded when the cruise has officially ended. That way you simply walk off at the time you have been assigned and your large bag(s) should be waiting for you in the baggage collection area of the cruise terminal.

I could write about baggage collection and possible pitfalls, but I believe the following stories will best inform you of things to be attentive to as you prepare your suitcases for collection.

> *We packed up the night before our cruise ended*
> *and everything was organized. The plan was to go*
> *for a leisurely breakfast and then walk off the ship*

with only my purse and a little knapsack holding our sleep wear, limited toiletries and our breakable souvenirs. We would not even keep a carry-on bag.

After I went to sleep, my husband did a final check of the drawers and closet. He thought I missed a few things and thoughtfully added some clothes he found in the wardrobe to the last suitcase and put it out into the corridor. He was pleased with himself for finding them and getting them into a bag before the bags were taken away. In the morning when we got up, I discovered what he had done. Those were our clothes for getting off the ship. We got off with him in his sleeping shorts and me in pajama bottoms and a t-shirt. We had to retrieve our bags from the baggage collection area before we could get dressed. I said to one of the cruise ship guys that we must look pretty stupid, but he told me it happens all the time.

Kim and Scott – Canada

***

You may not have heard a story like this one yet but we had in incident getting off the cruise. The last night of the cruise, we got ready for bed and were busy getting our bags packed so we could get them out into the hallway by 11pm. We only had the two big bags and both were going out into the hall.

We live a couple of hours from the cruise port and we had our car in a nearby long-term car park. Since we drove to the cruise terminal and would be driving straight home we never needed any carry-on bags, just the big suitcases. We thought, why bother carrying our stuff off since we would get a luggage buggy in the terminal when we picked up our bags. Not thinking, we packed everything and I mean everything but our toothbrushes. We put the bags in the hall and sat on the balcony in nothing but the ship's bathrobes, drinking a bottle of wine we had saved for the final night. Happy with our efforts, we finished the bottle and went to bed.

The next morning, we got up late and then we realized we had no clothes to wear off the ship. Our big bags were long gone. I called out to our cabin steward, who was in the hallway and asked him if he could help. The poor guy was trying to get all the rooms cleaned and prepared for the next group of people but he still made a few calls and got someone to help us out. That person went with a *fellow from security and they tried to find our luggage in the luggage area. Finally, after several hours, they came back and got my husband. They had some stretchy shorts and a t-shirt for him to wear. The clothes were obviously from one of the stores as they still had the tags on them. The idea was that he would find our luggage and get something for me to wear so I could leave the ship. He went out to the luggage area and found our bags and although he wanted to get back onto the ship, the security people in the terminal would not let him bring the bags back on and he could not return to our cabin. He took out some clothes for me to wear and they would be delivered to me. All this took time and the next group of cruisers were already getting on the ship.*

I was crying with the stress of everything by the time the clothes were delivered to me. The cabin steward could not have been nicer and told me not to worry about still being in the cabin. They had even arranged for me to have room service while I was waiting. What did my mega stressed husband pick out for me to wear? One of the semi-formal dresses I wore for a formal night, a hoodie and some running shoes. I was so happy to just get off the ship that I dressed quickly and left the cabin with the security guy accompanying me. I was at the elevator when the cabin steward came running up because I had been in such a hurry to get off that I had forgotten my purse in the room.

We were never charged for the clothing they brought for my husband to wear or the room service. We have never made that mistake again.

Meghan & Mike

Fast Get-Away

If you need to disembark quickly, you may decide to forgo checking your luggage and simply carry it off the ship. This is normally done by people who want to leave early/quickly and don't mind carrying all their luggage off the ship without assistance.

Getting Off the Ship

I would like to report that getting off the ship is always a seamless process but it is not. I have seen crowds, busy elevators, teeming waiting areas and long line-ups. I will address a few key points that may help you negotiate the process:

- Make sure you only have items that you can comfortably carry. Check everything else.
- If you need assistance getting off the ship, arrange for that assistance the day before your cruise ends. Do not wait until the last minute.

- If you are meeting up with friends before getting off the ship, select a meeting place away from the disembarkation point.
- Elevators can be very busy so if you can take the stairs, do so and save yourself a wait.

Collecting Your Checked Baggage

Some baggage collection areas (locations) have luggage belts, such as the type you will see at an airport, others just have a massive luggage area and each area is designated with a letter or number. When you get off the ship, look for the luggage belt or the corresponding designated area to find your luggage.

Double check the baggage tags to ensure you have the correct luggage. The ubiquitous black or grey luggage can look alike, and it is easy to make a mistake. I have been the victim of someone taking my bag in error and it was not a fun event.

Most cruise lines, in an effort to have ship departures flow in a smooth and efficient manner, have scheduled times for people to disembark. This always sounds so reasonable and efficient, but not everything goes according to plan and not everything is controlled by the cruise lines.

We have encountered delays by the baggage handlers and at Customs and Immigration. These groups are used to handling large numbers of passengers leaving cruise ships and processing usually goes well but expect that there may be delays. Try to avoid tight flight connections that require you to get off the ship in a timely manner, especially if you have to negotiate a customs and immigration process. The following are offerings spelling out the good and the bad.

> Disembarkation day is always sad for us but the cruise lines have it down to a science. Our luggage is removed from the hallway during the night so we just have our little back packs with us. We enjoy a leisurely breakfast on the ship and drink our coffees at a relaxed pace. We are then ready to get off the ship. Never a problem with our big bags. We have always found our luggage easily and leaving the arrival terminal is a piece of cake.
>
> Jim

***

> Exiting the ship was a horrific experience with us all herded slowly down the passageways. The elevators were impossible to use as everyone was trying to get on them all at once. When we finally reached the baggage area, there were thousands of bags all in a giant warehouse type area. We finally located our bags in two different sections even though we had the same color tags. The wheel was broken on my suitcase and I could not find

anyone to talk to about the damage. We barely made our flight.

(Name Withheld)

***

I prefer when customs and immigration people come on board and start to process people. It makes for faster handling. They check your passport, talk to you and issue you with a card. You then get off the ship and don't face long line ups. I wish all countries would do this.

Martin

***

The ship discharged us all pretty quickly but there was a hold up with the baggage guys delivering our bags. I was told they were not ship employees but a contracted company who were on some kind of work slow down. Hundreds of passengers standing around waiting for our luggage, while those guys took their time.

(Name Withheld)

We have never had a problem getting off a ship or picking up our bags. The cruise lines do a great job, but then why not? They do it every week and have loads of practice getting it down pat.

Stephen and Stefanie

***

Tell your readers to just chill out the morning the ship docks. Have breakfast and don't be in a panic to get off the ship. If you are among the last to leave, it is all quick and painless and your baggage is right there waiting for you. No crowds, no line ups.

Ginger - USA

Back-to-Back Cruisers

We just did back-to-back cruises. It was an amazing experience. It may have been our first time but it sure won't be our last. Time to tell the kids we are spending their inheritance!

William (location unknown)

I have taken back-to-back cruises and like those of you who may do the same, I had questions about the process. In our case, we were not staying in the same cabin and knew we had to pack up and move at the conclusion of our first cruise. We needed to know if we had to get off the ship and then check in again, or whether there was a more efficient process to save us time and effort.

Staying in the Same Cabin

If you are doing a back-to-back cruise and staying in the same cabin, you will find the process fairly seamless. You don't have to pack up and get off the ship. Everything can be left in your cabin as you prefer it. Generally, your cabin key card (which I will refer to as an access card), is programmed for the entire period of time you are slated to be in the cabin, but if not, a simple trip to guest services will have the card activated for the second cruise.

If you have made purchases that are being held by security, verify with guest services as to how that item will be handled.

Same Cabin but Different Packages

Some cruise lines might ask you to verify and address your onboard account particularly if you have different options on your second cruise that vary from those attached to your first. For example, if you had a beverage package and wi-fi on your first cruise, your access card will need to be changed to reflect the difference in the benefits you have associated with your second cruise. Usually in those cases, you are given a new card.

Cabin Change

In our case, we were changing cabins and found the process was extremely efficient. We packed all the items in the drawers and toiletries but left our hanging clothing in the closet. Our cabin steward took care of the rest. Our hanging clothing was loaded onto a heavy-duty rolling garment rack and our baggage onto a baggage dolly and they were taken to our new cabin while we were off the ship sightseeing.

Before leaving the ship, we had been given new access cards and told how we would circumvent the port check-in process upon our return. That way we were not caught up in the check-in procedures for the passengers who were just embarking. Overall, it was a smooth transition. We had the same benefits on both cruises so that aspect was not an issue.

Although I don't have a lot of experience in back-to-back cruises, I have posed the question to those who have had experiences with different cruise lines and most of them express the same sentiments. Generally, it is considered an easy process.

Testing, Visa or Other Requirements

On our most recent back-to-back cruises, there was a need to undergo testing for Covid prior to each cruise. We wondered how that would be handled. Would we have to get off the ship to be given a test? The cruise line made arrangements to test the back-to-back passengers on the ship the day before our first cruise concluded. They also ensured that everyone had the necessary Visas that were prerequisites for the countries we were going to visit and specifically, required for the country in which the cruise finished.

Passengers who failed the covid testing, or failed to have the appropriate documentation, could not continue and had to disembark at the conclusion of the first cruise.

River and Barge Cruises

We were on a river cruise and enjoyed every minute of it. The boat was smaller and it did not have a lot of the bells and whistles that the big ocean liners have, but we travelled past some wonderful towns and villages and waved to the locals who seemed more engaged. I am now a river cruise convert.

Iain - Wales

I decided to devote a short chapter to the world of river cruises as they have a distinct and wonderful vibe that differs from their big ship, ocean and sea going counterparts. The boats are smaller and the setting more intimate. In my port stop blogs, you will see that most cities started life on the banks of a river or the convergence of two rivers.

Water is a necessity for life and in ancient times, it was the main means of transportation and trade. Consequently, most major cities are located on the banks of a river. Not all rivers will accommodate large ships. I live in Ottawa, the capital city of Canada. It is located at the meeting point of two rivers but unlike Montreal, Quebec City or Vancouver, you will not see any large cruise ships docking here. You will however find day and evening river cruises.

When I think of river cruises, I tend to think of Europe where there is a proliferation of river cruises and they involve all the major navigable waterways. I will focus on those cruises in this chapter but caution my readers that there are river cruises in North and South America and Asia that are well worth booking.

Taking a river cruise has a distinct advantage in that the boats often dock in locations very near city centers which means you can get off the boat and walk to various sites. On many of these types of cruises, shore excursions are included as are other onboard perks that on a larger ship will result in extra charges. They tend to be all inclusive and move at a relatively relaxed pace. You will have the advantage of seeing the countryside on a more closeup and personal level.

One of the distinct advantages is the ability to see more of a country and get a better flavour of the culture as you see the homes and countryside close to the shores, whereas off the coast of a country, on a larger ship, you are not hugging the shoreline and view coastlines from a safe distance.

Food is often fresher as the cooks can obtain local foodstuff from the markets that morning in a quantity suitable for the clientele on the ship. Buying for 50 to 100 people as opposed to 5000 people.

We love river cruises as we are not caught up in the hustle and bustle of a big ship with 100 things going on all at once. It is quiet, calm and relaxed. There are also personal touches you won't get on the big ships. At one meal I mentioned I really liked a certain food and the next day, our waiter put it in front of me. The cook had picked it up at the local market that day!

Ivan - USA

One other comment relating to river cruising but with a twist, are the barge cruises. Usually smaller than the traditional river cruise vessels, barge cruises are smaller boats and often have under twenty passengers. The ones I received information about, had ten passengers or less and were tied to gourmet dining experiences.

These boats are narrow and most have a fairly relaxed itinerary wherein the boat can stop at any time in the day to allow passengers to participate in shore activities such as bicycling for a short distance, explore a local market or to have a picnic on shore. Barge cruises customarily traverse narrower waterways and canals and do not travel great distances as they generally stay in one country or region.

I Have Been on More Cruises

I like finding people who have been on multiple cruises because that usually means that they love cruising and they often have the best tips and stories. But I am always baffled by people who announce the number of cruises they have taken to justify an action.

On one cruise, while at the head of the line for the eggs cooked to order station, a woman squeezed her way past everyone and stepped in front of me. Noticing my quizzical look and hearing some muttered protests from the people behind me, she announced *"I have been on 30 cruises, so I know how everything works"*. Confused by this statement? Yes, me too. I am still trying to figure out why she thought that gave her the right to cut to the front of the line. First cruise or fiftieth cruise, it makes no difference in relation to bad behaviour.

We once had a couple tell us that we were sitting in their seats in the theatre. We apologized and moved over two seats. The couple behind us leaned forward and said that the seats were not reserved and that we should not have moved. The couple who had asked us to move, overheard the conversation and the woman said, *"We have been on 20 cruises and we always sit in these seats for all the shows"*. Ah, there is that number thing again. As if announcing the number of cruises legitimized them asking us to move so they could sit in their preferred seats. Had they simply asked us if we would mind moving, we would have done so without them having to resort to subterfuge.

Over multiple cruises, we have found those pesky sailing numbers always make an appearance, no matter what the activity. They continue to confound me because I fail to see the rationale for many of the declarations. Here are just a few I made note of over the years followed by my thoughts on the matter:

1. *That show was bad, I should know, I have taken 40 cruises.*
    The number of cruises you have taken makes no difference in forming an opinion about the quality of a performance. The show is either good or bad.

2. *I have been on 17 cruises and must sit by the window.*
    If one takes 17 cruises does a window seat become an automatic "*must*"? You either want to sit by a window or not.

3. *I have been on 20 cruises and I can tell the weather in advance of any cruise.*
    I am surprised the cruise lines have not snapped this guy up. He has a unique skill!

4. *This is the best cruise line. I sailed with this line 30 times and hands down it is the best.*

   When I asked him how many cruises in total he had sailed on, he told me 30.

5. *We have over 50 sailings under our belt so we are cruising experts.*

   Although suitably impressed that anyone has taken 50 cruises, I hold the opinion that people have different levels of cruising knowledge and expertise. I once met a man on a cruise who had encyclopedic knowledge of the ship and its history. It was his first cruise and he had researched the ship and line extensively.

The numbers game plays out in many ways but the best lesson given, that I was witness to, was on a Mediterranean sailing. We were invited to a gathering with the ship's staff to honour previous guests. There was a woman at the event who was standing with us in a little group that had formed. Bragging about the number of sailings she had with that particular cruise line she stated: "*You would be hard pressed to find someone with more days on this line than me*".

Shortly after her statement, there was an announcement of the collective number of sailings and then a special acknowledgement of an elderly man who had a staggering 10,000 plus days as a passenger onboard the cruise line. It turns out he was standing with us. While Dan did the math in his head as to how many years that worked out to, I stole a look at the woman who had a shocked expression. She had just learned a valuable numbers lesson. No matter how many cruises you have taken, it is highly likely that sailing on the same ship, there will be someone who has taken more.

They All Stayed Afloat

One of my favourite lines came from a fellow who told me that he had been on eleven or twelve cruises with five different lines. I asked him if he could share with me what he liked about each specific line. *"They all stayed afloat"* he dryly responded with a glint of humour in his eyes. I had to agree with him that such an accomplishment would certainly place any cruise line in good standing.

General Comments

We were sitting by the pool and a bunch of guys were there - all wearing bras. They wore them all day as some part of an inside joke or lost bet. One of them fell asleep and we are pretty sure he got a funny sunburn around the bra. The next day they were at the pool again and he kept his t-shirt on the whole time.

Chris - Canada

When going through some of the personal anecdotes that people provided to me for my book on cruising, I am reminded of how different people remember their trips. People talk about the places visited while others detail the ship, food and onboard events. Some of the best stories are the ones shared by people who recounted funny incidents that occurred while on a cruise. I write humorous travel books so naturally I gravitate towards those types of stories.

But one of my favourites is from a fellow who told me that at the time he took his first cruise, he could not remember the last time he had genuinely laughed. He was alone and on the cruise for a wedding of a family member. He told me that he belly laughed for the first time in years. In our e-mail exchange, I asked him if he would share the funny story that had him laughing. He said "*That is the strange thing, it was not one specific moment or one occurrence.*

374

It was throughout the cruise. I would find myself laughing over something with total strangers. Whether it was at the pool, in the elevator, at the bar or sitting at a table. There was always someone talking to me and making me laugh. It was like I was part of a community."

People travel for various reasons and cruising has a myriad of advantages. Good food, entertainment, lectures, fun events, group participation activities, solo options, dancing, music, and port stops. There is always something for everyone. My hope for all of you is that you enjoy your cruising experience and come away with warm feelings of laughter.

Enjoy your cruise and who knows, we may meet and share a tale or two!

Vacation Deaths and Other Horror Stories

Coming in September of 2025, my next book, *Vacation Deaths, and Other Horror Stories* deviates from my usual lighthearted offerings and details major crimes that have occurred on vacations.

www.ingramcontent.com/pod-product-compliance
Lightning Source LLC
Chambersburg PA
CBHW020917140626
46545CB00015B/87